About the Author

Bradley Rubenstein is a painter and writer who lives and works in Brooklyn, New York. His works are in the collections of The Metropolitan Museum of Art, The Detroit Institute of Arts, The Museum of Fine Arts, Boston, The Tang Teaching Museum, The Krannert Art Museum Teaching Collection at The University of Illinois at Urbana-Champaign, and The Teaching Collection at the Whitney Museum of American Art, among others. He has been the recipient of the National Endowment for the Arts Fellowship in Painting, the Pollock-Krasner Award, and a grant from the Emily Hall Tremaine Foundation. He has contributed interviews, essays, and reviews to *CultureCatch*, *Artslant*, *Battery Journal*, *M/E/A/N/I/N/G*, *The Brooklyn Rail*, *Sharkforum*, *ArtKrush*, *New Observations*, and *Art Journal*. Mr. Rubenstein is the author of *Press Eject and Give Me the Tape: Dialogues, Interviews, and Exchanges 2001–2020*.

THE BLACK ALBUM

Writings on Art and Culture

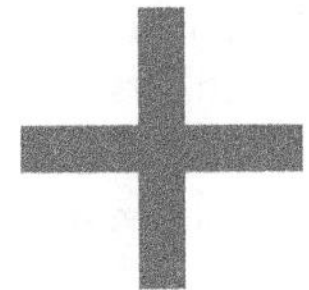

Bradley Rubenstein

BATTERY JOURNAL
Expanded Second Edition

The following contains works of satirical fiction; any resemblance to persons living or dead is probably coincidental. Due to the analog nature of this book, many of the hyperlinked references are lost. Where not noted, the reader is invited to recreate the digital experience and search other sources for quotations, references, and dates.

Edited by Anna Ehrsam.

Battery Journal, Brooklyn, New York
www.batteryjournal.org

Published by Meridian Art Press, Brooklyn, New York.
www.meridianartpress.com

Printed in the United States of America.

Publisher's Cataloging-in-Publication Data
Rubenstein, Bradley.
The black album : writings on art and culture / Bradley Rubenstein.
Expanded second edition. | Brooklyn, NY : Meridian Art Press, 2019.
LCCN 2019937239 | ISBN 978-1-7322219-3-2 (paperback)
ISBN 978-1-7322219-2-5 (ebook)
LCSH: 1. Art criticism. 2. Art critics. 3. Art and society. 4. Arts. 5. Satire
BISAC: 1. ART / Criticism & Theory. 2. ART / Popular Culture.
3. ART / History / General.
LCC N7475 .R83 2019 (print) | LCC N7475 (ebook) | DDC 701/.18--dc23

Library of Congress Control Number 2019937239

Contents

i   About the Author

xi   Acknowledgements

xiii   Publisher's Introduction

3   South of Heaven
Henri Matisse: *Matisse: Radical Invention: 1913–1917*; Museum of Modern Art, New York.

5   Sk8er Boi
Dan Colen: *Poetry*; Gagosian Gallery, New York.

7   Parallel Lines
Deborah Kass: *More Feel Good Paintings for Feel Bad Times*; Paul Kasmin Gallery, New York.

8   Roy's Keen
Roy Lichtenstein: *The Black-and-White Drawings, 1961–1968*; The Morgan Library & Museum, New York.

10   Staring at the Sea
Yoan Capote: *Mental States*; Jack Shainman Gallery, New York.

12   Sweet Leaf
Fred Tomaselli: Brooklyn Museum.

14   Stateless
Francesco Clemente: *A Private Geography*; Mary Boone Gallery, New York.

16   Aggressive Perfector
Joan Miró: *Miró: The Dutch Interiors*; Metropolitan Museum of Art, New York.

18   Confusion is Next
Raymond Pettibon: *Hard in the Paint*; David Zwirner Gallery, New York.

20   Lipstick Traces
Liz Markus: *Are You Punk or New Wave?*; Zieher Smith Gallery, New York.

21   Achtung, Baby
Anselm Kiefer: *Next Year in Jerusalem*; Gagosian Gallery, New York.

23   Tiny Little Pieces
Charles LeDray: *workworkworkworkwork*; Whitney Museum of Art, New York.

25   God Save The Queen
George Condo: *Mental States*; New Museum, New York.

27   Scary Monsters and Super Creeps
Jason Bard Yarmosky: *Elder Kinder*; Like the Spice Gallery, Brooklyn.

28   Slanted and Enchanted
Lynda Benglis: New Museum, New York.

29   Heart-Shaped Box
Pablo Picasso: *Guitars 1912–1914*; Museum of Modern Art, New York.

30   Sweet Love Falling Like A Pale Blue Light
Adam Marnie and Dawn Cerny: SEASON, Seattle, Washington.

34   Poker Face
Paul Cézanne: *Cézanne's Card Players*; Metropolitan Museum, New York.

35   Night in the Ruts
Karen Kilimnik: *my walk in the woods at night*; 303 Gallery, New York.

36   World of Skin
        Berlinde De Bruyckere: *Into One-Another to P.P.P.*; Hauser & Wirth, New York.

38   American Caesar
        Jasper Johns: *New Sculpture and Works on Paper*; Matthew Marks Gallery, New York.

39   Standing on a Beach
        David Salle: *New Paintings*; Mary Boone Gallery, New York.

41   Swimsuit Edition
        Willem de Kooning: *The Figure: Movement and Gesture*; Pace Gallery, New York.

43   Drums Along the Mohawk
        Mark Grotjahn: *Nine Faces*; Anton Kern Gallery, New York.

44   Pretty Tied Up
        Alexander McQueen: *Savage Beauty*; Costume Institute, The Metropolitan Museum of Art, New York.

46   Southern Man
        Cy Twombly: *Sculpture*; Museum of Modern Art; New York.

47   Wild-Eyed Boy from Freecloud
        Kal Spelletich: *Where's My Jetpack?!*; Jack Hanley Gallery, New York.

48   You're the One for Me, Fatty
        Lucien Freud: *Homage to Lucien Freud*; Metropolitan Museum of Art, New York.

49   Some Girls
        Aneta Grzeszykowska: *Lovetime*; Harris Lieberman Gallery, New York.

51   Shakespeare's Sister
        Nicola Tyson: Friedrich Petzel Gallery, New York.

53   Sound and Vision
        Gideon Bok: *Record Store*; Steven Harvey Fine Art Projects, New York.

54   Killing Joke
        David Moriarty: *Halcyon Daze*; CREON Gallery, New York.

55   Moby Dick
        Willem de Kooning: *de Kooning: A Retrospective*; The Museum of Modern Art, New York.

56   Beauty and the Beast
        Karen Heagle: *Let Nature Take Its Course and Hope It Passes*; I-20, New York.

57   Walk Like an Egyptian
        Matthew Barney: *DJED*; Gladstone Gallery, New York.

59   Horses
        Susan Rothenberg: Sperone Westwater, New York.

60   Rebel, Rebel
        Eva Hesse: *Eva Hesse Spectres 1960*; Brooklyn Museum, Brooklyn.

61   The Thing
        Mira Schor: *Painting in The Space Where Painting Used to Be*; Some Walls, Oakland, California.

62   Alphaville
        Allison Schulnik: *Mound*; Zieher Smith, New York.

63   The Revolution Will Not Be Televised
        Sanford Biggers: *Sweet Funk—An Introspective*; The Brooklyn Museum, Brooklyn.

64   Waltzing Mathilda
        Peter Williams: *Midnight Waltz in D Minor*; Paul Kotula Projects, Ferndale, Michigan.

65   Thunderball
      Jonathan Meese: *Hot Earl Green Sausage Tea Barbie (First Flush)*; Bortolami Gallery, New York.

67   Atrocity Exhibition
      Maurizio Cattelan: *All*; Solomon R. Guggenheim Museum, New York.

69   Snow Blind
      Paul McCarthy: *The Dwarves, The Forests*; Hauser and Wirth, New York.

70   Naked
      Edgar Degas: *Degas and the Nude*; Museum of Fine Arts, Boston.

71   Red Sails
      Howard Hodgkin: Gagosian Gallery, New York.

72   Take a Look Around
      Lola Montes Schnabel: *Love Before Intimacy*; The Hole, New York.

73   Violent Femmes
      Sanja Iveković: *Sweet Violence*; Museum of Modern Art, New York.

75   Temptation
      Damien Hirst: *The Complete Spot Paintings 1986–2011*; Gagosian Gallery: New York, London,
      Paris, Beverly Hills, Rome, Athens, Geneva, and Hong Kong.

76   Dark Christmas
      Various artists: *Dark Christmas*; Leo Koenig, Inc., New York.

77   Bat Out of Hell
      Joyce Pensato: *Batman Returns*; Friedrich Petzel Gallery, New York.

79   Bulls on Parade
      Jean Dubuffet: *The Last Two Years*; Pace Gallery, New York.

81   Gigantic
      Rachel Kneebone: *Regarding Rodin*; Brooklyn Museum, Brooklyn.

83   On Some Faraway Beach
      Liz Markus: *The Look of Love*; Zieher Smith, New York.

84   Celebrity Skin
      Eric Fischl: *Portraits*; Mary Boone Gallery, New York.

86   Small Faces
      Various artists: *The Renaissance Portrait from Donatello to Bellini*; Metropolitan Museum of
      Art, New York.

88   Tripping Daisy
      Terry Winters: *Cricket Music, Tessellation Figures, & Notebook*; Matthew Marks Gallery, New
      York.

90   Halber Mensch
      Georg Baselitz: Gagosian Gallery, New York.

92   When Darkness Doubles
      David Lynch: Tilton Gallery, New York.

93   Night Dark Night
      Mira Schor: *Voice and Speech*; Marvelli Gallery, New York.

95   Black and Blue
      Ron Gorchov: Cheim & Read, New York.

96   The Van Gogh Boat
      Keith Haring: *1978–1982*; Brooklyn Museum, Brooklyn.

97   Cuts You Up
Robert Yoder: Platform Gallery, Seattle.

98   Blister in the Sun
Dana Schutz: *Piano in the Rain*; Friedrich Petzel Gallery, New York.

99   Karma Chameleon
Francesco Clemente: *Nostalgia/Utopia*; Mary Boone Gallery, New York.

100   This Wreckage I Call Me
Martin Kippenberger: *The Raft of the Medusa*; Carolina Nitsch Project Room, New York.

101   Slow Burn
Rodney Dickson: *Painting*; Klemens Gasser & Tanja Grunert, Inc., New York.

103   Rubberband Man
Richard Prince: *14 Paintings*; 303 Gallery, New York.

105   Sign of the Times
Various artists: *Signs & Symbols*; Whitney Museum of American Art, New York.

108   Station to Station
Alighiero Boetti: *Game Plan*; Museum of Modern Art, New York.

111   L'Age d'Or
Edouard Vuillard: *A Painter and His Muses, 1890–1940*; The Jewish Museum, New York.

112   Be Here Now
Angela Dufresne: *Parlors and Pastorals*; Monya Rowe Gallery, New York; CRG Gallery, New York.

114   Almost Famous
Richard Phillips: Gagosian Gallery, New York.

117   Five Easy Pieces
Jackson Pollock and Tony Smith: *Sculpture: An Exhibition on the Centennial of their Births*; Matthew Marks Gallery, New York.
Tony Smith: *Source*; Matthew Marks Gallery, New York.

119   50 Shades of Gray
Pablo Picasso: *Picasso Black and White*; Guggenheim Museum, New York.

121   Master of Puppets
Bjarne Melgaard: *A New Novel by Bjarne Melgaard*; Luxembourg & Dayan, New York.

124   Call Me Ishmael
Barnaby Furnas: *If Wishes Were Fishes . . .*; Marianne Boesky Gallery, New York.

126   Luxe, Calme, et Volupté
Henri Matisse: *In Search of True Painting*; Metropolitan Museum of Art, New York.

128   Family Affair
Dieter Roth. Björn Roth; Hauser & Wirth, New York.

129   Daydream Nation
Various artists: *NYC 1993: Experimental Jet Set, Trash and No Star*; The New Museum, New York.
Julian Schnabel: *1978–1981*; Oko, New York.

131   Public Image, Ltd.
Jean-Michel Basquiat: Gagosian Gallery, New York.

133   Voodoo Problems
Peter Williams: Foxy Production, New York.

135 Funtime
Various artists: *Gutai: Splendid Playground*; Solomon R. Guggenheim, New York.

137 Nights Without Armor
Karen Heagle: *Battle Armor*; Churner and Churner, New York.

139 Holywood
Paul McCarthy and Damon McCarthy: *Rebel Dabble Babble*; Hauser & Wirth, New York.
Paul McCarthy: *WS*; Park Avenue Armory, New York.

142 Pretty in Pink
Cary Leibowitz: *(paintings and belt buckles)*; Invisible Exports, New York.

144 Saturday Night Special
Michael Williams: *Paintings*; CANADA, New York.

147 The Walk Home
Julian Schnabel: The Brant Foundation Art Study Center, Greenwich, CT.

149 The Recognitions
Michel Majerus: Matthew Marks Gallery, New York.

153 Fade to Grey
Jasper Johns: *Regrets*; Museum of Modern Art, New York.

155 Body of Evidence
Maria Lassnig: MoMA PS1, New York.

158 Bête Noire
Susan Bee: *Doomed to Win/Paintings from the 1980s*; A.I.R Gallery, New York.

160 Mallrats
Walter Robinson: *Figure Studies*; Lynch Tham Gallery, New York.

162 The Shape of Things to Come
Henri Matisse: *The Cut-Outs*; The Museum of Modern Art, New York.

164 Tick, Tick, Bang
Various artists: *The Forever Now: Contemporary Painting in an Atemporal World*; Museum of Modern Art, New York.

166 Kicking Against the Pricks
Peter Williams: NOVELLA, New York.

168 Peel Slowly and See
Bill Jensen: *Transgressions;* Cheim & Read, New York.

170 The Immigrant Song
Jacob Lawrence: *One-Way Ticket: Jacob Lawrence's Migration Series and Other Works*; MoMA (Museum of Modern Art), New York.

172 Physical Graffiti
Leon Golub: *Riot*; Hauser & Wirth, New York.

174 Written on the Kitten
Jean-Michael Basquiat: *BASQUIAT: The Unknown Notebooks*; Brooklyn Museum, Brooklyn.

176 This is What Tomorrow Looks Like: On Painting
Albert Oehlen: *Home and Garden*; The New Museum, New York.
Albert Oehlen: *"Home and Garden" Annex*; Gagosian Gallery, New York.
Magalie Guérin: *Project Room*; Lyles & King, New York.
Brenda Goodman: *Selected Work 1961–2015*; College for Creative Studies, Center Galleries, Detroit.

Brenda Goodman: *Painting is Not Doomed to Repeat Itself*; Hollis Taggart Galleries, New York.
Erin Smith: *The Right Place at the Right Time*; Amy Li Projects, New York.

178   Zombie Birdhouse
Keltie Ferris: Mitchell-Innes & Nash, New York.

180   The Whiteness of the Whale
Frank Stella: *A Retrospective*; Whitney Museum of American Art, New York.

183   Where Darkness Doubles Light Pours In
Mira Schor: Lyles & King, New York.

185   More Pricks Than Kicks
Philip Guston's Nixon Drawings; Hauser & Wirth, New York.

187   Wide Awake in America
C. Michael Norton: *When Paintings Awake*; David&Schweitzer Contemporary, Brooklyn.

189   Love in the Ruins
Anselm Kiefer: *Transition from Cool to Warm*; Gagosian, New York.

191   Things Past: Brenda Goodman at David&Schweitzer
Brenda Goodman: *In a New Space*; David&Schweitzer Contemporary, New York.

193   Vir Heroicus Sublimis
Cy Twombly: *Coronation of Sesostris*; Gagosian, New York.
Per Kirkeby: *Paintings and Bronzes from the 1980s*; Michael Werner, New York.
Mary DeVincentis: *Dwellers on the Threshold*; David&Schweitzer Contemporary, New York.

197   Men In Rooms: Bruce Nauman at MoMA PS1
Bruce Nauman: *Disappearing Acts*; MoMA PS1.

199   The Palace at 4 a.m.
Giacometti: Soloman R. Guggenheim Museum.

202   Guided By Voices
Hilma af Klint: *Paintings for the Future*; Soloman R. Guggenhiem Museum.

205   Hesitation Marks
Judy Glantzman: *1979–Today*; Betty Cunningham Gallery.

207   Dandy in the Underworld
Dana Schutz: *Imagine Me and You*; Petzel Gallery.

209   Also available by Bradley Rubenstein

Acknowledgements

The author would like to thank the following for their editorial contributions:

Andrea Alessi
Trong G. Nguyen
Mark "Dusty" Petracca
Steve Holtje
Wesley Kimler
Phong Bui
Gennifer Levey
Taylor DeFoe
Michael Lee Nirenberg
Ashley Booth Klein
Natalie Hegert
Charlie Schultz
Kat Georges

Publisher's Introduction

About *Battery Journal*

Battery Journal is

1. a journal for contemporary art and culture.

2. a platform for related manifestations: multimedia and polyvalent projects.

3. a collaboration between artists, writers, and intellectuals.

A battery is a portable container in which chemical energy is converted into electricity and used as a source of power. *Battery Journal* is "where the meaning is held," and a generator for new forms and ideas. *Battery Journal* is an art and cultural journal with an innovative approach to presenting cutting-edge contemporary art and cultural theory. Dedicated to covering all modes of production—from sculpture, painting, installation, performance, film, and sound to architecture, literature, and science—we feature writing by and about some of today's most incisive thinkers. Each issue presents articles and reviews from a range of progressive perspectives.

The Black Album: Writings on Art and Culture is a collection of writing by painter and writer Bradley Rubenstein. There was once a time when art, technology, science, and poetry collided with politics. Zola and Cézanne. Fénéon and Seurat. Balzac and Rodin. Jean Arp and Hans Arp. Anarchy and beauty combined. In our current moment it seems that we might be well served to remember this past; when art and culture are driven underground, new ideas emerge. Taking Joan Didion's collection of criticism, *The White Album*, as a point of reference, Rubenstein creates a new vocabulary for critiquing an age where art has wed technology, fiction has become reality, and images, like words, are not always meant to be trusted. Like Robert Smithson, Rubenstein eschews a personal writing style, instead using science fiction, comedy, and other genre styles to create a lively, continuously changing narrative.
—Anna Ehrsam, Publisher

Anna Ehrsam is an interdisciplinary artist, art historian, and educator who works across a variety of mediums. Her work embodies infinitely permutable forms, performances, sounds, text, images, and video. She has lived and worked in New York City for over twenty years. The objective of her work is to develop and expand textual languages including form, color, light, sound, text, and context. Using their intrinsic physical, metaphysical, and relational properties to make concrete and ephemeral phenomenon, she creates intimate artifacts, installations, images, drawings, and documents. Ehrsam is guided by the concepts of beauty, truth, and knowledge as liberating forces.

THE BLACK ALBUM
Writings on Art and Culture

Bradley Rubenstein

BATTERY JOURNAL
Expanded Second Edition

"I am a camera with its shutter open, quite passive, recording, not thinking . . . Some day, all this will have to be developed, carefully printed, fixed."
—Christopher Isherwood, *Goodbye to Berlin*

"I'm the subject. I'm also the verb as I paint, but I'm also the object. I am the complete sentence."
—Barnett Newman

"I write entirely to find out what I'm thinking, what I'm looking at, what I see and what it means. What I want and what I fear."
—Joan Didion

South of Heaven

Henri Matisse: *Matisse: Radical Invention: 1913–1917*; Museum of Modern Art, New York. Published August 5, 2010; *CultureCatch*.

Henri Matisse usually brings to mind bucolic scenes of rest and calm, but here we finally meet the artist who matched Cézanne and Picasso in his ambition to discover and convey a new, distilled way of seeing through painting; an artist driven to strip-mine nature in order to find an essential ore of pure form. Invention was everything, and he was not above letting his subjects suffer a little in his desire to attain it. The show begins, appropriately enough, with a painting, *Three Bathers* (1879–82), by his idol Cézanne. Cézanne's grotesque yet compelling nudes serve as a prototype for Matisse's attack on the human form, but that is all. Matisse, unlike Cézanne, is all about feeling the figure, retooling it, and giving it back to us in a new form. Flattened fields of color, like flesh stretched over the canvas, and sinewy, whip-like lines describe new forms. *Le Luxe II* (1907–08), a large nude woman and her two female supplicants, and *Bathers with a Turtle* (1908), with its weird pre-pubescent hybrids, are lush and beautiful, and edged with enough kink to rival Picasso's *Demoiselles d'Avignon* (1907). The coltish girl-woman on the painting's proper left reminds us of nothing so much as Lolita on the beach.

In the second and third galleries the knives come out and the real work begins. In both his sculpture (*Back II*, 1911–13), and paintings (*Portrait of Yvonne Landsberg*, 1914), Matisse cuts, scrapes, abrades, and slashes paint and plaster to carve out (both literally and figuratively) the figure. Unlike Cézanne's nearly OCD horror of staining the canvas, Matisse first gives us the portrait of Ms. Landsberg; then he goes to work on it like a surgeon, cutting in and carving out, abstracting the figure by showing us what it looked like to him. We see the process, the work involved, and for a brief moment we are in the head of the artist, looking through his eyes.

Head, White and Rose (1914) is Matisse's response to Braque and Picasso's Cubism, and perhaps one of the most psychologically fraught works he would ever paint. Nominally a picture of his daughter Marguerite, it is a densely worked and layered piece of creation and destruction. Marguerite's head is reordered with thick black lines, a black dog-collar hides the scar of a childhood tracheotomy, and the thick, dark surrounding space serves to engulf and contain her, rather than recede into background. A profound sense of longing and possession pervades the piece, as if he felt that if he stopped painting her, she might disappear. Not even her pretty pink and blue striped blouse can lighten the mood of the portrait—and why should it? It was painted at the outbreak of World War I, and a sense of existentialist fear has begun to enter the work. He becomes both Dr. Jekyll and Mr. Hyde, torn between the need to dissect the human form and the need to protect it (remember the tracheotomy). The urge to take apart, though, has begun to wane in the face of the real taking apart of the world. *French Window at Collioure* (1914), perhaps the most abstract work of his career, gives us a window, but one with a view of darkness, silence, and the unknown—a landscape of total eclipse, of a dark night that would last for years. We have the sense that the black, which begins to invade his works from this point on, has crept in through this window, left open just a minute too long. Louis Aragon wrote, "Whether or not the painter intended it, and whatever that French window once opened onto, it remains open. It was onto the war then, and it's still onto events to come that will plunge men and women into darkness . . ."

All of this is back-story, of course, to *Bathers by a River* (1909–17). *Bathers* gives us a veritable catalog of his themes and techniques in one large frieze, from lush patterned greenery to simplified, stark figuration, anonymous and isolated. Matisse both absorbs and deconstructs Cubism here, giving us a 360-degree view of the human figure, but resists the temptation to overlay the action, allowing us to imagine either four separate figures or different aspects of one. But there is a fifth element, small, yet significant; a snake slithers up mid-canvas, bisecting the composition where a black panel abuts a white. There was a serpent in another garden that brought to its inhabitants the gift of the knowledge of good and evil—of light and dark. They saw that they were naked; they became human. We could take the obvious view of the serpent as symbol, that Matisse's Arcadia has been corrupted, that the innocence with which he sought to deconstruct the human form has paled when compared to the atrocity exhibition of maimed soldiers returning from the front. Or, perhaps, we can imagine the little serpent as Matisse: The Artist playing God in the Garden of his canvas, offering us that divine ability—to see for ourselves the darkness and the light.

Sk8er Boi

Dan Colen: *Poetry*; Gagosian Gallery, New York.
Published September 24, 2010; *CultureCatch*.

When we are young we think as children do; we see the world as full of promise, often mistaking signs for wonders. We start by faith, and consummate by vision, at least according to St. Augustine. When we grow older we put away childish things—or, in the case of Dan Colen, who is having his first exhibit at the Gagosian Gallery, exhibit them.

Mr. Colen's show doesn't so much occupy the gallery space as sulk against the walls. One meets these guarded, obdurate, art objects head-on. *The Sweetest Thing* (2010), a freestanding wall—brick, concrete, steel, and re-bar—is the first obstacle one encounters upon entering the first room. A passing reference, perhaps, to Minimalist sculpture via Gordon Matta Clark, subbing as an homage to the passing of his friend, the late Dash Snow, who Mr. Colen commemorated in an earlier work by faithfully recreating Mr. Snow's studio wall, *trompe-l'oeil* style. Colen's referencing of his earlier work pulls a neat sleight of hand—one reaches out to touch the piece, expecting to find painted Styrofoam, and is met with brick. By pulling us in to what we think we know, then cheating us out of the payoff, the piece manages to attract and repel, much like an Olsen Twin. In contrast to the eerie and sublime *Dash's Wall*, a surreal, prophetic, and wry bit of insider art, we are given just the wall—brick, concrete, etc.—without any the magical transformation by metaphor and faux technique.

In the second gallery Colen gives us a row of 13 parked Harley Davidson motorcycles, *Cracks in the Clouds* (2010), which he painted and wrapped himself after a photograph of a row of 13 parked Harleys he saw on a street. These bikes have toppled oops-fashion, like dominos, and now lie on the floor in a fallen row, like a Carl Andre sculpture. Mr. Colen has shown his memetic skills in the past, recreating graffiti on walls, canvases with ersatz tags, and, most skillfully, deconstructing Walt Disney animation cells. While his bike detailing here might not be up to Jesse James's standards, as a sculptural recreation of *The Last Supper* it by far surpasses the ironic-disaffected-youth set pieces of his past.

The third gallery proves a bit harder to reconcile but challenges in a more complex way. Three paintings, very large, rent a lot of very valuable Chelsea wall space but are dominated by *Overture* (2010), an inverted half-pipe, which looms like the Arc de Triomphe in the center of the space. *A Love Story* and *Another Country* (both 2010) are in Colen's signature chewing-gum medium. Extruded and smeared skeins of melted chewing gum are layered on the canvas, building up an impastoed surface reminiscent of Jean Fautrier's *Hostages* series. The drying gum arrests the gesture of the artist's hand (or it looks like in some cases a trowel), the gum oozes and sags of its own weight; the sickly pastel colors give the works a kind of trippy, cartoon feeling. Colen may be taking the piss out of Ab-Ex painting, but unlike, say, Richard Prince in his recent paintings, he has a lighter hand.

The Space Between Nothing and Everything (2010), in oil on canvas, is an articulately rendered depiction of confetti, traced from a photograph. While it is a beautiful painting, with its nods toward Willem de Kooning and Brice Marden, it seems to cry out for a more substantial meaning. What it most brings to mind is a motif from Bret Easton Ellis's *fin de siècle* novel *Glamorama*; where the settings are described as "sets," constantly filled with the swirling debris of confetti from after-parties; the air cold and dank and smelling of shit. Like Mr. Ellis, whose writing has been hailed, derided, and finally assimilated into the cultural canon, Mr. Colen's painterly objects and sculptural works try to straddle two worlds—

critiquing the superficiality of contemporary culture, while trying to imbed themselves into that very system. The tragic and continual beauty of youthful works is their unabashedly misguided arrogance. These works may suffer a defanging by being shown at the grown-up's table of the Gagosian Gallery, but to judge Mr. Colen's odes to adolescence (the show is called *Poetry*— think *Basketball Diaries* or *Blood and Guts in High School*) too harshly or quickly would be to miss the boat. The reluctance to put away childish things may be a requirement of genius, and one of the pleasures of looking at art is to find a renewal of vision; to see the world from another point of view, no matter how dismal.

Parallel Lines

Deborah Kass: *More Feel Good Paintings for Feel Bad Times*; Paul Kasmin Gallery, New York. Published October 8, 2010, *CultureCatch*.

There is a great Roy Lichtenstein painting from the 1960s called *Image Duplicator* that shows a comic book mad scientist with a thought bubble that reads, "What do you know about my Image Duplicator?!" Whether this mythical machine ever existed outside the realm of Lichtenstein's imagination is beside the point—dozens of artist from the '60s through the '90s used image replication and deconstruction as their primary motif, from Jasper Johns and Lichtenstein and Andy Warhol through Sherrie Levine and David Salle and Jeff Koons. Deborah Kass has largely followed this model, with the twist of appropriating the appropriators—using Warhol's images (already appropriated from newspapers and magazines) and then combining them with Jewish themes and pop icons (for example, Barbara Streisand in *Yentl*), giving the works a post-modern, feminist, and political slant that most artists of her generation, with the possible exception of Cary Leibowitz, didn't have.

While Ms. Kass's works along these lines were often witty and thought-provoking, they eventually ran into the wall of post-modern-art-about-art: the referencing of styles eventually became a style, the endgame of an endgame. In her recent exhibition at Paul Kasmin Gallery, *More Feel Good Paintings for Feel Bad Times*, Kass seems to have found a way out of this *cul-de-sac*, opting for fairly straightforward text pieces that evoke through their painterly style as well as provocative use of language fragments. The tone is lighter, the colors evoke a trippy '60s psychedelia, and the works cohere into a more organic whole instead of a cultural history lesson. *Oy* (2010), a remix of Ed Ruscha's *Popeye*, is brilliant: the simplicity of its editing combines with a respect for Rusha's deft painterly touch, to merge seamlessly. *Popeye*, a pop icon, is gently and subversively transformed in the viewer's mind—the tin of spinach replaced by a jar of gefilte fish.

In other works, colored bands reminiscent of Ellsworth Kelly or Brice Marden are layered with text (*Being Alive, C'mon Get Happy*, both 2010), bringing to mind the Partridge Family bus. Her sense of color is astute, spot-on with a sense of time that evokes the past without being nostalgic or sentimental, much as the television show *Mad Men* captures the spirit of the same period. In a certain sense Kass's works operate on the same premise as *Mad Men* does, celebrating and critiquing at the same time. And that is the ultimate success of this work: we are drawn in by the familiar, the style of type and colors that we are by now familiar with—and then, by an apt reworking of message, are left with a different experience than we expected. How we respond to this mix of art and culture icons is very much a personal choice; Kass has opened up her work and allows us to read our own story into art's history.

Roy's Keen

Roy Lichtenstein: *The Black-and-White Drawings, 1961–1968*; The Morgan Library & Museum, New York.
Published October 12, 2010; *CultureCatch*.

One of the many visual images to become embedded in our collective minds from the World Trade Center attack on 9/11 is the showers of paper falling from the Twin Towers. Paper memos, faxes, and archived letters—things that, a decade later, seem quaint, having been replaced by emails, texts, and tweets. Of course, though it is a wild stretch to compare this event to any art-historical watershed moment, one might, tentatively, compare it with the papery revolution of Cubist collage. There was a moment, in the early half of the twentieth century, when the use of text and images from popular media such as advertising and newspapers sought to replace the high art materials of stone and paint, overthrowing notions of what comprised an artwork and its relationship to culture and politics. Nearly half a century later, Roy Lichtenstein and other artists whose movement would be labeled "Pop" expanded on these notions of "high" and "low" materials and images.

In this excellent exhibit at the Morgan Library, we see that unlike some of his contemporaries such as Jasper Johns and Andy Warhol, Lichtenstein conceived and executed a mini-oeuvre of works on paper whose intent and ambition for drawing seems to rival that of Braque and Picasso. While Lichtenstein's Pop Art contemporaries found icons in everyday life and elevated their subjects to the status of minor deities (Warhol's *Marilyn*, for example), Lichtenstein, as this show suggests, used the transient nature of paper (it ages quickly, it rots, it is far more delicate than canvas or marble), as well as techniques simulating printing in magazines and newspapers (Ben-Day dots) and sought to achieve a measure of the avant-garde with which the Cubists imbued their collages. Where Picasso used the torn and clipped fragments of newsprint, rearranged and decontextualized to represent the provisional nature of contemporary culture, Lichtenstein painstakingly simulates these techniques through *pochoir* (stencils), *frottage* (rubbings), and various projection methods to trace images such as *I Know How You Must Feel, Brad!* (1963) and *Bratatat* (1962). Lichtenstein plays this conceit two ways: he undermines the notion of the high-art status of the drawing as preparatory sketch, or study, as he elevates the low-rent status accorded to collage by careful mimicry of mechanical technique.

We see this two-fold approach in his choices of subject matter as well. For example, *Woman in Bath* (1963) takes the subject of the female bather, an Impressionist favorite, and interprets it through something resembling a Calgon ad. The faint echoes of the political (and here we are left to our own interpretations of what his political stance might have been) are heard in images of large pointing fingers *a la* "Uncle Sam Wants You" and jet fighter pilots with thought-bubbles saying "Target Destroyed!" With American involvement in Korea and Vietnam an of-the-moment topic, these motifs can't be easily written off as aesthetic caprice any more than Picasso's references to Balkan engagements.

In the end, though, the lasting importance of these drawings lies not merely in their revolutionary appeal. Lichtenstein treated these works on paper as a category separate from his painterly enterprise, and in this sense he is a little retro in his approach. One is reminded of artists as diverse as Boucher, Ingres, and Daumier, who made definitive bodies of graphic work; artists who combined tradition and innovation in subtle ways, which by their stand-alone nature sometimes rival the paintings on which their reputations stand.

It is always a pleasure to see works in the Morgan Library, which, like the Frick or the Metropolitan Museum, adds a grandeur and history to the experience of looking at art. Although it might seem a little taxidermic to look at the work of a Pop icon in this setting, it does provide a sense of retrospective context to a moment in twentieth-century art.

Staring at the Sea

Yoan Capote: *Mental States*; Jack Shainman Gallery, New York.
Published October 30, 2010; *CultureCatch*.

In 1886 the French sculptor Fredrick Auguste Bartholdi sent aboard the ship *Isere* a large statue based on a portrait of his mother. For nearly a decade he had been working on this large-scale piece, which was to represent American Liberty, a gift from the French to the American people. By now this icon has become a familiar image, the "face" of liberty in the United States, but one must wonder sometimes how the artist came to represent this abstract concept, for a country he hadn't visited, in such a remarkably clear way.

Cuban artist Yoan Capote has given us some equally arresting icons for our America in his exhibition *Mental States*, though unlike Bartholdi he has traveled back and forth many times between New York and his native Havana. This sense of travel has imbued his work with a look that is a little less distanced, with a more familiar art vocabulary, but also creates a sense of displacement, both on the part of the artist as well as for where the art will fit in—to what culture, for what audience. Much of the works impact lies in just this no-man's-land.

A piece called *In and Out*, for example, is a brick-and-mortar sculptural recreation of the American flag—its rough sincerity offers references to both Jasper Johns and Betsy Ross. Two bronze tree-like forms, with long trunks that morph roots into human feet shod in penny loafers, remind one of Robert Gober—though the obvious metaphor of "pulling up one's roots" wears its heart on its sleeve in a way that Gober's work never does.

An enormous set of scales, set unbalanced, is entitled *Beauty and Intellect*; a minimalist set of bronze boxes, which open to reveal human sexual organs and fingers, is entitled *Beautiful People*. These rehearse familiar surrealist tropes, except that one feels that, to the artist, these are not so much surrealist as they are simple depictions from his experience. This gives these works an edge, an odd sense that we are looking in a mirror expecting to see ourselves yet surprised that the face in the reflection isn't ours. These works succeed to a large degree based on our familiarity with the references and Capote's interpretations of them.

The truly remarkable pieces in the show are not the high-production numbers, but, like *In and Out*, paintings reflecting his *Arte Povera* (poor art) approach. *Ilsa* and *Stress*, two oil on jute landscapes, exemplify the *Povera* methodology, gleaning a maximum effect through an economy of means—in this case, fish hooks, nails, and boating hooks. *Stress* depicts the midtown New York skyline in dirty grays and whites, much like a well-read newspaper photo. Heavy impasto paint is demarcated by clusters of rusted fishing hooks that bristle out from the surface, drawing the eye close and repelling it at the same time. This attraction/repulsion meshes with the city skyline: from a distance one is drawn in; once there, one is pushed out. This trope of course is a perfect metaphor for the immigrant view, although if *Stress* were the only work here, this might seem thin gruel for thought.

Ilsa, the show's standout work, plays this same game, but the rules have somehow changed. It is essentially a vast seascape, with rolling waves and a small expanse of clear sky; we are drawn into and over the water, defined by the tangled hooks, and struggle to peer past the horizon. We puzzle over the hooks again, and the emptiness of the canvas allows us this. The sea is a harsh mistress, after all. Think of The Old Man, or that other fisherman who became a fisher of men. It takes a great deal of faith to cast one's empty hook upon the sea, and even more belief that it might return filled. This is the eternal dream of the immigrant, imagining what might be "there," and the ultimate success of this painting is that it conveys that dream so well. Capote carefully leaves the horizon blank, but as we stand in front of the endless sea, we might conjure some better future place. Our city lights might be breaking over the horizon, or our whale, or our last great fish.

Sweet Leaf

Fred Tomaselli: Brooklyn Museum.
Published November 10, 2010; *CultureCatch*.

There is a wonderful scene in Pink Floyd's film version of *The Wall* where Bob Geldof, having ingested a significant quantity of everything, trashes his hotel room, carefully shaves his head (and, memorably, his eyebrows), and then proceeds to obsessively arrange the shards and fragments of the mayhem, as well as the surviving pills and drug paraphernalia, into patterns on the carpet. Fred Tomaselli has created a coherent body of collage works over the years, deploying an astounding array of painstakingly layered images embedded with an equally astounding array of drugs embedded in their resin surfaces. LSD, speed, aspirin, anti-depressants, Ecstasy, marijuana leaves, and psychedelic mushrooms are carefully aligned in patterns reminiscent of the psychedelic art of the 1960s, and also of the trashed-hotel-room-floor-sculpture of Mr. Geldoff.

Tomaselli has developed something of an audience for this work over the years. Many admirers note the labor-intensive qualities of his work, which harks back to the Pattern and Decoration movement; others are quite taken with seeing art made out of actual drugs. While Damien Hirst has also cast a veritable pharmacy of pills in resin in his sculpture, Tomaselli has attempted to elevate the medium to a pictorial art form, often with mixed results. In this show, his efforts have paid off and we are finally able to discern clarity of vision in the work, which may have been missing in the past.

One or two early works transcend the original formula (drugs arranged in a pattern, laminated in plastic) and possess a quiet resonance. *Untitled Rug* (1995) and *Black and White All Over* (1993) use the requisite caplets and leaves to mimic a Navajo rug and an Amish quilt, respectively. The juxtaposition of drugs and spirituality, and the relationships of the two, are perhaps obvious statements, but they show an underlying motif that Tomaselli has developed further in his work, with greater depth and subtlety than the early pieces reveal. Hanging near these two early pieces is *Night Music for Raptors* (2010), a simple depiction of an owl, made from hundreds of cut-out paper eyeballs. The title hunter, who hunts in the dark and is able to rotate his head, is perfectly depicted through the metaphor of the panoptic eye. There is a nod to the Italian proto-surrealist Arcimboldo in this piece as well, giving it a wonderful sense of art-historical nuance.

References to Islamic art, Op and Pop Art, Medieval decoration, and Audubon Style field guides abound, and are most effectively employed in works that have a darker edge. The rows of pills and cut-out photos of butterflies suggest something out of Buffalo Bill's dungeon in *The Silence of the Lambs*, or from John Fowles's novel *The Collector*. The theme of beauty in stasis becomes a worn trope in the weaker of the works (*Field Guides*, 2003), but dazzles and provokes in *untitled (Expulsion)* (2000).

untitled (Expulsion) brings together threads of Biblical lore in an updated style reminiscent of Bosch. Our Adam and Eve flee paradise, cast out by rays of dope, suggesting an ironic Eden as Opium Den. In the context of the Brooklyn Museum's collection of Bierstadt's, Duran's, and other Hudson River School artists, this updating of the Biblical Landscape is well timed and well placed, giving the painting an historical context.

It is particularly refreshing in this season (so far) of bombast and over-hyped installations to see the work of an artist dedicated to handcrafting precise, labor-intensive works on a small scale dealing with big, philosophical topics. Striving to make art about nature and transcendence is, apparently, still a relevant source, even if it requires a little "enhancement" in our modern times.

Stateless

Francesco Clemente: *A Private Geography*; Mary Boone Gallery, New York.
Published November 17, 2010; *CultureCatch*.

Francesco Clemente has always traversed various boundaries in his work: the geographical, personal, and sexual have all been routed through his various explorations in a multitude of media. His exhibit *A Private Geography* at Mary Boone uptown, his best in many years, proves no exception to this rule. It may be misleading to say that his work is all about the breaking down of perimeters. Instead, he renders them porous through his work and peripatetic lifestyle: He lives and works in New York, Italy, and India through various parts of the year, and works in painting, sculpture, prints, and most successfully pastel, drawing, and watercolor. Failing global economies, bad politics, and wars dominate our news; clearly the civilized world as we know it has gone to fuck; yet to judge by the luminous watercolors and pastels in this show, Clemente has emerged from them all quite unscathed.

True to the ideal notion that an artist's boundaries end at the edge of the canvas, Clemente gives us a world view as seen from the inside. And an astounding view it is. William Shakespeare wrote, "all the world's a stage," and in a suite of recent watercolors, *Actors of the Terriero* (2006), Clemente depicts it. A butterfly rests on a quill pen, poised over a scroll, unfurling over a pile of skulls (*Actors of the Terriero II*); two helmeted heads are impaled on a pike (*Actors of the Terriero VII*)—shades of *Hamlet*. A crimson robe (*Actors of the Terriero III*) and crown (*Actors of the Terriero XIV*) whisper *Macbeth*. Genet, Wells, Homer, and Beowulf . . . the list of references seems limitless: chains, spikes, bound hands, boats, and animals lend their various metaphors to the bestiary that is in Clemente's own personal steamer trunk. Another series of watercolors, *After Attar's Conference of the Birds* (2010), traces elements (birds, fire, timepieces, etc.) from Farid ud-Din Attar's poem of 30 birds and their metaphorical travels toward enlightenment.

Less engaging, perhaps because of its literalness, is a series of digital prints based on collaged maps of the world. They are reminiscent of Julian Schnabel's *Navigation Drawings*, though not as successful, perhaps lacking the touch of artist's hand that is so integral to Clemente's work. That said, they do provide a map of the mind of the artist, so to speak. Bits of antique New York maps locate the Metropolitan Museum of Art and the Brooklyn Museum (as well as Bellevue Medical Center, formerly known for its "Lunatic Asylum"). An Indian map indicates the Ran Nasar Museum; in another, the road to a Roman theater. Clearly, finding the loci of art is never far from his mind in both Clemente's internal and external roaming.

The largest work, *Irons and Rainbows* (2010), combines pastel and watercolor, Clemente's strong suits, and reminds us of his importance to the Transavangardia movement of the '80s. Individually framed pieces are linked in the form of a jigsaw puzzle, a perfect metaphor for his internal sense of mapping, and alternate pastel and watercolor in the tessellated surface. The individual elements join to form an iconic depiction of an imaginary Kali: picture a D/s Nina Hagen circa the Palladium Years, holding the leashes of two women, who hold the leashes of two more. A daisy chain, so to speak, representing the endlessness of the Universe; supported by vignettes of eggs turning into birds, snakes, and a weeping eye. A rainbow arches over and through all the drawings, formally uniting all the elements. A master of Symbolism, Clemente doesn't really explain the elements as much as present them to us, a fitting metaphor for the nature of the universality of art as a language.

Clemente the explorer isn't so much Columbus as he is Bowles; rather than seeking to co-opt the styles of the cultures that he samples, as he has done in the past, he now has absorbed them and reinterpreted them through his own aesthetic vocabulary. Not since his moving, and similarly idiosyncratic, series *The Stations of the Cross* in the early '80s has he proved so strong a teller of painterly travel stories. We find Clemente finally playing to his strengths, the ability of his work to both transfix and transform us, taking us along on his nomadic voyages, and leaving us off safely back home.

Aggressive Perfector

Joan Miró: *Miró: The Dutch Interiors*; Metropolitan Museum of Art, New York.
Published November 22, 2010; *CultureCatch*.

Two years ago the Museum of Modern Art presented *Joan Miró: Painting and Anti-Painting*, a retrospective of the Catalan artist's work from 1927 to 1937. This small slice of the painter's *oeuvre* proved to be one of the best and most intelligent shows of that year, parsing Miró's long and often repetitive years of work to get to the period that not only made him an important figure for his time, but made him an important painter for ours. Now, the Metropolitan Museum follows up this event by winnowing further the scope of works of that period and gives us just three works, called *The Dutch Interiors*, magnificent proto-surrealist pieces from his most fertile research into image deconstructing, along with preparatory studies, sketches, and most importantly two of the original Dutch masterpieces upon which they were based.

The paintings were begun after a trip to Amsterdam, where he acquired the postcard reproductions that he worked from. His rhetoric at the time reflected that of the Dadaists militaristic attacks on High Art. "I imagine to attack every day more and more thoroughly, making my victims die cleanly, without agonizing nerve spasms," he wrote of this project. "A dry blow, like lightning." One pictures Miró as the character of Dexter, from the television show, whose nocturnal dissections on his living victims he describes as "exploring" them, and yet who recoils at all the messy blood-splatter. What drove Miró in these works and is brilliantly documented in large museum wall texts and diagrams, was something akin to an autopsy of the works, whose smooth, flawless surfaces hid intricate details and nuances that he wanted to exhume for his own. About *Dutch Interior I* (1928) we learn, "[He] was seduced by the ability of the Dutch painters to make dots as tiny as grains of dust visible, and to concentrate attention on a tiny spark in the middle of obscurity." Here in one sentence we find the territory Miró will continue to mine with such success in his later *Constellations* series. His version of Marenz Sorgh's *The Lute Player* debones the musician and stretches the figure diagonally across the canvas, flaying him *a la* Hannibal Lector. The effect, however, conveys not horror but a sensuous abandonment to the music. Sorgh's lute player has a doe-eyed listener at a table laden with plump fruits, her attention rapt. Miró has turned the pleasure of playing for her into the pleasure of just playing, making this a personal recital, or if we might go further, a private performance for us.

In *Dutch Interior III* (1928), Miró cuts away the necrotic trappings of art history like a good surgeon. With his precise brushwork and hard-edged forms he eliminates atmospheric shading, flattens the planes to eliminate depth of field, and pins together the figure as if reconstructed by an interior logic. We *see* elements of a woman—breasts, arms, hands—but we *feel* the sinuous reach of her arms, the arch of her body. The splayed limbs and disjunctive anatomy suggest a reconstruction of the form, not as "idealized" but as "ideal." Harmony of (human) form trumps harmony of composition and reminds us why the Surrealists took so quickly to Miró, adopting him as one of their own. This little painting leads the way to Picasso's deconstructed women as well as to Surrealist parlor games such as "The Exquisite Corpse." Little touches like the small white dog and arrow give an absurdity to the work and point to future artists including George Condo and Peter Saul. Indeed, for an artist so driven to destroy painting, it turns out that Miró did quite a lot to resuscitate it.

The abundance of studies and sketches in the show, as well as a few ancillary paintings, adds greatly to the laboratory feel that Miró was trying to conjure. It also belies the simplicity of the final works. His fetishistic focus on "every little dot" or "reflection" is made manifest; lines, arrows, and points draw the eye through the carefully modeled yellow field. In the end, though, all of this background material, while useful for interpreting the symbols and signs of the *Dutch Interiors*, merely reinforces what the paintings already tell us: Miró was a consummate painter's painter, driven by inner need to reinvent an art for himself. If the result looks so clear and simple, it is because he did it so well.

Confusion is Next

Raymond Pettibon: *Hard in the Paint*; David Zwirner Gallery, New York.
Published November 27, 2010; *CultureCatch*.

Satire, that first cousin of Irony, has long held a high place in both literature and the visual arts. Voltaire, Boswell and Dr. Johnson, Daumier and Hogarth paved a road for the free critique of politics, social interactions, and the breaking down and understanding of class, race, and economic structures. Raymond Pettibon, who three decades ago began his career creating cover art for Post-Punk bands like The Minutemen and Sonic Youth, continues this tradition in the recent exhibition at David Zwirner.

Like his artistic influences, Pettibon combines text and image to convey a dystopic view of our late capitalist culture's obsessions with celebrity, violence, sex, and sports. His trademark slashing calligraphic line art and fragments of Marcel Proust, William Faulkner, movie lines, and Biblical passages portray America seen through a glass darkly, of mediated culture.

In the '90s Pettibon made the leap from graphic illustrator to something akin to the Bret Ellis or Charles Bukowski of the L.A. art world. His noir commentary seemed a perfect fit for the times; his screeds on paper bore an eerie similarity to the surreal "Buckethead" rant of Charles Manson. That was then and this is now; and now the cacophonous spew of pulp that is titled *Hard in the Paint* bears only a pale resemblance to the satirical wit that was Pettibon at his best. He still has his moments here: a huge decapitated head floated on an empty field of white, swirls of hair done up in some retro-'50s style dominates the composition *No Title, (5,000 strokes . . .)* (2010). The drawing calls to mind the surrealist notebook scribbles of Louise Bourgeois as well as Da Vinci's Deluge drawings. *No Title (The Invisible Man's . . .)* (2010) reads "Four years at least hopefully eight" and shows a black man, who bears a passing resemblance to Barack Obama, either wrapping or unwrapping a mummy-like bandage around a seated figure. Is the mummified person a surrogate Obama, *a la Invasion of the Body Snatchers*? The paranoia of the Tea Party Movement, the Birthers, anti-Muslim groups, etc. is alluded to with subtlety and innuendo.

This is not the case in the second gallery of the show, where this clusterfuck buries Pettibon's wit beneath a clutter of sophomoric graffiti. A wall text begins, "Obama Nig" followed by "Norman is that you," and then "My Negro Problem and Yours" on a second line. Further deconstructed ramblings follow. These eschew any attempt at coherency—and further, eliminate any direct connection to a visual element—leaving us to search the images in the gallery to make the connection (if there is one) between what we are reading and what we are looking at. A drawing of a Dalmatian dog, a zebra, and a monkey are pinned below these lines. No, really, I'm not kidding. What, if any, conclusions are we supposed to draw?

The unfortunate effect of this conceptual slackness is that it draws our attention to look harder at the individual drawings. *No Title (She must know . . .)* (2010) makes reference to the Mona Lisa, but the execution is lacking the razor sharpness on which his reputation has been based. Tired rehashes of baseball players, vintage cars, and other Californian staples seem dashed off, lazy, and worse, cranky. More the work of an aging hack illustrator than a Young Turk, they grouse "Piss off" rather than hiss "Fuck you." They no longer appear hungry, just anorexic.

Punk gave everyone the opportunity, for however brief a moment, to critique themselves and society, much like a Restoration comedy. For once being on the outside was no longer an excuse for inaction. There was no outside anymore. Pettibon, and others like him, took the words and music which was being made and gave us the image. The failure of this work now, thirty years later, is perhaps because that spirit is no longer in us, as it is no longer in him. But we can't say we weren't warned. In a work he made in the '80s he draws a Clint Eastwood figure, circa *Fistful of Dollars* (cowboy hat, poncho, cigar), and a text which reads, "Don't cry Boy. You'll understand. Even your goddam childhood idol has got to eat."

Lipstick Traces

Liz Markus: *Are You Punk or New Wave?*; Zieher Smith Gallery, New York.
Published December 5, 2010; *CultureCatch*.

Punk was about color. Puce, fuchsia, chartreuse. The colors of spray paint; the colors of cheap nail varnish and hair color. Colors abhorrent to Nature. Color represented individual choices, perhaps the last individual choice that the disempowered could actually make. The legions of those that came after missed the boat, and black became standard issue, no doubt due to the misguided apotheosis of the gormless retard Sid Vicious as the poster-boy for the movement. Liz Markus, as witnessed by her solo exhibition *Are You Punk or New Wave?* at Zieher Smith hasn't forgotten the primary role that color played in those years.

In the past Markus has used thin washes of subtle hues to pay homage to a wide variety of her artistic peers and heroes. Television idols, Color Field Abstractionists, and '80s art world "superstars" like Julian Schnabel and Jean Michel Basquiat.

Her choice of technique and subject matter always seemed a perfect fit, well-meshed, if only because they were knitted together by her genuine admiration for what she depicted. How else to explain the success of her paintings of Nancy Reagan done as if painted by Jules Olitski? To be a fan, an aficionado, was not a hobby, in her view, it was a calling. Maureen Tucker once said that The Velvet Underground had about 100 fans—but that all of them went and started their own bands. Markus has long followed this dictum, openly worshipping her idols, while never imitating them. Her work has trumped that of lesser talents, too many to list, whose wan pictures of Kurt Cobain or odes to Slayer never really rise past the level of fanzine illustrations.

Here, in her large paeans to Punks, color plays the vital role it once held, with results both witty and elegiac. Paintings of a ghostly Johnny Rotten-as-Elvis-as-painted-by-Warhol depict twinned Rottens (*Double Rotten I, Double Rotten II*, 2010). Her hand-painted version of Andy Warhol's silkscreened silver screen idol is both a homemade tribute to both musician and artist, as well as sly nod to Warhol's early hand-drawn ink illustrations of his gods, like Truman Capote. Markus eschews image reproduction as a postmodern trope in favor of something deeper, and more personal. In the paintings *Basquiat* and *Basquiat 2* (2010) she portrays the football-helmet wearing painter in earthen hues and then in faded tones, suggesting something once seen and then remembered. The poignant portraits don't seek to emulate the brash style of the artist's work, but rather pay homage to the artist himself, whose frailty was masked under the armor of his own aggressive style of painting. In these works Markus is not afraid to wear her heart on her sleeve, communicating something personal or even private, instead of presenting a rote lesson in the deconstructing of a pop image.

In another body of work actual pages of ads from magazines like Artforum are given a splashy treatment of silver glitter. Ads for once-important-now-forgotten artists, as well as some of her artistic forbearers like Sturtevant are pasted to the canvas surface like Xeroxed handbills for The Ramones at CBGBs; the text for the shows is redacted with the glitter. While not without their own aesthetic merits, these collaged pieces seem haunted more than haunting. One looks to see if she might have included an ad for herself amongst them, like any good punk would have. Her long suit is her sense of searching for a real emotional connection, so crucial in the music and art of the punk moment. The Minutemen asked, "Do You Want New Wave or Do You Want the Truth?" Markus clearly demands the second.

Achtung, Baby

Anselm Kiefer: *Next Year in Jerusalem*; Gagosian Gallery, New York.
Published December 9, 2010; *CultureCatch*.

The brilliance of Mel Brook's film *The Producers* is that the plot turns on the creation of a musical so horrifyingly bad that no one will see it—whose very appallingness is, of course, exactly what the audience was hungering for. Thus, *Springtime for Hitler* is born. We might be tempted to feel thinking along those lines went into the production of Anselm Kiefer's recent exhibit *Next Year in Jerusalem*, a crowed, operatic, and at times jaw-droppingly distasteful spectacle.

Kiefer's long career, beginning with his conceptually based performance works of the early '70s, has always walked a fine line between heart-on-the-sleeve apologism and ironic deconstruction for the National Socialist movement, the Holocaust, and a *huispot* of misguided German idealisms. Judgments about his work have often been somewhat less than pronounced because it would be unthinkable that Kiefer sought to praise, rather than bury his country's political and aesthetic past. We now find, though, with larger and larger production values, and the imprimatur of grand international exhibitions (notably the Louvre), that Kiefer's ambitions may be exceeding his moral grasp. How else to explain the centerpiece of the show, a huge, metal, walk-in gas-chamber/meat locker, filled with dozens of black and white photos of the artist dressed in his father's Nazi uniform, Sieg Heil-ing us through the front door? The photo is exhumed from an early Kiefer performance project where he visited regions and countries occupied by the Nazis, and, dressed in Dad's old togs, executed the traditional Nazi gesture (*Occupations*, 1969). An interesting bit of regression therapy, then, perhaps, but the motivation is questionable now. How do we reconcile his resurrection of this image for international consumption now? Exhibiting this image, as well as executing this gesture in Germany today, is illegal. Is this redux version a commentary on American politics, or is it rather a tasty bit of naughtiness, coy yet creepy?

Theodor Adorno wrote (and it is worth quoting at length), "To anyone in the habit of thinking with his ears, the words 'cultural criticism' (Kulturkritik) must have an offensive ring, not merely because, like the automobile, they are pieced together from Latin and Greek. The words recall a flagrant contradiction . . . [yet] the critique of culture is confronted with the last stage in the dialectic of culture and barbarism: to write a poem after Auschwitz is barbaric, and that corrodes also the knowledge which expresses why it has become impossible to write poetry today." In other words, we are fucked if we try and fucked as human beings if we don't. Yet it is this very ambition to transcend our immediate collective pasts that art strives for, and on this very moral ground that Kiefer has finally fallen victim to hubris.

Huge vitrine sculptures (*Die Sefiroth*, 2010; *Die Schechina*, 2010; *Flying Fortress*, 2010) conflate bits of Theologica Germanica, Judaism, and Gnostic mysticism in a superficial, piecemeal way. Like Damien Hirst, but dustier. It is, in fact, more imperative after Auschwitz (or Hiroshima, or My Lai, or 9/11) for our art to transcend, to take a stand. That it is barbaric is inevitable; truth is a primal thing. Equivocation, which is fey and untrue, is what Kiefer gives us, disguised as a history lesson.

Fortunately, as in the past, when Kiefer is stripped of his theatrical trappings, he proves to be a painter, and one to reckon with. Samuel Beckett, writing on the work of Watteau, could have been speaking of Kiefer's desolated landscapes (*San Loreto*, 2009–2010): "Nature and the human denizens, the unalterable alienness of the 2 phenomena, the 2 solitudes, or the solitude

& the loneliness, the loneliness in solitude . . . the loneliness that cannot collapse into solitude." Scarred, ashen, blackened vistas; ruins the color of night, or the Third Reich's Scorched Earth. Kiefer pieces them back together, resurrecting Expressionist Degenerate painting styles, and the heroic landscapes of Caspar David Friedrich. Kiefer, in a sense, is creating a golem painting. With these works we are not distracted by the heroic Sturm und Drang, but moved by the simple act of seeing, or so we might believe, what Germany looked like to a two-year-old Kiefer in 1947. At least we can hope, lest we also have found our Hitler.

Tiny Little Pieces

Charles LeDray: *workworkworkworkwork*; Whitney Museum of Art, New York.
Published December 28, 2010; *CultureCatch*.

Even in the metric age we still measure animals and things in hands and feet. So acute is our need for a haptic experience of our surroundings that the measure of the man, so to speak, is the measure of the universe. In the beautiful retrospective of the sculptures of Charles LeDray, currently on view at the Whitney Museum of American Art, we find this basic tenant upturned as we enter a Lilliputian world of very tiny things.

LeDray has spent the better part of two decades crafting a world of everyday objects, faithfully replicated in miniature. Entering the galleries of these minute versions of pottery, men's clothes and uniforms, teddy bears and furniture one finds oneself suddenly Gulliverized, made aware of one's clumsy corporeal bigness. The fourteenth-century Saint Augustine wrote: "Look and see; feel and see . . . see with your eyes . . . see with all your senses. Because [Christ] was seeking the inner sense of faith, he apprehended also the outer senses."

It is not such a stretch to attribute such a liturgical reading to LeDray's works as it might seem. Little versions of what resemble Psalm books (*Dispatch #1*, 1992, *Work Book*, 2004) and the Homely Protestant-like *Sturbridge Cobbler's Bench* (2000) lend themselves to such a Puritanical reading of LeDray's oeuvre. The very nature of his disciplined, fingers-to-the-bone method of production almost seems to illustrate the dictum "idle hands are the Devil's workshop." In fact *Ring Finger* (2004) gives us that finger worked to the bone; a carved bone replica of a human digit wearing a wedding ring. "Worked to the bone" and "to death do us part" are slyly intertwined. *Wheat* (2000) another bone piece offers the transmogrification of the Communion Host's transubstantiation into our own bone machines. Even at his pithiest we cannot shake the religious underpinnings of LeDray's work. *Family* (1985), two pint-sized plush teddy bears riding a donkey to their first Christmas is a clever Nativity rendered heartbreakingly cute.

Other toy-like pieces of teddy's and a comical kitty licking herself (*Pretty Teacher*), as well as several vitrines filled with his signature small ceramic works offer a slightly different riff on the theme of "work." Multi-tiered glass cases are packed with hand-thrown vases, plates, bowls, etc., some black and white, some faithfully recreated with colored glazes and hand-painted designs. One imagines a make-believe tea party. LeDray draws us into the world of children, whose imitation of adults is play, dressed in the trappings of grown-up work. Children learn through the simulation of adult behaviors and activities, a metaphor on some levels of how LeDray's sculptures function; art, imitating craft, imitating art. The tactile materials—velvets, clays, buttons and cloth, though rendered untouchable through their art-object status—hold such a primal place in our collective memories that although we can't actually touch them, we can imagine we feel them.

Lest we feel too burdened with a feeling of our own Sloth in the face of such industry, LeDray gives us the witty *Straightjacket* (2005), with its nod to Jack Nicholson in *The Shining*, banging away at his typewriter "all work and no play . . ."

The show concludes with *Men's Suits* (2009), an installation of small, diorama-like rooms which resemble floors of a men's department at Bloomingdales. Tiny suits, ties, clothing racks and hangers occupy two of the little sets, while the third, comprised of hampers, pallets, boxes and bins gives us Filene's Basement. Panels of fluorescent lighting hang low, illuminating the three floors of the store, creating an eerie feeling of emptiness, casting us into the role of night-shift security making the rounds. This piece, more complex psychologically, weaves all the elements of LeDray's process into one tableau. We see the racks and piles of little handmade replica clothing, the bins and boxes, carts and racks, and can imagine ourselves browsing through the tie selection. All this work, far from making Charles a dull boy, has made him a fascinating artist.

God Save The Queen

George Condo: *Mental States*; New Museum, New York.
Published January 26, 2011; *CultureCatch*.

As might be expected from the hyper-prolific Condo, his retrospective Mental States at the New Museum is a bawdy, sprawling affair. Since the early '80s Condo has continued to develop a body of work which both appropriated and expanded on artists as diverse as Picasso and Velasquez, Guston and Gorky, while striving for a hybrid sort of Pop Surrealism, peppered with subject matter like Crucifixions and Shakespearean dramas. Condo has more often than not hit his mark by accidently landing in a zone of comical, dark, whimsy. This fine exhibition backs him on this gambit by studiously trying to elevate his work to Old Master status.

Condo fills two floors of the New Museum, with examples of work from different periods of his career. As a fisher of images, Condo has always cast a wide net. The subjects of his paintings veer between Picassoid butlers, comic Christ, and the anonymous anthropoids, which Condo has dubbed "Pods." They are all unified, however, with a kind of loose, viscous, cartoony hand. His deep ties to the history of painting, and his innate sense of taking the piss out of it can be best seen by his two most recent projects: Condo's cover for Kanye West's *My Beautiful Dark Twisted Fantasy* came in five different versions; his recent portraits of Queen Elizabeth II in even more warped, yet somehow perceptive, variations. We can see what we are up against when trying to pin down such a protean artist. While he has drawn from a deep vein of art historical forebears, he has also been a canary-in-a-coalmine for both his contemporaries, artists such as John Currin and Lisa Yuskavage, and a younger generation of painters like Dana Schutz.

Condo's early forays into an appropriated Cubo-Surreal style (*The Madonna*, 1982) led to a deeper understanding of painterly abstraction. Works like *Dancing to Miles* (1987) forged a biomorphic, synthetic, all-over way of painting which was often compared, quite aptly, to Gorky and Matta. This connection was very important, as some of Condo's strongest works date from this period, done at a time in the late '80s and early '90s when Neo-Expressionist shrillness was on the wane. Eventually, though, Condo seems to have shifted his focus from such formalist concerns and returned to what had by now become a signature style, a meshing of late Cubism and *Mad* magazine's Spy vs. Spy.

Theophile Thore, writing about the work of Watteau, could have been describing Condo's paintings and their concerns over the last decade:

"To superficial observers, [he] does not seem to adhere closely to nature. This, however is his supreme merit . . . his mysterious and poetic landscapes, in his dazzling, bright skies, in the incomparable . . . figures, with the delicate and deft extremities, in the exquisite coloring of his women's complexions . . . they painted princesses, and he painted shepherdesses; they painted goddesses, and he painted women; they painted heroes, and he painted monkeys!"

Keep in mind Watteau's Pierrots and Gilles when contemplating Condo's goofy yet tortured *Macbeth*, or his more recent portraits of *HM Queen Elizabeth II* (2006). Compared to Lucien Freud's official picture of the Queen, which is a caricature in its own right, Condo gives us a popeyed Regent in garish, theatrical make-up and wig—a Paranoiac-Critical study of royalty, or shades of The Sex Pistols ("they made you a moron"). Like Watteau, his powers of transforming observed reality into something subjective, and highly personal are most effectively used on the intimate, theatrical subject. In a survey such as this it is sometimes hard to sort the wheat from the chaff although the New Museum has done an effective job gleaning. We are treated to a few too many gilded sculptural variations, more reminiscent of Koons than de Kooning.

What we ultimately take away from this exhibit is the sense of search for a contemporary way to weave together elements of past styles and subjects at a time in our history that is rapidly rendering those very elements obsolete. Condo has struck a Faustian bargain here by allowing himself to stand with the giant by posing as something of a court jester to them. He hits his targets quite often, but more importantly when he misses, he misses them in interesting ways.

Scary Monsters and Super Creeps

Jason Bard Yarmosky: *Elder Kinder*, Like the Spice Gallery, Brooklyn.
Published February 17, 2011; *CultureCatch*.

From kouros sculptures to the late self-portraits of Picasso, when artists depict the very young or the very old, questions of intent and psychology always arise, grafting themselves to the work of art. Jason Bard Yarmosky turns the tables on the usual practice of showing the blossoming of youth or the dying embers of old age by combining the two in an oddly intriguing, though deeply unsettling way.

Yarmosky paints portraits of the elderly, with an eye to the vicissitudes of old age, yet dresses them up in attire reminiscent of the boxed Hallowe'en costumes of the Spider-Man variety. On the surface they appear to be riffing on the character of the creepy old neighbor on *Family Guy*, or, more sinisterly, John Wayne Gacy and his collection of clown costumes. Harmony Korine's recent *Trashhumpers* is populated with a similar species—young actors with the prosthetic makeup of old men, wiggling dildos and drooling onto their pajamas. Here, a football-helmeted codger cradles a scotch while standing in his boxers (*Tight End*, 2011); in *Cowboy* (2011), a dark shadow obliterates the face of a potbellied man in a Stetson and vest.

There is a combination of innocence and perversity to these characters. They speak both to a sense of lost innocence and to the adult who wears the trappings of childish things in order to take innocence from the young. On a deeper, psychological level they might address questions of neoteny. Freud saw neoteny as important: the study of the undifferentiated organism, born with the potential of cognitive development, but lacking a full consciousness. Jung, too, spoke of the pure *eternus*, the boy/man: unacculturated, yet capable of feeling stigma. The little boy who refuses the passage into adulthood. Peter Pan.

While Balthus painted little Lolitas, ensconced in high-backed chairs with their knickers exposed, Yarmosky's girl/women tend toward an aging Amazonian type. *Ballerina* (2010) wears a Valkyrian helmet, *Princess* (2011) a set of Playboy bunny ears. With their sagging waddles and pendulous breasts, they seem like haunted versions of some past life. No less ominous in their undertones, though. We are reminded of those characters in *Red Dragon* and *The Dead Zone*, the mothers who create the monsters. Psychopaths themselves, they castrate and humiliate, though somehow *they* never end up being the subjects of hilarious pedophile jokes on tv cartoons.

Somehow these reflections take us far too into the darkness. And if we are to believe Yarmosky (and we want to believe), these are images also reflecting the fleeting joys of life, the eternal childhood we all carry with us. We know better than to take the word of an artist at face value, but to not in this case would deny the odd beauty he depicts. Joyce Carol Oates once wrote, "a scar is a memory stitched in flesh." And while not all our scars are on the outside, our lives are inscribed on our faces and flesh. That Yarmosky covers the roadmapped skin of his subjects with the trappings of youth may not be as insidious as it might seem. Merely a metaphor for our ceaseless, losing, battle with time.

Slanted and Enchanted

Lynda Benglis: New Museum, New York.
Published February 26, 2011; *CultureCatch*.

Since the late '60s, Benglis has been making objects and creating performance works that nominally were developing a feminist slant on Minimalist and Process art—nominally being the key word here. Although her work incorporated many of the basic tenets of the movement, there was always something inherently sexual permeating the material nature of her work. Beginning with her early latex pour pieces, *Fallen Paintings* (1968), which removed the medium from the canvas and let it pool sensuously over the floor, to the more literal *Smile* (1974), a cast-lead double dildo that she famously posed with—inserted—for an *Artforum* ad, these early works, as well as single-channel videos (*Female Sensibility*, 1973) and sets of Polaroids.

Unlike her male peers, who were obsessed with boxes, tunnels, cages, and colossal Cor-Ten steel monoliths, Benglis focused on the inevitable entropy inherent in her material. A crucial choice: she worked with metals, polyurethanes, latexes, etc., that is, media that begin as liquid and then harden.

Critical to really understanding Benglis's work is grasping how much the concept of stasis is involved. She froze the moment where something was fluid, organic, a pure potentiality, and then captured the latent tendencies of the matter when it had reached its potential. And stasis, indeed, is sexy. In an extended series of polyurethane, bronze, and aluminum pieces, she explored the making of monumental sculpture determined only by the limits of material. Even the titles suggest the erotic and sublime: *Wing* (1970), *Come* (1969-74), and *Eat Meat* (1973).

In her lesser efforts, as well, she manages to manipulate wax, cloth, and wire in ways that evoke a visceral feeling. The tableau *Paula's Props* (1975), with its architectural columns, lead Jesus, and real and faux flora, suggests dungeon decor more than a Robert Kushner installation. To give the works the credit they are indeed due, it is instructive to compare them to the somewhat overblown theoretical works of Morris, whose incessant nattering on about prisons and panopticons couched a similar penchant for an art of the physical. Benglis's five-part work *Phantom* (1971) is a phosphorescent foam series installed in a separate room. Torrents of glowing foam spill from the walls, like forensically black-light-lit semen in trajectory. They evoke waterfalls, tendrils, ectoplasm, Michelangelo's *Dying Slaves*, or Rodin's *Balzac*. Walking into the darkened room becomes an encounter for all the senses— the subtle change of light as the material loses its phosphorescence, the smell of the urethane, the disorienting light. They are complete amongst themselves, perfect forms; yet the viewer's presence seems to activate them (even if it doesn't, really).

In her most recent series of black patina bronzes (*Figure 2, Figure 5, Figure 6*, 2009), Benglis uses industrial spray insulation and wire to create forms that evoke the shapes of countries and continents, as well as bullet-riddled, black flags waving above the ashes. Haunting, given our political clime, yet their primeval sensibility suggests hope, eternal.

Heart-Shaped Box

Pablo Picasso: *Guitars 1912–1914*; Museum of Modern Art, New York.
Published March 14, 2011; *CultureCatch*.

In the course of only a few years, Pablo Picasso and his friend and colleague Georges Braque revolutionized painting through the development of Cubist Abstraction. Around 1912 or 1913 Picasso seems to have made a leap from the two-dimensional collages—a technique Braque had pioneered—bringing his own personal style of metamorphosis into three dimensions. Picasso's art, which seldom left the tether of a human or figurative referent, found a perfect metaphor in the form of the guitar.

The anthropomorphic shape of the instrument alone oozes sex (think Hendrix, Page, or White), and its assembly process echoes the cut-and-paste method of Cubist collage picture making. Picasso was always in the process of morphing figures into objects and back again—like a shape-shifting necromancer with ADD.

What is striking about this exhibition is how Picasso managed to wrest such a melodic quality out of the purely visual components. He was, by all accounts, tone-deaf, knew the lyrics to only one or two popular songs (a fragment of sheet music for a sugary pop song, *Sonnet,* appears in one collage here), and, unlike Braque, never learned to play any kind of musical instrument. The focus of the exhibition is, of course, on the two versions of the seminal guitar constructions. One, the prototype, is in cardboard; the other, in cut sheet metal. The cardboard *Guitar* (1913) was arranged in several configurations before the final metal arrangement was realized. Its variable modes of installation characterized Picasso's improvisatory way of working during the 1912–14 period covered in the exhibition.

Andre Salmon wrote of this new work when he first saw it: " . . . Picasso, leaving aside painting for a moment, was constructing this immense guitar out of sheet metal whose plans could be dispatched to any ignoramus in the universe who could put it together as well as him . . ."

The influence and impact of *Guitar*, at that time, cannot be underestimated. In fact, its importance from inception can be measured by noting the luminaries who flooded his studio to see it: the Russian Constructivist sculptor Vladimir Tatlin, Jacques Lipchitz, Duncan Grant, Clive and Vanessa Bell, art historian Roger Fry, and Gertrude Stein. xx . . .

In a sense, this interplay between fluid and fixed sculptural methods prefigured much of modern sculpture. Carl Andre, Frank Stella, or Sarah Sze are all indebted in some amount to *Guitar.* In two demure figurative works *Head of a Girl* (1913) and *Head of a Man* (1913), we are entreated to see the workings of Picasso's thought process. Here he takes the dressmaker's or guitar craftsman's paper pattern and applies it to a traditional set of "husband/wife" portraits—the kind a Rubens or Rembrandt might have painted. Signs and the markings of the guitar are just hinted at in the shapes of the lips and ears in the man's portrait . . . and wood-grained hair in the girls. Again we have a metamorphosis in the sense of diagrammed sensation—a being between states, and in flux. A sense of touch as description or index: this is soft, this is hard, this is smooth, this is rough, etc.

Already Picasso cannot resist the temptation to morph the inanimate instrument into something more living. These symbols for human characteristics, notations, or signs become interchangeable in a Mr. Potato Head way—equivalences in a sense. A feeling of god-like humor pervades these pieces, as if, after working on his guitars, and with some spare parts left over, Picasso felt it not too far of a stretch to make a man, too.

Sweet Love Falling Like A Pale Blue Light

Adam Marnie and Dawn Cerny: SEASON, Seattle, Washington.
Published Spring 2011, show catalog.

[Cast]

Adam Marnie/Boy on Subway
Dawn Cerny/Girl on Subway/Girl in Hotel Room
Robert Yoder/Man in Hotel
Bradley Rubenstein/Hotel Clerk
Ian McShane/Male Prostitute at Gas Station
Robert Colvert/Gas Station Attendant
Marion Bartlett/Caril Ann's Stepfather
Velda Bartlett/Caril Ann's Mother

[Second Unit]

Betty Jean Bartlett/Marion and Velda's Daughter
Robert Jensen/Carol King's Boyfriend
Carol King
C. Lauer Ward
Clara Ward/C. Lauer Ward's Wife
Merle Collison/Traveling Salesman

[Scene I] Handwritten in margin: "I am not going to lie to you I kind of hate myself now"

[Soundtrack: Bruce Springsteen "Nebraska"]

[Male V.O.]:

And it's a story that might bore you but you don't have to listen, she told me, because she always knew it was going to be like that, and it was

[Jump Cut]

[Hotel Room]

We pan in on Girl, sitting on bed, wearing only panties, smoking, box of tissues in her lap. She takes one and:

GIRL: I jumble up words and letters. I can't tell when words are left out or unnecessary or spelled so poorly specialists need to be called in—to say nothing of my humiliating tendency towards grammar. It can take a half an hour to write one paragraph. It can be especially painful when it comes to articulating something I really mean—So now I confess my deepest shame is being put with the English as a second language kids, the autistic kids, and the kids with developmental problems for special tutoring . . . that no matter how hard I worked—never seemed to make things more easy. My deepest shame is tied up with a fear of not being able to communicate with ease—and then being singled out for it. Remember how over the summer I railed against Alex for using his "personal language" as being selfish and lazy—maybe I was just jealous.

Not that I think either of you give a fuck if I miss-spell things or make grammatical errors—I think that it is valuable for me to confess because I think that my struggle and desire to connect is largely at the root of the shame I am interested in.

This last weekend on the train down to Portland D.W. and I are on the same car as this bachelorette party—these women were fucking cunts. They started with tanning, moved to make-up, went to waxing, diets, after a few drinks started bashing the sexual proclivities of their so-called friends. They never listened to each other, they never connected, and there was at no point personal confession let alone any verbal self-reflexive articulation of how evil they may have sounded to the other 15 people (and 4 kids) on the train car. It was so startling to me that I started thinking about the delicacy of shame in our societal eco system. At its worst shame is a crippling affliction that rules your ego and leaves you filled with anger at the world. Shame, at its best, is a measured way of being

PAGES MISSING

[Judy comes up looking for the baby. She looks around the side, over the edge, and even up in the air. Punch is looking very sheepish at the side of the booth.]

Judy: Mr Punch, where is the baby? What's happened to the baby?

Punch: He was such a noisy baby.

Judy: Mr Punch! What have you done with the baby?

Punch: He fell out the window. [Punch uses his hands to mime the action.]

[Laughter]

Judy: [Repeating Punch's actions.] You threw him out the window? Mr Punch, you can't throw the baby out the window!

[Laughter]

I'm going to have to teach you a lesson. [She starts chasing Punch around the booth hitting him with her spoon.]

Punch: Stop it! Stop it!
[Punch dodges. Judy hits the side of the stage instead and looks around for Mr Punch.]

Judy: Mr Punch! Where have you gone? Come back here! You haven't learnt your lesson yet.

[Punch then pops up on the other side of the stage with his stick. Punch and Judy exchange blows.]

Punch: Now me teach you a lesson!

Judy: Mr Punch, that's not the way to do it. Stop it! Stop it!

[Laughter. Applause.]

[Soundtrack: Church of Misery "Badlands"]

PAGES 27–40 MISSING

Subway car. Boy and girl seated. Boy (Trent Reznor/Kurt Cobain type) wearing T-Shirt that reads: YOU CAN FUCK ME WITHOUT A CONDOM BECAUSE I'M DEAD INSIDE ALREADY

DELETED SCENE

[Girl's V.O.]:

Shame is a strangely graceful system of checks and balances—one's consciousness checking in with ideas about good and evil. Overcoming it is a profound act of tenderness and in the face of the deepest of fears. It is this reconciliation of shame and fear (the thing that I consider the "hole" or the unknown) that tenderness, grace, forgiveness bring. One cannot experience that kind of tenderness if they don't admit they have fucked up. It is in the abstract space of the hole or the grotesque that I can begin to reconcile my relationship with reality. I think this is why I keep coming back to the Pieta—the gruesomeness of Mary, a mother, holding her son's bloody body on her lap after he had been crucified after so many milky images depicting The Madonna and Child. She holds him like a baby and greaves although the act of his death was of a gift, a sacrifice—all we can see is one body tending to another.

The flowers and the vase strike a similar cord: an offering. Offerings are not exclusively made when something is "wrong" (a death, a fight, sickness) they are also made to appease (Thank you very much for having us to dinner, that was very nice of you, fuck you very much) The vase is a hole, a vessel, sometimes a means for decoration but mainly a means for presentation of an offering.

[Smash Cut]

[Offscreen]

"Fuck you."

"No, fuck you!"

"NO. FUCK. YOU."

[Soundtrack: Glass breaking, sobbing]

(beat) "Are you proud of yourself now?"

[Fade to Black]

SCENE MISSING/Handwritten on separate page: "Keep up the good work! :-)"

[Gas Station]

We see Boy at the counter, buying cigarettes. Talking to ATTENDANT.

BOY: I don't know. Killing just stopped being fun anymore.

BOY begins to cry. And we:

Page 51

(Handwritten in margin: "Why didn't you call me you fucking prick! I NEVER should have [indecipherable]")

[V.O./Boy from Subway]

I am working on moving past the surface . . . that is, the surface is not labored over and fondled. Form: cobbled, or slouchy. I am wondering about something for people to stick their hands in . . . like a vase filled with . . . Mentos? I don't know? Xanax? Condoms? I keep thinking about your experience. Or your hands in a vase getting the car keys. I remember finding washed out porn magazines in some bushes behind the school with some friends—and feeling delight and creepy—thinking about the people who "stashed it" and the men who were posing. I remember in the 5th grade when Josh Townsand passed the dictionary to me while keeping his finger pointing at the word "cunt" but never said anything to me. Josh died in Afghanistan two years ago and after reading about it in the New York Times I wrote his twin brother an email that makes me cringe every time I think about it. I think about overhearing a group of guys say I was a "faggot," teachers asking me to dance during the slow songs at Jr. High dances, Davin Kovel telling everyone I went to the retard room for tutoring, or punching Matt Shaw's face when he was beating up someone smaller than him—how he called me a cocksucker for the next four years and making me cry really hard in science class. Now I think about how I connect strongly with too many people because I would rather die than make someone feel bad or left out—this makes me a liar and I feel shame about that too, but still I turn to her, my eyes interested, and

[FADE TO BLACK]

Credits roll:

Poker Face

Paul Cézanne: *Cézanne's Card Players*; Metropolitan Museum, New York.
Published March 19, 2011; *CultureCatch*.

The Metropolitan Museum of Art's small survey of Cézanne's Card Players series highlights three versions or variations of the seminal painting. Although it is indisputable that much of Cézanne's concerns in this group of works—indeed in much of his painting—were formal ones, here we see into these pieces something of the psychology that Picasso and Giacometti called "Cézanne's anxiety."

We might see this as his anxiety over trying to depict the human figure, from the point of view of The Modern Artist. Making and unmaking at the same time; taking apart elements of the body and reassembling them in much the same way that the Industrial Age began to compartmentalize and utilize a growing human workforce. Man might only be created once, yet in the Machine Age, once formed, could be endlessly modified.

Cézanne's project from the outset had been to take the rational and scientific elements from the Impressionists' School and elaborate on them, with his own idiosyncratic notions of form. The Impressionists had taken ideas from contemporary scientific theories, which had analyzed sunlight, discovering that instead of being a single ray, consisted of a complex wavelength spanning a spectrum from red to violet, like a rainbow. For them this had opened up new systems of color, and many artists, like Seurat and Signac, devoted their careers to capturing the nuances of how light envelopes and describes the objects we see. In order to achieve these effects they set down small patches of pure hue, simulating the fleeting effects of light on surfaces outdoors. In doing so, they ameliorated 500 years of studio-constrained painting by working directly from nature.

Cézanne developed these ideas further; his *Card Players* reject the received notions of the time, such as accepted false theories of perspective and composition. He believed that the Impressionists lacked a certain amount of discipline and could not build a strong enough aesthetic to rival schools of the past. Color alone was not enough for his project; Form would also have to be attacked in order to restructure the feeling of shape in a pictorial space.

The three variations of *Card Players* don't represent three distinct persons at the table. Nor do we get much of a sense of an impending drama or event occurring or about to happen. In fact, in much the same way that the cards are presented turned away from us, the personalities of these men are kept in check, largely hidden like a hand of cards. There is, as in much of Cézanne's work, particularly when the subject matter includes women and bathers, a persistent, embarrassed concern with the figure on display. In the paintings here, Cézanne shows such reserve that we begin to see the figures less as peasants at play and more as abstract forms. This, in large part, allows the sense of painterly space to open up, giving us a fresh view, a new way of seeing. By taking apart the elemental aspects of a traditional figure–ground composition, with its perspectival illusionism, Cézanne has shown us that we might better see into his painting by following its elements piece by piece through the work, like Hansel and Gretel chasing a trail of breadcrumbs.

Eugène Delacroix, writing on the works of Shakespeare, could have just as easily been describing Cézanne's methodology: "He adds or subtracts, adapting his material to suit his purpose, giving you people created out of his imagination, but real for all that. This is a sure sign of genius . . . his inventiveness is inexhaustible, he knows how to combine the *true* with the *ideal*."

Night in the Ruts

Karen Kilimnik: *my walk in the woods at night*; 303 Gallery, New York.
Published April 6, 2011; *CultureCatch*.

We can feel the slipping away of old forms of knowledge, of practice, of gathering the necessary information. How vast was our collective iconography once. Ancient ceramic and stone epics from Greece and Rome, Prussia, and Egypt. Vivid Christian depictions of the Middle Ages; stories told through symbols: the Ox for Luke, the Lion for Mark, the Eagle for John. The serpent, the peacock, the cross and crown. Masaccio's *Adam and Eve* or Goya, with his *Caprichos*, transmitted something essential about our existence—a record, getting a bead on something, and lesson, all at once. Picasso's *Guernica* was possibly the last work to make such a statement. Or Julian Schnabel's series *The Recognitions*.

At 303 Gallery, Karen Kilimnik shows *The Hellfire Club Episode of the Avengers* (1989), an installation based on the sixties television series. The installation is an assemblage of Xeroxes, photographs, velvet, and black-and-white drawings of British manor houses. Kilimnik filters the iconography of the television show through her own perspective—gleaning gold frames, mirrors, eerie cobwebs, and an axe, presented as if relics from another era.

This sense of retrospection is apparent even in her more recent photographs. *my walk in the woods at night* (sic) is a spooky image of a moon glowing through a forest of trees. *Dirty Snow/Oscar de la Renta gown* might be a commentary on the fleeting nature of style. A *memento mori* or vanity piece. Kilimnik shifts back and forth through icons and styles (including her own) in a restless attempt to find the knowledge, the subject, the information. This to-and-fro-ing gives us a kaleidoscopic view of both the artist's mind at work as well as our own disconnected way of seeing today.

The problem with trying to depict such disparate subject matter, especially as filtered through the medium of old reruns, is that we have lost much of the essential vocabulary needed to decode and understand the information we are seeing. We are prone to dismiss this condition by blaming television, the internet, media in general, Hollywood, etc. And we might not be totally wrong. But these are not the guilty parties. The media have been tried, so to speak, many times and been found wanting, though not necessarily guilty. They all, in their intrinsic ways, possess aspects of production that involve the exercise of judgment, intellect, creativity, and taste. The Gentle Reader will please note that this is a column for an online magazine.

We can't dismiss the work of Kilimnik out of hand. (Nor, indeed, do we want to. It is good.) But missing at its heart is a sense of belief in itself, in our age.

When we read of Cennino Cennini saying specific prayers for the mixing of specific colors and glazes, we are tempted to laugh. To be amused by his quaint sincerity. Lest we mock too quickly, was he not also, in his own way, seeking the same knowledge—information— necessary for his painting that Kilimnik is seeking for her work? Maybe we are asking too much. After all, we will ultimately get the art and the artists that we deserve for our time. And Kilimnik, like all artists since forever will seek out the information she needs.

World of Skin

Berlinde De Bruyckere: *Into One-Another to P.P.P.*; Hauser & Wirth, New York. Published April 19, 2011; *CultureCatch*.

"What a piece of work is man! How noble in reason! How infinite in faculty! In form and moving how express and admirable! In action how like an angel! In apprehension how like a god! The beauty of the world! The paragon of animals! And yet, to me, what is this quintessence of dust? Man delights not me, no, nor woman neither . . ." Hamlet's despair. The existential dilemma. Before his untimely death at the hands of a trick gone bad, the Italian filmmaker Pier Paolo Pasolini (*The Gospel According to Matthew*, *Accattone!*, and *Salò*) captured the ruins of post-WWII Italy—and the metaphoric inner decay of its people—by showing the beauty of man corrupted. Belgium artist Berlinde De Bruyckere pays homage to Pasolini and the history of Northern Renaissance masters in the exhibit *Into One-Another to P.P.P.* currently at Hauser & Wirth, New York.

In his films, Pasolini presents his distrust of all things beautiful—his desolate housing project settings, his rent-boy pretty actors, even his choice of material, all seemed to point to an inherent vice in the fabric of humanity. Beauty, no matter how divine, his works seemed to say, will be paid for eventually. Blood In. Blood Out. This reckoning was at the heart of the Northern European Renaissance also. In contrast to the Italians with their celebration of Beauty, their glorification of the figure, and their theatrical scenes, artists such as Dürer, Rogier van der Weyden, and Jan van Eyck depicted a harder, colder, more tempered view of humanity.

De Bruyckere has combined Pasolini's interest in Catholic ritual, Renaissance painting (though he also had a fondness for Francis Bacon), and literature into a series of drawings and sculptures that depict life-sized figures in various states of flayed grandeur. In three pieces entitled *Into One-Another to P.P.P.* (2010–2011), life casts of dancers writhe, twist, and sprawl, exhausted, like the cast-off flesh of St. Bartholomew, or Buffalo Bill's victims in *The Silence of the Lambs*. Gray, exsanguinated, and waxy, the flesh of these beings reflects the pallor of a van Eyck or van der Weyden painting. *Into One-Another II* (2011) is a tangle of flayed flesh and tree branches, suspended on a makeshift stretcher; presumably a fresh kill dragged out of a watery grave, much like the first victim Detective Starling encounters. Like Buffalo Bill, De Bruyckere seems driven to create not out of a sense of hatred for humanity, but out of an internal sense of what Ideal Beauty really is.

Taking things apart and putting them back together, *a la* Rodin or Dr. Frankenstein, drives the sculptures. In her accompanying drawings, De Bruyckere ventures into the animal kingdom, combining the figure with such animal elements as deer antlers. *Romeu My Deer* (2011) and *The Wound* (2011) suggest lessons learned from Joseph Beuys, who said of his references to stags, bees, and hares:

> The hare is directly related to birth . . . For me the hare is a symbol of
> incarnation. In reality, the hare does what man can only do mentally:
> digging inside, digging a construction, a grave . . . Humans are able to think,
> to propose ideas, not to produce honey . . . In this way the deathly nature
> of thinking becomes vital again . . . human thought can be alive, although it
> can also be intellectualized to the point of death through the same process,
> and may remain dead, expressing its cadaverous nature in politics and
> pedagogy.

De Bruyckere, like Beuys, points to an alternate view of humanity; though tortured in execution, it suggests the potential of rebirth, transformation, and hope.

American Caesar

Jasper Johns: *New Sculpture and Works on Paper*, Matthew Marks Gallery, New York.
Published May 6, 2011; *CultureCatch*.

Woody Allen once said that he didn't want to achieve immortality through his art; he wanted to achieve it through not dying. The octogenarian Jasper Johns has seemingly pulled off the ultimate hat trick, managing to do both. *New Sculpture and Works on Paper* at Matthew Marks Gallery, New York presents the already-immortal Johns's third major show since the death of his legendary dealer Leo Castelli.

The works presented here are ambitious; cast bronze rectangles contain myriad symbols both personal and historical, as any Johns's painting of the past would. Not to say that these are typical Johns's works, rather, they might be called typical *late* Johns's works. His last exhibit of paintings, entitled *Catenary* (a catenary is the curve that a rope or chain makes when hanging from two points), seemed to mark a self-imposed good-bye, with their dignified references to the cosmos, his own painting, and a goofy reference to the way a fishing line hangs from the pole (as in "Gone fishin'. So long, see ya tomorrow . . ."). In his new work we hear the same funereal march, but it is a little more insistent. Johns's paintings, beginning with the early Flags and Targets always contained a note of seriousness within them, with the lush reticence of their frozen brushstrokes. They marked an end of an era in art (though a beginning of a new one in his); his pictures of "things the mind already knows" were elegies for something lost. The poetry that others found in his work wasn't that he could take an old idea and make it new— rather, he could take new ideas (about art, or life) and make them seem eternal.

What lends a certain amount of pathos to these sculptures is how insistently they drive home the idea of *permanence* (bronze) and *immortality* (they resemble nothing so much as a Greek funerary *stele*, an Egyptian tomb frieze, or the black monolith in *2001: A Space Odyssey*. During the Dynastic Periods in Egyptian art themes of animals, nature, and warfare were carved on tomb walls to accompany the dead of high status or great wealth on their journey. These three themes can be viewed as the expression of a Pharaonic world-view; a Divine ruler guaranteed the functioning of this mortal realm by dominating these forces, keeping them in balance. The images in these reliefs were depictions of rituals and offerings (wine, animals, etc.) that would provide the dead Pharaoh with everlasting sustenance. Here Johns's mimics the registers of this ancient form, but rather than stock his *steles* with rich fare, he gives us numbered panels. At first we might think our visual cupboards are bare; then we remember that numbers were always one of Johns's stocks-in-trade. Repetition (of numerals, of alphabets) was, for Johns and his colleagues, an approach to a transcendent form of seeing. In these recent works we are again reminded of his Cheever-like sensibility, the gift of seeing something metaphoric in the most rote and mundane. A philosophy of boredom. David Foster Wallace summed up Johns's work when he wrote: " . . . something that's dull or opaque . . . provide[s] enough stimulation to distract people from some other, deeper type of pain that is always there, if only in an ambient low-level way, and which most of us spend nearly all our time and energy trying to distract ourselves from . . . true freedom means being conscious and aware enough to choose what you pay attention to and to choose how you construct meaning from experience. Because if you cannot exercise this kind of choice . . . you will be totally hosed."

Standing on a Beach

David Salle: *New Paintings*; Mary Boone Gallery, New York.
Published June 2, 2011; *CultureCatch*.

It was not that long ago that David Salle seemed to strike a collective nerve with his simulations of paintings: for some, he resurrected Painting; for others he fucked its necrotic corpse. Among critics he was praised for revivifying the art form, along with his colleagues Julian Schnabel and Eric Fischl, and vilified by feminist critics for his reified soft-core porn subject matter. Artist and writers such as Peter Halley and Mira Schor drew up highly articulate sides in the battlefields that Salle called paintings.

At Mary Boone Gallery, Salle emerges from over a decade of forays into film, set decors, and Rosenquist-like billboards with a new series that grafts together elements of his earlier works with panels depicting an empty seascape set with Adirondack beach chairs.

In works such as *Time is a Frame* (2010) and *The Mennonite Button Problem* (2010), Salle employs the trope of amateur porn photography and combines the blurry images of lingerie-clad women in uncomfortably torqued positions with blankly limned pictures of meat and boats. Twenty years ago such post-modern painterly shenanigans seemed wildly misogynistic (meat=women=object) to some; to others it represented the end-game of visual depiction—one of these things is not like the others (to paraphrase *Sesame Street*.) Perhaps the idea of redoing his own works is part of a strategic effort on Salle's part. How better to show how bankrupt our collective image bank is than by cribbing from his own work? What strikes a note of pathos, though undoubtedly unintentional, is just how far our porn has come in the internet age. One imagines trying to explain to young viewers what is going on here and having to answer their imploring queries: "Why isn't the naked lady moving?" or, "Why isn't she sucking six cocks?" The media that Salle once seemed to navigate with such knowing skill has far outstripped him. He is hoist on the petard of his own irony.

In the painting *Camus* (2010), Salle employs two motifs he used to great effect in the past: The name of the author of *The Stranger* is deployed over an image of a reclining woman, a riffing on his painting *Tennyson* from the eighties. Salle also incorporates a red velvet rope, dipping in front of the picture plane, as if to keep us, the riff-raff, at bay. A real light bulb protrudes in front of a panel of photographic tree branches, glimmering like a dying sun peeking through a wintery forest. Haunting. Yet, somehow, in spite of himself Salle seems to have hit on a kernel of art in this work. Like his add-on panels of the empty seascape, which remind us of Meursault killing the Arab on the sickeningly hot beach, we feel a gnawing emptiness in front of these works. Not empty in the sense that Salle might wish us to feel; that is, hollow from the dizzying array of things and images we are assailed with every day. Rather, we feel a void not filled by the empty calories that these anemic gestures contrived as art give us.

Our empathy is piqued by knowing, irony of ironies, that Salle *meant* these works to be seen as real art all along. Like Meursault, he is ultimately unrepentant for perpetrating these objects upon us, and, in the end, we must be grudgingly appreciative of the patience that it took him to drive home his point. Looking past the wooden chairs out into the empty sea, we feel his absolution. "As if that blind rage had washed me clean, rid me of hope; for the first time, in that night alive with signs and stars, I opened myself to the gentle indifference of the world. Finding it so much like myself—so like a brother, really—I felt that I had been happy and that I was happy again. For everything to be consummated, for me to feel less alone, I had only to wish that there be a large crowd of spectators the day of my execution and that they greet me with cries of hate."

Swimsuit Edition

Willem de Kooning: *The Figure: Movement and Gesture*; Pace Gallery, New York.
Published June 10, 2011; *CultureCatch*.

The Pace Gallery exhibit *The Figure, Movement and Gesture* focuses on his painterly transformation from abstraction to figuration and back again. "The figure," de Kooning once said, "is nothing unless you twist it around like a strange miracle." Twist it he did, contorting it into pastoral landscapes, creating a new style of painting and blurring the boundaries of representation and abstraction.

The legend of de Kooning has overwhelmed our collective memories, our subconscious, and become the *sine qua non* of "the artist's artist," tortured, scrabbling to the top. Although this may have served him well once, it obscured our vision. Seeing these works dispels some of the myth and allows us to see for ourselves their importance.

De Kooning spoke of his work as "slipping glimpses," moments captured in paint, caught while he tried to nail down reality—a reality as he saw it. This "de Kooningism" (English was his second language) was his way of trying to define an art practice that eluded the vernacular of his time.

His ways with paint were the old ways, and his attacks on panel and canvas (the stuff of sails) were bound to stagger toward the heroic. He had jumped ship from the old country, a stowaway, and escaped the drunken, child-abusing mother only to come to the new world and marry the painter Elaine Fried, another alcoholic succubus. He was fascinated by popular culture and American beauties, both on and off the silver screen. They didn't even have to be real, as his paintings of Minnie Mouse and Betty Boop-like celluloid hotties attest. It is no wonder that the theme of Women dominated his pictorial activities. The high-heeled fire-crotch *Woman* (1969), an outstanding oil on canvas, seems so fresh and pulsing we might be tempted to mistake it for a portrait of Lindsay Lohan. A large oil on paper, *no title* (1970–77), has the goofy sexiness of Betty Rubble.

De Kooning moved to the Hamptons from Manhattan in 1963. In his new studio, he painted figures that were different from his urban-influenced, wild-eyed, and toothy harpies from the 1950s. In contrast to the dark charcoal and black enamel that bound the corpulent Monroe-esque earlier works, brushstroke and color were freed in his new beachcomber-inspired babes. As he began to describe motion through paint (girls digging clams, splashing in the surf), the distinction between figure and ground diminished, until woman was no longer differentiated from landscape.

This is the focus of de Kooning's work from the late sixties onward: sweaty, tanned, semi-clad girls on Long Island beaches. It may seem silly now; we've been weaned on beach girls (the East Coast ones are hip, I hear). Pink skin too fair for the sun; tanning flesh with sand dusting it like a cinnamon-sugar doughnut, sunbaked and oily. Salty. Wet. Sweaty. Cocoa butter and Coppertone. But that is us, and we are not (yet) 60, with memories of the Netherlands (do they even have beaches?) and that stowaway journey to a faraway, unimagined country. Imagine, if it is even possible, how de Kooning must have seen those girls on the beach and wanted to make them his through paint. We don't, actually, have to tax our imaginations. *Montauk II, Montauk V* (1969), and *Two Figures III* (1968). The closest thing we'll ever see to pure fucking lust on canvas.

De Kooning, whatever his genius or shortcomings as an artist (that is not our place to judge today), had one saving grace throughout his career: frank, utter sincerity; sometimes brilliant, sometimes awkward and misplaced. Unlike Pollock, he was unafraid of letting his passion rule his brush. We must be grateful, for he let us in, shared all. Yes, this is a show of great Art, but de Kooning gave us more; paint breaking like great waves on some wilder shores of love.

Drums Along the Mohawk

Mark Grotjahn: *Nine Faces*; Anton Kern Gallery, New York.
Published June 14, 2011; *CultureCatch*.

For nearly a century the search for the Primitive, the essential, untouched-by-civilization essence of Man, drove artists as diverse as Ensor to Picasso in their Modernist depictions. Apparently, this Conradian pursuit has not been completely exhausted, as the recent works of Mark Grotjahn at Anton Kern demonstrate.

"It was a distinct glimpse: the dugout, four paddling savages, and the lone white man turning his back suddenly on the headquarters, on relief, on thoughts of home—perhaps; setting his face towards the depth of the wilderness, towards his empty and desolate station." Conrad's narrator, Marlowe, in paddling down the Congo in search of Kurtz, finds that he brings the seeds of corruption to the innocent savages that he has come to survey. In a similar vein, Grotjahn, with these paintings, seeks to bring a sense of purity, geometry, and order to the simple depiction of a human face but shows that such a task is insurmountable (at best) and fuck-headed (at worst). Grotjahn has for several years been creating paintings that search for an almost antiquated sense of symmetry and order. A geometry that is predicated on a very Modern sense of balance as its First Principle. His *Butterfly* paintings, largely monochrome, sought to create a sense of proportion that ultimately was, like their titular, short-lived inspiration, undermined by the impossibility of such perfection.

In these works, such as *Untitled (Lotus Paul Signac Face 41.31)* (2010), Grotjahn begins with a rough sketch of a human face (whether or not he actually has depicted a likeness of the French Post-Impressionist artist is probably beside the point) and then proceeds to scarify, with paint, strokes that begin to resemble a peacock feather pattern over the portrait. Does he mean to suggest a semblance between his own OCD working method and the pseudo-scientific formulations of Signac? Or is this ritualized overpainting some sort of Freudian death-of-the-father painterly act? Picasso internalized what was then known as Primitive Art: Iberian and African sculpture, Egyptian tomb statues, etc. and then transformed them, albeit with great prejudice, into individualized works. *Les Demoiselles d'Avignon* comes to mind. Braque, his partner in Cubism, took such activity with a grain of salt, stopping short of absorbing Picasso's superstitious practices but still using some motifs found in African art. What we find with Grotjahn is a return to the colonialization of art, as embodied by Conrad (or, in the visual arts, his contemporary Ensor), where the artist grafts his own interpretation of "the Primitive" over an underlying structure of already-generic Western Art (read: the portrait). *Untitled (Geo Abstract Reveal Face 41.61)* (2011) is as good an example as any other. The Futurist/Cubist/Rayonist strokes pile up, like tribal tattoos, until the original premise of the painting is obscured beneath a train wreck of paint.

It isn't that these paintings are bad. That is the unfortunate part. It is, like the project that they nominally seek to illustrate, that they aren't clear. Or, rather, maybe we have reached a point in history that has rendered the possibility of such clarity impossible. We can admire Grotjahn for attempting such a journey—much as we admire Conrad/Marlowe for his—with the understanding that it was pointless, doomed to fail, from the outset. The horror. The horror.

Pretty Tied Up

Alexander McQueen: *Savage Beauty*; Costume Institute, The Metropolitan Museum of Art, New York.
Published June 14, 2011; *CultureCatch*.

Polonius said it best: "Clothes maketh the man—but make sure they are quality, not flashy . . . and above all to your own self be true . . ." For those who have been buried under a rock for the last fifteen years, or, perhaps more likely, locked in their Master's dungeon, McQueen's sartorial splendors may come as something of a shock. To those of us who have followed the career of Aimee Mullins (below-the-knee paraplegic, model/actress/athlete), admired Prince Charles's Savile Row suits, watched Björk on the red carpet, or seen Lady Gaga (Six Million People Can't Be Wrong), this exhibition may seem more overdue than revelatory. Oh, yeah. *Alexander McQueen: Savage Beauty*, is at New York's Costume Institute through August.

How do we describe the protean McQueen? He drew his fashion inspiration from a deep well of art, but what he produced became Culture. Not since Coco Chanel or Halston have we seen a designer whose attention to detail—from the fabric, to the hat, to the shoes, to the presentation—rivals that of McQueen. He appeared almost *sui generis* (unless one might consider that the Marquis De Sade mated with Chanel and kept the subsequent issue chained under the Council House kitchen sink for sixteen years). McQueen served his apprenticeship sewing "Charles is a Cunt" into the linings of the Prince of Wales's Savile Row suits while designing his first collections. His models—at his shows, as well as on their Met recreations— were fitted with BDSM accoutrements: bruises on arms, ligature marks on wrists, etc.

It only got better from there. His choice of the model Aimee Mullins, a longtime participant in the performances of Matthew Barney, as his first inspiration for shoe design speaks volumes. McQueen designed not only the shoes she wore, but also the legs, as she is a double amputee. McQueen carved the shoe-leg combo to complement her ensemble, *No. 13* (spring/summer 1999), adding an additional two inches to her height for the runway show. Clothes maketh not the man, indeed, but legs are a different story.

McQueen had sensitivity to period and tone: Victorian photography, with its subtle hints of death masks and spirit photography provided the milky washed-out tones of an early "line." We use this term loosely; McQueen was only bespoke. McQ, that House that exists today, bears as ghostly a semblance to his work as does the spirit photo to the subject.

Bondage, Punk, Scottish tartans followed, each year bringing new inspiration, yet all tied together (no pun intended). *It's Only a Game* (spring/summer 2005), included a series of Obi-inspired (American) football uniforms, which morphed East and West and was inspired by *To Sir, with Love*. *Widows of Culloden* (autumn/winter 2006–2007) gives us a holographic Kate Moss, engulfed in flowing white, twirling eternally, the ultimate Goth waif. With a soundtrack from *Schindler's List*. Further references punctuate his collections, such as to *Story of O*, and *Taxi Driver*. An early collection, *Taxi Driver* (autumn/winter 1993–1994), introduced "bumsters," which reveal the end of the spine and top of the arse, his favorite part of the body.

No detail escaped his shows—too many to list. Handel's *Sarabande, God Save the Queen*, and Björk all bring a texture of sound; haunting, when queuing through the rows of gimp-masked mannequins. As one who attended early shows of McQueen's work (fuck, they'd let anyone in back then, apparently), I was always struck by how much attention he gave to hats and masks and veils. As if to both obliterate the predominant fashion for supermodel faces, as well as to revive the punk ethos of identity. We were all ugly; we were all the same. That was the thing that McQueen brought to the runway: stiff little fingers attitude.

This served Lady Gaga well. Shy, not particularly beautiful, McQueen designed headwear to both obscure and protect her fragility, armor for her expulsion into public life. Lady Gaga was perhaps his finest creation. The alien and armadillo shoes, the slave veils. If he designed it, she wore it, and it became another icon.

Fashion and death and tragedy are often intertwined. Just close your eyes and try to remember the color of Jackie's pillbox hat.

Southern Man

Cy Twombly: *Sculpture*; Museum of Modern Art; New York.
Published July 14, 2011; *CultureCatch*.

Men, like trees, wrote Abraham Lincoln, are best measured when down. With the passing of Cy Twombly last week at age 83, we may finally begin to count the rings.

Sculpture, now at The Museum of Modern Art, is an opportunity to examine the lesser-known three-dimensional works of the American painter.

Twombly is best known for his scratchy, graffitied canvases, whose subject matter ranged over centuries of classical myths, great battles, and, in his final series *Bacchus*, giant wine-colored flowery shapes. His signature style, a combination of handwriting, scribbles, and Ab Ex gestures, can be sampled at MoMA in *Leda and the Swan* (1962), hanging near the start of the exhibition. Last week's eulogizing of Twombly brought forth great ejaculations of praise for his influence on artists from Beuys to Basquiat. Numerous articles noted his long-held interest in Poussin (he is paired with him at the Dulwich Picture Gallery in London currently) and his attempts to capture something of the architectural theatricality of Poussin's paintings in his own work. Looking at his seemingly random, effete scratchings, one might be tempted to ask, Poussin? On what fucking planet?

His sculpture is a different kettle of fish. Solitary, dramatic forms, comprised of found objects like wood, wire, and plastic flowers (*untitled*, 2005) huddle together in the small museum gallery. It is Delacroix who best explains Twombly's relation to Poussin when he writes "Poussin . . . planted his figures side by side, like statues—he did this habit of making small models so as to get the shadows correctly? But although he may have gained this advantage, I should be more grateful to him if he had attained a more closely linked relationship among his figures."

Works like *By the Sea* (1988) and *untitled/Funerary Box for a Lime Green Python* (1954) could have been on Delacroix's mind. Small pieces of wood (Twombly's sculpture, unlike his paintings, have an intimate, human scale) are patinated with white paint ("White paint is my marble," Twombly said once). Seeing them arranged together like little puppets on a stage gives one a feeling of story and narrative that Twombly's paintings purport to have but often lack. We also see Twombly's sense of wit concerning history with a cut-out heart in the ice-cream-soda shaped *untitled* (2005), which has SNAFU scrawled across it. SNAFU, a military acronym for "situation normal all fucked up," reminds us of Joseph Heller's *Catch 22*, as well as Twombly's own history—he combines references to his stint in the Army as a cryptographer as well as his own bisexual proclivities. Seldom has his work exhibited such witty intimacy.

And this is what makes this show such a wonderful final tribute to the artist Robert Hughes called "The Third Man" of post-Abstract Expressionist art. Along with Jasper Johns and Robert Rauschenberg, those hunter-gatherers of all things mundane and beautiful, Twombly had an innate sense of the romance of the everyday object, elevating it to Art through his manipulations. What a racket we make, who are doomed to cease and leave no trace behind.

Wild-Eyed Boy from Freecloud

Kal Spelletich: *Where's My Jetpack?!*; Jack Hanley Gallery, New York.
Published August 2, 2011; *CultureCatch*.

The flight to Tokyo from London makes one stop, in Moscow. The layover is interesting. You can't see much from the air or the airport. Dismal and cold. There is a First-Class lounge where you are served tea and ice cream. There are lots of magazines, but none are in English. In the toilet the ceilings have little open slats, which make you think there might be hidden cameras. You're a little scared.

Before flying was a means to an end, it was a sensation, a thought. The desire to fly was to experience weightlessness, a release from corporeality. The "flying-machine" made man superhuman. For Kal Spelletich, flight's future promise may be gone, but not forgotten. Where are the jetpacks? The flying cars, the escape pods, anti-gravity boots and moon colonies? This is the future, your future, but not the one that was promised.

Keith Haring wrote, with regard to his own pre-Steampunk, Neo-Primitive aesthetic, "Contemporary man, with his blind faith in science and progress, hopelessly confused by the politics of money and greed and abuse of power, deluded by what appears to be his 'control' of 'the situation' . . . believes in his 'superiority' over his environment . . . he has lost touch with his own meaning." Along with his friend and colleague Jean Tinguely, whose works prefigure Spelletich's, Haring sought to subvert the notion of "progress" and "mass culture" by creating artworks that reduced these ideas (power, progress, longevity) into stylized monograms whose very temporality (for Haring, graffiti, for Tinguely, self-destructing machines) undermined the notions of Art with a capital "A." Tinguely, Jean Dubuffet, and later Haring and Kenny Scharf, set precedent for groups of artists like Survival Research Laboratories, Collaborative Projects (Colab), et al., whose practice did not revolve around making artworks, per se, but rather objects whose existence was meant as an intervention, somewhere "between Art and Life," as Robert Rauschenberg eloquently phrased it.

Antoine de Saint-Exupéry, the French writer and aviator, wrote that "one of the miracles of the airplane is that it plunges a man directly into the heart of a mystery." Spelletich's *Unidentified Harley Davidson Throat Singer* (2011) and outboard-motor propelled jetpacks illustrate the improbability of flight and thus show us the mystery. They simulate the real objects, which we (now) take for granted, although, indeed, they are miraculous. Thus, we see how deeply our collective psyche has been transformed in a mere one hundred years, by flight, as well as our other technologies. What depth of imprint it has left on our very souls.

It has been the role of the artist to point to elements of our lives that may seem trivial, if only because they are so often overlooked, so ingrained have they become. Pop Art did this. Performance Art in the seventies. Dada in 1917. Punk. Steampunk. The list goes on. There is a need for this kind of work, and whether we call it Interactive, Performance, Sculpture, or Environmental (Burning Man is a great example), it is and will remain, for the foreseeable future, the best gauge we have for measuring how far we have come, as well as a compass to point in the directions we might yet go.

You're the One for Me, Fatty

Lucien Freud: *Homage to Lucien Freud*; Metropolitan Museum of Art, New York.
Published August 12, 2011; *CultureCatch*.

You are pretty sure you have a handle on things—a bead on the situation, so to speak. You know the speed that light travels (299,792,458 meters per second). This is of some help. You know, more or less, where you are: what universe, what planet, what continent, what street, what room number. You are focused on reading this. That will keep your mind occupied for well over one minute. Your body, however, is operating on another level altogether. Several, as a matter of fact. At the same time. None of which are you really concerned with right now. Your brain tells your heart to beat, your blood is oxygenated. You are digesting. Producing and accruing shit and piss. At some point, before you finish reading this, you will realize that you have become wet.

Few artists have managed to capture the gross beauty that is the human. Lucian Freud (December 8, 1922–July 20, 2011) was one of them. His was not an art of our higher aspirations or perceptions of ourselves, but a candid depiction of our animal existences. At the Metropolitan Museum of Art, seventeen of Freud's works sketch a selection of his studies of the human in its pure corporeal state. The oil paintings, sixteen from anonymous private collections, were originally to be exhibited as *British Paintings After World War II*, but at Freud's passing last month, the museum quietly installed the paintings and renamed the exhibit *Homage to Lucian Freud*.

Naked Man, Back View (1991–92) is the Met's seminal Freud, a rear-view nude of the performance artist Leigh Bowery crushing a small stool. Pound for pound, it is fair to say that no artist has described as much human topography as Freud. His lolling, academically inclined nudes of fat queens, corpulent business tycoons, hefty slags, and his own daughters provided enough frisson of modern psychology to cover for the fact that his true obsessions lay in the flesh; it keeps them still from being sucked into the dustbin of aesthetic oblivion.

Freud made his way as a young man from cosmopolitan Berlin to urban London. His early work belied his interest in the purely physical, with a nod to the elder (Grandfather Sigmund) Freud, dabbling as it did in minor surrealist themes and Northern European Renaissance-styled portraits (*A Young Painter, 1957-8*). Largely, though, Freud owes much of his fame to the cult of personality that surrounds him—rake (alleged father of twenty-six children), gambler (extravagant, yet bad), epicure, etc.—more than to great talent. As William Rubin noted of Barnett Newman, his career turned on his ability to be urbane and irresponsible without spreading malice. Céline wrote, though not of Freud, but it applies:

There wasn't much to be said for me, but my manners were all right, and I was self-effacing; deference came easy to me, I lived in constant fear of not being on time but took good care never to get ahead of anybody. In short, I had delicacy . . .

Delicacy may not be the first word that jumps to mind when viewing *Evening in the Studio* (1993), but it comes close to explaining how Freud managed to navigate a 50-odd-year career. The eleventh-century monk Ælfric wrote that art should be created *"pro Gloria Dei,"* which we might stretch to mean "for a greater end than our visual delectation." For a work of art to be a Work of Art it must rise above the mere visual grammar and syntax of paint and become a Painting. Lofty, yes, but who are we, after all, to debate an eleventh-century monk?

Well, here we are, at once awkward and exhilarated. Yes, you say. Here we are.

Some Girls

Aneta Grzeszykowska: *Lovetime*; Harris Lieberman Gallery, New York.
Published August 27, 2011; *CultureCatch*.

From Charles de Gaulle airport to JFK is eight hours, but the time change and constant daylight make it seem longer. On our last night in Paris we went to dinner, a very boring party, and then bought drugs and went to a club called Boy or Toy. From there we took a taxi to the airport, finishing the drugs on the way and Amelie tucking the gun she bought at the club into the cab's upholstery to avoid problems checking in. On the plane I sat between Lars von Trier and Philip Seymour Hoffman, who were both sucking morphine lollipops. Arne Glimcher and Robert Downey, Jr. were seated behind us and alternately kicked the back of our seats and discussed James Franco's new show very loudly. We were told we couldn't smoke, even though we were seated in First Class, so I went to the toilet with Uma where we did a couple of quick lines and then shared a cigarette after she disabled the smoke detector with a tampon. Back in my seat someone offered me a Rohypnol, and I swallowed it dry and spent the rest of the trip home staring at the cloudless sky.

We live in the age of Meta. Meta-Criticism, Meta-Literature, Meta-Art. Aesthetics in the digital age have made us first question the structure and order of things, the nature and shape of reality, then allowed us to gently move into territory more fluid and amorphous. Reality, as we see it digitally, on television shows, or in the news, is a porous thing. Our lives and stories intertwine with others, creating an interesting moment in history where we share information more fluidly, though with less certainty as to what is "real." Aneta Grzeszykowska, the Polish photographer, is making her U.S. debut at Harris Lieberman in an exhibition entitled *Lovetime*, an *homage* to the feminist precursors she admires and emulates. In 2007 she debuted a series of color photographs based on Cindy Sherman's black and white *Untitled Film Stills*, carefully replacing Sherman with her own image, like an eager understudy vying for a choice role. Like Sherrie Levine, one could question whether this was a strategy of displacing the inherent aesthetic value of the "original" in the age of "the mechanical" or a coy ploy to shill inexpensive versions of the originals at lower prices while retaining a patina of artistic integrity.

Grzeszykowska, whose works are included in The New Museum's *Ostalgia* show, are featured at Harris Lieberman in an exhibit that lays bare her real feelings by placing images of herself collaged onto archetypal shots of her artistic heroes. Feminist performance/photographer/installation artists like Ana Mendieta, Birgit Jürgensen, Francesca Woodman, Hannah Wilke, Helen Chadwick, and Theresa Hak Kyung Cha used their work to comment on issues of identity, violence, and feminism in the male-centric art world of the Seventies. Here, they share a Meta-Space with a nude, pregnant Grzeszykowska, who cuddles up to them, becoming both protective mother and needy child in the collages. The fact that the six artists Grzeszykowska chose came to unfortunate and untimely ends lends a surreal, slightly melancholic air to the book that these pieces comprise. *Lovebook* (2010) is displayed open on the wall, allowing the pieces to form an open narrative—we are left to our own devices to decide if she is avenging angel or the issue of such a rich history of feminist art.

Clock (2011) is a 12-hour video that is comprised of stills of Grzeszykowska performing choreographed dance combinations, which are synched with the hours of the day. The image of the artist is multiplied to correspond to the changing hours, with replicate Grzeszykowskas multiplying with the minutes. Of the works presented, *Lovebook* is stronger, if only because the narrative implied is so nuanced. This is not a new strategy, the mixing of fictional realities with an artist's narrative. Bret Easton Ellis, in a moment of pique at his friend and colleague Jay McInerney, had Patrick Bateman roof and rape Alison Poole (one of McInerney's characters from his novel *Story of My Life*) in *American Psycho*. Mallarmé dedicated "Prose" (1897) to a person named Des Esseintes. Des Esseintes was a character from Huysmans's *Against Nature*. "Prose," by the way, was a poem.

Shakespeare's Sister

Nicola Tyson: Friedrich Petzel Gallery, New York.
Published September 9, 2011; *CultureCatch*.

A screenwriter bursts into his agent's office. "I have a great idea for a new picture," he enthuses. "We do a remake of *The Wiz*, only with white people." Cliché Hollywood joke, sure, yet spot on, with regard to current received ideas of making art. The Reboot, Redux, the Remix—pretty much any fucked-out form of production—has replaced genuine individual expression. Part Matisse, part von Sacher-Masoch, part Mary Shelley: the work of Nicola Tyson draws from a wide range of inspiration while managing to pull off that most important feat in art, remaining uniquely her own. Tyson is exhibiting her recent paintings and sculptures at Friedrich Petzel through November 5, 2011.

Tyson's drawings, in the early nineties, were simple, small, black and white, mounted in groups. Abstract heads and bodies floated in little boxes, resembling a strip of film or a contact sheet. They had a cinematic quality that, at that time, resembled the work of Cindy Sherman. Like Sherman, Tyson created images that related in some ways to Leonardo da Vinci's physiognomic caricature studies. Grotesques, but of a psychological sort, as if she were trying to describe what these characters felt like on the inside. Her early paintings elaborated on some of these ideas, with figures that combined an imaginary anatomy with references to bondage and mutant sex, like a cross between *Salò* and *Alien: Resurrection*. The critical response of the time compared her work to Francis Bacon, perhaps because of her stage-like settings, but this seemed off the mark. Where Bacon created literary, somewhat obscure theatrical tableaux, Tyson dove deeper into the psychology of her subjects.

In the early twentieth century, Fritz Kahn created a series of books describing the physical body through visual metaphors drawn from industrial culture—factory lines, combustion engines, refineries, etc., that sought to give a visual depiction of a new psychological understanding of the modern human being. Freud, too, tried to describe new ways of comprehending the internalized being trapped in the body. Tyson combines elements of both in her recent paintings, working in a particularly British tradition of satire. In *Figure with Sphinx* (2011) she stages a tableau straight out of *Oedipus*. *Figure with Pigeon* (2011) has a gnome-like creature wrapped in swaths of cloth (resembling something out of Victoria's Secret, but shredded) and the titular pigeon, resting on a hot-water bottle. It brings to mind other figure-with-animal compositions with weird twists, like Titian's *Portrait of Charles V with Dog*. In *Figure Creeping* (2011) Tyson refers back to the eighteenth-century caricaturist James Gillray, who described his work as "Mock Sublime Mad Taste"—which pushes the satirical impulse toward something more anarchic, much like Malcolm McLaren and John Lydon would with the antics of the Sex Pistols 200 years later.

In a second gallery Tyson presents a series of small sculptures on plinths. The traditional presentation contrasts with the contingent feel of the pieces themselves. Fabricated out of self-hardening modeling compound, the diminutive works bear the fingerprints and marks of their creation. Highly abstracted, though not abstract, the little creatures resemble white swans, preening, laying eggs, and sleeping. One swan has been cast in bronze, and patinated black, making the whole of the group resemble some small puppet-show staging of *Swan Lake*. They project an eerie psychological element, with their immediate handmade facture;

they sway between being Degas-like studies and the work of mental patients. Hauntingly and ephemerally beautiful, they bring to three dimensions what the paintings can only show one facet at a time.

We ultimately come to identify with Tyson's project. We believe in the sincerity and depth of her probing; she penetrates the fine line between what can be seen (the exteriority of the subject) and what can be shown (its interiority). The promise of her earlier work is being fulfilled; we are now given the story, as well as the actors. As her homunculi lurch and creep across the canvas, we are drawn into their heads, and by proxy, into Tyson's.

Sound and Vision

Gideon Bok: *Record Store*; Steven Harvey Fine Art Projects, New York.
Published September 16, 2011; *CultureCatch*.

We were once young, loaded, and gaveth not a fuck. We cut huge rails on an album called *Unknown Pleasures*; sorted weed together on something named Led Zeppelin. When we listened to the music, we looked at the covers and imagined the strange and luminous beings that created these sonic universes. Creatures like Brian Eno, who probably wore clothes of pure ocelot, owned a talking panda . . . had furniture made out of live girls. We were allowed to imagine. And it was one huge collective act. Gideon Bok captures something of this time in his exhibition *Record Store*.

Many artists have used music as both subject and metaphor in painting. From references in the Dutch genre scenes of Hals and the *Jazz* cut-outs of Matisse to the syncopated color rhythms of Mondrian, music has proven a deep well from which to draw inspiration—providing correspondences, or poetic analogies with multiple references that tie the aural to the visual. Bok, unlike many of his contemporaries (for example Christian Marclay), remains firmly rooted in the traditions of painting while choosing to explore forms of musical influence. In the past Bok's work focused on interior spaces, such as his studio, which he depicted with a Giacometti-like, skeletal paint handling. Reminiscent of Frank Auerbach or Leon Kossoff, Bok recorded the process of painting by erasing, overpainting, and reworking—building up layers of paint and meaning as a way of showing the activities that happened in the space. The end result of those paintings suggested a document, like a photograph that had been printed and reprinted over and over on the same sheet. It is worth noting that one of the early features of those studio "portraits" (besides bottles of Jack Daniels) was his phonograph and record LPs.

Here, though, Bok has narrowed his focus to the albums alone, presenting sets of oil on MDF panels mounted in rows: *Welcome to the Monkey House* (n.d.), *Into the Pink* (n.d.), *Exile* (n.d.). The subject is the record sleeve, which lies horizontally, creating a trapezoidal shape within the LP-sized panel. He paints with a rough, expressive hand while listening to the album he is depicting, linking the paint handling with its musical counterpart; Kandinsky attempted this synesthetic experience also in his work. Bok notes that he has been influenced by Erwin Panofsky and Merleau-Ponty, with particular regard for their theories of phenomenology and perspective. The collection of albums also calls to mind how closely we are all linked through what we believe is personal taste yet is really assumptions made by groups of people, not mere individuals. We are joined together by sensibilities. Liking the same things. Bok elaborates on or obscures the original cover art (in itself an art form of the past), showing how our "perspective" of the work shifts by our perceptions of it.

There is a great story in Keith Richards's autobiography, *A Life*, where he describes tooling around London in the sixties in his Bentley. He wanted to listen to music while he drove, so he had a stereo built in to the back seat. (This was way before iPods.) He then had to hire someone to sit in the back and change the 45s every few minutes. Bok's paintings have something of that sense of nostalgia to them. In the age of digital music, it all looks very different now even though the songs remain the same.

Killing Joke

David Moriarty: *Halcyon Daze*; CREON Gallery, New York.
Published September 24, 2011; *CultureCatch*.

(Audience Applause) . . . ok . . . so a guy calls into work. He tells his boss he can't come in that day because he's sick. The boss says, "Ok. No problem. Take the day off. How sick are you, anyway?" The guy says, "I just fucked my sister." (Laughter) . . . Thank you.

Sigmund Freud said, "A joke is a contract of mastery at another person's expense." Meaning, essentially, we laugh at the misfortunes of others while admiring our own, more fortunate, position. Jokes reveal, and play with, our inner fears (see above: social faux pas), relationships to power and money (see above: talking to the boss), and social taboos (see above: incest). Shakespeare's comedies often reveal more of the human condition than did his tragedies. Humor in art is a rare thing, especially in painting, as quite often the viewer is never sure if the whole enterprise is a joke. David Moriarty's exhibition *Halcyon Daze* manages to be witty, yet not mean-spirited. Moriarty combines narratives, or fractured fairy tales, as it were, and weaves together scenes and characters from pop culture, art history, and his own imagination seamlessly.

In *Britneys* (2008), Britney Spears, wearing a white dress, sits in front of another Britney Spears dressed in the manner of Thomas Gainsboroughs's *The Blue Boy*, smoking a pipe. This strange, pastoral image is framed (and framed again) by *trompe l'oeil* trellises and gilded picture frames. The whole scene is a series of receding depictions, like Alice down the rabbit hole, which creates the impression that we aren't looking at an attempt to show an alternate reality, but, rather, we are being told a story that probably wasn't all that true to begin with.

In *My Christmas* (2008) we get Elaine de Kooning—possibly two of them—nude and one wearing a sun bonnet, lounging flirtatiously in front of stacks of colorfully wrapped and ribboned boxes. One Elaine fondles a faux wood-grained frame, which is engraved with "My Christmas," a play on how Pablo Picasso used to sign his works with fake nameplates in the canvas. Goofy, for sure, but the writer Jacques Vaché wrote about "the theatrical and joyless futility of everything"—a pretty close description of this giant stack of Christmas boxes and Elaines. Remember, Elaine, wife of Willem de Kooning, was a painter who was as well known for her giant shoe collection as she was for her paintings of buffaloes . . . (Applause/Audience laughter) . . . HECKLER: "You suck!" . . . Shut up Dad, you're drunk, go home . . . so, anyway, maybe the whole thing is making fun of de Kooning's generation of artists, with their existentialist pretentions cloaking their avarice, or maybe it is just the setup; Moriarity's sense of humor precludes spoon-feeding us punch lines.

(Applause)

Joan Miró wrote in a letter to his art dealer that he wanted to "assassinate painting" in the 1930s, meaning that he was about to embark on a series of humorous paintings and drawings that used artistic conventions to create wry, funny commentaries on the act of painting. Miró's sense of humor was a little more acerbic, though no less perverse than Moriarity's. *Bunny, Beers, Babe* (2009) is, well, just that. A bunny rabbit, with its references to Joseph Beuys, *Alice in Wonderland*, and Japanese suits of armor, hands the titular girl a frosty beverage. Three-dimensional lettering spells out "As Is," storybook style, like an obscure narration. "As Is," like "Runs Great" signs at used car lots, sets the tone for this piece—where better to find guys in funny suits that are going to tell you stories that probably aren't true. Well, maybe in an art gallery. (Laughter) Thank you . . . (Applause)

Moby Dick

Willem de Kooning: *de Kooning: A Retrospective*; The Museum of Modern Art, New York. Published September 25, 2011; *CultureCatch*.

Vincent van Gogh once said, "The fishermen know that the sea is dangerous and the storm terrible, but they have never found these dangers sufficient reason for remaining ashore." As apt a metaphor as any for the 70-year-long journey that was Willem de Kooning's career. De Kooning was born in Rotterdam in 1904. He stowed away on a ship as a young man, sailing to New York, where he became arguably one of the most important American painters of the twentieth century. *de Kooning: A Retrospective* at The Museum of Modern Art, NY, traces the course he navigated through the art of his time.

From his early training as a decorative painter in Holland, a housepainter in Hoboken, and a commercial illustrator in Manhattan, de Kooning moved on quickly to investigate the burgeoning movement known as Modernism. Early on he befriended the artist Arshile Gorky who became his primary influence and mentor, friend, and sometimes rival. Along with Gorky, de Kooning began to explore ways in which to abstract the figure *Pink Angels* (1945), as well as to make early forays into purely non-objective works such as *untitled (The Cow Jumps Over the Moon)* (1937–38). His constant determination, and relentless perfectionism (he seldom considered a work finished) came to embody an archetypal image of the mid-century painter. A Captain Ahab in search of an elusive Modernist image.

De Kooning's process of building a painting was intertwined with the movement that it depicted as well as the movement involved in the act of painting. He often rotated the painting while working on it—attacking if from all four sides. While working on a nominally figurative work *Woman* (1951), he considered the figure/ground relation from every angle. At times he would draw with his eyes closed, with his left hand, or with both hands at once. He especially liked to draw while watching television, trying to capture the instantaneous movement on the screen. "My drawings are fast, like snapshots," he said. His paintings were slow; he painted, scraped off, repainted, sanded, and painted again. He often worked for years at a time on a single canvas. But most of all, de Kooning was a colorist. No other artist of his generation was as able to dissect the form and reassemble it with such spectacular results. *Clam Diggers* (1963) reveals glimpses of feet, teeth, a hand; the bright hues—yellows, reds, blues, all deployed throughout the field of the image—create a visual tension between the linear configurations and the chromatic contrasts. Focus on one, and you lose the other. This struggle was paramount for de Kooning, who saw the act of painting as a search for an image that, to his mind, at least, could never resolve itself on canvas. Nothing in his *oeuvre* illustrates this better than . . . *Whose Name Was Writ in Water* (1975). The bright color is a ruse, covering some essential struggle for Truth. Melville may have said it best: "Nature absolutely paints like the harlot, whose allurements cover nothing but the charnel-house within . . . Wonder ye then at the fiery hunt?"

Beauty and the Beast

Karen Heagle: *Let Nature Take Its Course and Hope It Passes*; I-20, New York.
Published October 3, 2011; *CultureCatch*.

"Tiger, tiger burning bright / In the forests of the night / What immortal hand or eye / Could frame thy fearful symmetry?" Though she is probably not immortal, it would seem Karen Heagle has stepped up to William Blake's challenge.

Her large, beautiful, and radiant painting *Inexperienced/Insatiable* (2011) is but one of many depictions of sublime animals, of both the predator and prey varieties, in her current exhibition.

Heagle's tiger wades into a stream or river, head lowered, and glows from within (lushly painted stripes and golden-hued fur) and from without (a reddish light is cast over the whole scene, as if from a setting sun). This fearsome beast stands guard over the rest of the exhibit, which consists mostly of still lifes of prey animals, such as deer and rabbits.

Heagle has, in the past, made reference to heroic figures in her paintings; here she presents a more subtle, nuanced series of works that draw from great *nature morte* artists of the past. We see shades of Chardin and Soutine, as well as Flemish and Dutch *vanitas* works, in *Rabbit, Copper Pot, Lava Lamp* (2011); the titular lava lamp is a modern update, though with its constantly morphing waxy insides, it is a perfect metaphor for the vicissitudes of life. Nothing is constant but change.

Studio Still Life with Partially Disemboweled Deer (2011), the show's standout work, brings together elements of the hunt and the artist's studio: a dead deer, hanging by one hoof; a Savarin can remind us of Jasper Johns; the dark, nighttime setting is a nod to Philip Guston and his night-studio scenes. All of this is woven together by the workbench—studio or kitchen furniture? We might be led to believe that Heagle sees both. The whole *mise-en-scène* is framed by a leaded glass window (its pattern reminds us of Johns's *Flagstone* paintings), which casts a feeling of religiosity over the proceedings. Heagle reminds us of the sacredness of the hunt, with its codes of respect for life (we don't kill more than we need) and a reverence for the act of painting itself. Like Guston, many of Heagle's works depict elements of the studio as a constant theme. Heagle, like Soutine, though, breathes more life into her works, allowing Nature to triumph over Art.

Heagle's brushy, wet, painterly style bears some relation to Frans Hals, particularly *Fisher Girl* (1630–32) in the Metropolitan Museum's current Hals show. She breathes life not just into an old genre of painting, but into the dead animals she portrays. It is this constant back-and-forth aspect of her work that intrigues us and holds our attention. *Self-Portrait in Armor* (2011) depicts the empty suit of armor, a stand-in for the artist. Has she taken it off, so to speak, to show the sincerity of her work? We are also reminded of suits of women's armor (yes, those have a long history), in particular the diminutive helmet (also at the Met) purported to have belonged to Joan of Arc.

Another Dutch artist, Piet Mondrian, once wrote, "One day the time will come when we shall be able to do without all the arts, as we know them now; beauty will have ripened into palpable reality. Humanity will not lose much by missing art." Though Mondrian made some beautiful paintings, his was a project set to freeing the spirit by diminishing the visual experience. The House of Art has many rooms; in those rooms are many mansions, and Mondrian's work no doubt resides in one of them. We are fortunate, however, to have artists like Heagle, who allow us beauty and the sublime.

Walk Like an Egyptian

Matthew Barney: *DJED*; Gladstone Gallery, New York.
Published September 26, 2011; *CultureCatch*.

The opening pages of Ovid's *Metamorphoses* describe a time before the ages of silver, bronze, and iron, when Spring was everlasting, and nectar flowed in streams; mankind was "without a law," did right always, and lived contentedly. This was definitely not the times described in Norman Mailer's *Ancient Evenings*, the libretto for Matthew Barney's project of the same name, which he has been working on since 2007. We might be wise to take the writer's words with grains of salt, however. The novel, though not without moments of wit and brilliance, is on about the same level as a certain Bangles song we can name, but won't, when it comes to Egyptology. The exhibition of Barney's project avoids being pinned down quite so hard by being 1.) an element of his larger series of performances and installations, and 2.) quite beautiful.

Set in ancient Egypt, Mailer's novel chronicles the seven stages of the soul's progression through death and rebirth according to Egyptian mythology. While Mailer's narrative focuses on the transformation of the human body, Barney enacts the recurring cycles of reincarnation through the use of an automobile, creating a contemporary allegory of death and rebirth within the American industrial landscape. The sculptures on view are both formally and conceptually related to the 1967 Chrysler Crown Imperial from *Cremaster 3*. Revolving around three generations of American automobile design, the *Ancient Evenings* narrative is rooted in the reincarnation of its leading protagonist, the Chrysler Imperial.

The centerpiece of the exhibition, *DJED*, is a monumental cast-iron sculpture that was poured during a live performance of the opera's third act in 2010. The primary form of *DJED* is the undercarriage of the Chrysler Imperial, modified to evoke the pillar-like hieroglyph of the Egyptian god Osiris's power. Osiris was the god of the afterlife, and sculptural representations used an attached beard to represent his appearance. The axles and drive shafts of Barney's *DJED* (2009–11) allude to this in an oblique, metaphorical way. Similarly, the scatter-sculpture *Sacrificial Anode* (2011) refers both to the way we receive Egyptian art (in pieces) as well as to an understanding of old forms of representing the figure.

Artistic conventions at the time required representing the human body in its most complete form. Ancient Egyptians respected the divinity of each of its individual parts. Egyptian mortuary texts associated portions of the human anatomy with particular deities, and certain amulets and votive offerings to the gods were often created in the shapes of abstracted limbs or organs. Vital organs, such as the brain or heart, were removed at death and embalmed separately to ensure their function in the afterlife, and replicas were occasionally provided in their place to guarantee the deceased's spiritual abode.

The British sculptor Henry Moore once noted, "Size and monumentality are not the same thing. What I found in Egyptian [art] was a monumentality of vision." In spite of the grandiosity of the Sphinx and Pyramids, Egyptians highly regarded detail in art and short stature in physique as hallmarks of divinity. They associated the physical characteristics of *achondroplasia* (a form of dwarfism) with the sun-god Re. Myths told how Re died every evening as the sun set and was reborn every morning—reincarnated as a preternaturally wise child-god.

In many ways Barney's projects have been focused on this sense of death and resurrection. What is of interest in this new cycle of performance works is how he transforms the contingent nature of the performances (the two I have seen have both involved rain and things that didn't work properly) into sculptural works of subtle monumentality. In some ways Barney follows in the tradition of Joseph Beuys, whose sculptural works also carried a great deal more metaphorical weight than his performances.

Horses

Susan Rothenberg: Sperone Westwater, New York.
Published October 11, 2011; *CultureCatch*.

Jasper Johns, with his *Flag* and *Target* paintings of the 1950s, helped to change the way that we looked at paintings. He showed us that there are never truly distinct and separate categories of names for what we see and (as he phrased it) "things the mind already knows." Everything is always contingent on something else. His works begged questions such as "What is the image *of*?" "What is contained *in* the picture?" and "Where does the role of the artist end, and where does the viewer's job begin?" Susan Rothenberg was asking some of these same questions in the late '70s. In her nominal images of horses, she presented us with some of the most visually complex puzzles in art since Johns. What we assumed were abstracted depictions of an equestrian nature were anything but. Shadowy horsey outlines, painted with horsehair brushes on grounds made of ground hooves—they gave us everything but a horse. Rothenberg long ago evolved from such painterly philosophizing, focusing instead on a brand of abstraction that hovered somewhere between Monet's large-scale, Impressionist landscapes and Alberto Giacometti's nervous figurative portraits.

At Sperone Westwater, Rothenberg revisits some of her earlier painterly concerns, adding onto, rather than reverting to, the questions she once addressed. She continues her investigation into image making, extending both her thought process, and ours, in her exploration of light, form, and color, of images of human body fragments, dogs, and ravens. Juxtaposed against heavily scumbled backgrounds, bodies become shapes and outlines, creating a tension between figuration and abstraction that harkens back to the early horse paintings.

Rothenberg continues to use animals as surrogates for the human body, transforming the representation of the figure into a cipher, which operates much the same as Johns's *Numbers* and *Alphabet* paintings. For example, the silhouette of a black bird with open beak in *Raven* (2009–10) is depicted against a white, heavily worked background. In *Ring Necks, Covering* (2011) she paints two doves at the perimeter of the canvas, perched on branches that extend outside the picture plane, bisecting it diagonally, setting up pictorial tension. *White on White Head* (2010) gives us the profile of a large head outlined in gray and black, which refers obliquely to the work of Philip Guston—another artist who, in the late '70s, was influential in the New Image movement, which Rothenberg pioneered.

Although it would seem, on the surface, that this combination of flat ground and abstracted figuration would leave little room for narrative, it is in our nature to create stories around the images we see in paintings—and Rothenberg leaves enough room for us to do our job as viewers. What Rothenberg does, by removing the object of the painting and leaving a silhouette, or visual hole, is to create a space (literally) that we can fill. Ravens, with their references to Poe; other animals; and decapitated heads are ripe with narrative potential. Frank Stella called these areas in a painting the "working space" of the painter, and that is as good a description as any of what is happening in these works. Rothenberg is not merely rehashing the modernist phenomenology of Minimalism, or Post-Pop art, she is building on the vocabulary that developed out of these movements. She is writing, if not a new chapter in art's history, at least a damn good story.

Rebel, Rebel

Eva Hesse: *Eva Hesse Spectres 1960*; Brooklyn Museum, Brooklyn.
Published October 21, 2011; *CultureCatch*.

In 1969 Eva Hesse participated in *When Attitudes Become Form*, a benchmark exhibition of Minimalist art. This was a watershed moment for Hesse. What the participants in this show demonstrated with their work was that experience—that of the artist and that of the viewer—could be given shape through language, line, color, and pre-existing shape (primary ones such as circles and squares were popular) and that experience could acquire meaning as aesthetic objects. In essence, these artists demonstrated that the recording of their process of thinking about art and making objects was the artwork. Although it is this work that Hesse is known and remembered for, we are fortunate to be able to view her lesser-known paintings from the early '60s at the Brooklyn Museum.

Hesse no doubt saw these earlier works as transitional, coming as they did between the end of the Abstract Expressionist movement and the flourishing of Pop Art, but she did attempt to explain their meaning to some extent. In 1959 she wrote in her journal, "Paint yourself out, through and through, it will come by you alone. You must come to terms with your own work and not with any other being."

In three gray "self-portraits," Hesse may be identified by her straight dark hair. Iconic, highly simplified images in which Hesse eschewed likeness, instead attempting a psychological study of the self as seen from the inside. In *No Title* (1960) she depicts herself as a bald and sickly figure—presciently foreshadowing her early death from a brain tumor.

The major painting in the exhibition, *No Title* (1960), gives us a double self-portrait, but of a Bride and Groom. The Bride, veiled and holding flowers, the Groom something that looks like Gollum from the *Lord of the Rings*. The Bride sits in a chair with her elbows bent as if she is about to rise. Gollum moves in front of her, beckoning her to follow—perhaps a reference to the Bride's passage from virginity into matrimony, willing, yet haunted by doubt.

Though the paintings here are a small part of her body of work, they show a sensitive intellect and a painter fully in command of her pictorial vocabulary. Schools, dogmas, and styles (such as Minimalism) were but other ways that an art object was fit into the stream of history—and even by the time of *When Attitudes Become Form*, the sense of avant-gardism had become institutionalized—a pre-requisite for any artist graduating from art school. (Hesse attended Yale School of Art with Richard Serra, Chuck Close, and Mel Bochner.) However, these early paintings show us that the real avant-garde may have already happened, and if it did, these works were largely ignored. In Hesse's paintings, like those of Van Gogh, Signac, Gauguin, et al., we see a testament to the constant renewal of art, in spite of art's entrenched notions of progress. A history of art should one day include works like these, ones that were overlooked, ignored, or best thought of as outside the arc of an artist's history. A secret history, or as James Joyce wrote, conceived in "silence, cunning, and exile."

The Thing

Mira Schor: *Painting in The Space Where Painting Used to Be*; Some Walls, Oakland,
California.
Published November 1, 2011; *CultureCatch*.

Mira Schor understands clarity of ideas. Her exhibition *Painting in The Space Where Painting Used to Be* demonstrates that. This robust show of five works dramatically combines her own history as an artist with elements of a history of Modernist painting quite succinctly. Schor has integrated a fierce intelligence and precision in language with a lush painterly hand. No mean feat, that. Her multi-disciplined approach to art making and adherence to Painting as High Art places her among the most interesting artists working today.

Here we have something like a story of art, a meta-narrative, starting with *Lack* (1997), the painted word brushed into a dark ground. Part "In the beginning there was the Word," part Post-Modernist Lacanian theory writ personal, she begins a story about beginning a story. That is, demonstrating in paint the process by which an artist conceives an idea and renders it visible through plastic form. Thought made flesh, so to speak. Schor's brush surface recalls other painters, such as Rembrandt and de Kooning, who sought a similar result from oil paint. Borges said that there were only two narratives in storytelling: *The Odyssey* and the Crucifixion. If we adhere to this, then Schor has embarked on a Homeric journey, though, in this case a mental voyage of discovery.

Do you want a cup of tea? Or an aspirin? Or a Serafem? Don't be embarrassed. Keep a grip on it. Don't worry. Everything's going to turn out okay in the end. Treats are in store.

In her essay "Modest Painting," Schor outlines her program for painting. She writes, "Modest painting does not aspire to historical importance through physical domination of the viewer or the room in which it is placed via monumentality of size." Her aspirations may be modest, but the depth of these pictures and the seriousness of purpose they exhibit are far from minor in impact. Schor, a feminist artist and thinker, has long eschewed less immodest paths for her artistic discourse. She has weathered the decades of artists who achieved higher profiles through second-rate performance involving pulling things out of their snoopies, or scatter-sculptures of used tampons. Schor has instead focused on leveling the playing field—by bringing her work, and her ideas, to life through paint.

In *Thinking of "Thing"* (2011) and *Thing* (2011) she draws the artist mentally composing a picture, and in the subsequent painting, a luminous white ground inscribed with the word "thing," she presents us with the result. In this picture she produces a painterly object that both respects the traditions of painting and embraces the modernist conceptual ideas of artists like Lawrence Weiner and Joseph Kosuth.

Schor's complex ideas about art making, and specifically the role of the painter, are summed up in the final two works in the exhibit. *First Idea* (2010) and *The Space Where Painting Used to Be* (2010) are self-portraits, of a sort. Schematic stick figures—or cartoons along the lines of Philip Guston's late self-portraits—read, pace, recline, and most of all, think. Lines diagramming the sight lines from eye to book to thought balloon show the process by which an art idea becomes an art object.

Schor gives us a glimpse into the headspace that creates, bringing her journey, and by proxy ours, full-circle. From thought to expression. Schor takes us from that space where painting was to where its possibilities lie.

Alphaville

Allison Schulnik: *Mound*; Zieher Smith, New York.
Published November 9, 2011; *CultureCatch*.

On April 1st they isolated the strain of Virus HC-35, which became known as The Flu. On May 5th President Manson declared a State of Emergency, cleared the protesters from Zapruder Park, and issued orders for the Continuous Curfew. And the deaths came in millions. By June the food had run out, and we began to hunt the neighbors. By July the neighbors had run out, and we stayed confined to the 69th floor.

Two days ago we ate Amelie. Now Katya is sitting in the living room, counting the last of the drugs on the table. Enough Neroin and Serafem to last only one person for the rest of the month. "You know, darling," I say, "You are very beautiful. I am seriously considering turning you into a lampshade." Katya's dark eyes narrow. "Don't be silly," she says, "we don't have electricity." The headaches are continuous because of the recycled air and hunger. I have not had my period in three months. "It's not the side effects of the cocaine," I say, with something like affection. "I'm thinking that it must be love." Katya looks up, her eyes bright, smiling. She whispers, "This ain't rock and roll. This is genocide."

Offred mused, in her *Handmaid's Tale*, that the art of the future would resemble nothing so much as the art of the past. (Fred had brownish, academic portraits hanging in his private office.) Maybe. But the art of the future will likely resemble the art of the future. Allison Schulnik makes a compelling argument for what that future art might look like.

In her paintings and sculptures (at Zieher Smith) she presents a worn, derelict population of clowns in *Idyllwild* (2011). (Picture the psycho clowns painted by Red Buttons meet the clown paintings of the psycho John Wayne Gacy.) This is set amongst half-starved, rabid-looking animals, such as *Dempster* (2010)—mangy and hissing—and *Standing Gin #3* (2011)—with black, mutant eyes staring menacingly—as well as flowers, wilted and irradiated, arranged in still lifes. *Very* still lifes. Like the floral arrangements at some mass funeral or the bouquets left outside tenement playgrounds or doorsteps commemorating soon-to-be-forgotten victims of the next horrific and mindless urban violence. In Memoriam to Identity.

Schulnik writes, "My fixation on these characters is not intended to exploit deficiencies, but to find valor in adversity." Indeed, that is exactly what makes these dystopian denizens so spot-on for our historic moment. Even now, Lower Manhattan is beginning to resemble Schulnik's landscape. Filled with hunters and gatherers, waiting for a dirty bomb, a meteor, or a tribe of talking apes. Peopled with people like *Yogurt Eater* (2011) or *Blue Head* (2011). Schulnik depicts these pitiable and potentially virulent creatures that we have already come to know and adds just enough of the unknown to make them more alien still. None of Schulnik's characters carries any placarded manifesto, but if they did, their message would be very clear: We're the future / Your future / No future for you.

The Revolution Will Not Be Televised

Sanford Biggers: *Sweet Funk—An Introspective*; The Brooklyn Museum, Brooklyn.
Published November 12, 2011; *CultureCatch*.

Gil Scott-Heron, who is considered the godfather of Hip Hop music, was born in Chicago in 1949. A fiercely intelligent and precocious youth, he attended The Fieldston School in New York, one of five African American students in his class. Scott-Heron was expelled, at one point, for playing the piano in his dormitory. Rebellious, and often feeling like an outsider because of his race and economic standing among his fellow students, he focused on poetry and literature (particularly the work of Langston Hughes) and music (Blues) as an outlet for his ideas. His poem "Whitey on the Moon" was released on his first album *Small Talk at 125th and Lenox* (1970). A commentary on the economic inequities he saw at the time, it reads in part: "The man jus' upped my rent las' night. / ('cause Whitey's on the moon) / No hot water, no toilets, no lights. / (but Whitey's on the moon) / I wonder why he's uppi' me? / ('cause Whitey's on the moon) / I wuz already payin' 'im fifty a week. / (with Whitey on the moon)." Sanford Biggers, whose exhibition *Sweet Funk—An Introspective* is at the Brooklyn Museum, was born in 1970.

Like Scott-Heron, Biggers gathers the imagery and sounds of Blues, the rhythm and movement of break dancing, and the costumes and theatricality of blackface routines and turns them into a very personal discourse on race and culture in our time. The exhibition centers on a large installation of a tree growing through a player piano (*Blossom*, 2007), which grows through the museum's fifth-floor rotunda. With passing references to "a tree grows in Brooklyn," nature versus culture, and Buddha's enlightenment under the bodhi tree, it drives home its point by intermittently playing "Strange Fruit," the ode to black victims of racism made famous by Billie Holiday.

In a separate room, a two-channel video creates a dreamlike carnival depicting a traveling minstrel. He incorporates his signature lighted sign (a bright-red grinning mouth with marquee light bulbs for teeth) called *Cheshire* (2008) into a fractured narrative of a man dressed in a red, white, and blue suit (played by Ricardo Castillo) who travels by train through a city and into the countryside. The actor emerges from an ocean, applies makeup backstage, sits with a young boy on the train, and dances in a church—ultimately ending up sitting under a tree in a park, where the grinning sign hangs from a branch. References to minstrel shows, the Underground Railroad, Hip Hop culture, and southern lynchings are abundant—but the disjointed pacing of the narrative prevents an overly didactic reading. Poetry triumphs over adversity, Biggers seems to imply.

Biggers is less successful when the objects he creates are static. *Lotus* (2007) is a seven-foot diameter circle of glass mounted in a steel frame. The glass is etched with a flower shape, the radiating petals actually comprised of diagrams of decks of slave ship quarters. An overly didactic explanation on a wall label explains how *Lotus* combines references to Buddhist equanimity and Western cruelty; interesting, probably, but the references to botanical etchings and whatnot weaken any political message.

There is a sense of urgency lacking in many of the smaller pieces. Though interesting constructions in their own right, the sense of conveying a message is overwhelmed by their determined artfulness. Tree branches, pianos, and Salvation Army blankets point to things greater than the sum of their parts, but Biggers doesn't push the metaphors as hard as he could have. However, when his pieces work (*Blossom*) they strike with precise wit.

Waltzing Mathilda

Peter Williams: *Midnight Waltz in D Minor*, Paul Kotula Projects, Ferndale, Michigan.
Published November 17, 2011; *CultureCatch*.

One of the problematic legacies of Modernism was its emphasis on originality, youth, and the myth of the artist who sprang *sui generis* into a recognizable, signature style. There were rare exceptions, such as Picasso and Matisse, who remained in the canon and were allowed to mature and develop their works past their youthful experiments and achieve a late body of work. Admittedly, the fact that they lived to be ninety sort of bludgeoned the historians and critics into pretty much accepting whatever they did just because they refused to die. On the other hand, de Kooning lived just as long, and his constant morphing of styles proved to be equally as protean but not as accepted, and his later painting was more or less dismissed until well after his death. What gets overlooked in this now familiar pattern of looking at artists is the fact that most of them go through a period of adolescence after their initial "breakthrough" works, and then they slowly hone their style. This period of artistic growth, often overlooked, is usually the most interesting of an artist's career.

Peter Williams's current show at Paul Kotula Projects catches the artist in this period of his development, and at the top of his game. Williams's paintings of the last twenty years or so were alternately sharp, witty, or darkly satirical. With time he has grown into a much more personal and somewhat melancholic style, shedding inhibitions and allowing his paint to convey the expression of his personality and ideas in a beautiful synthesis. This is not to say that he has lost any of the edge that his earlier works had—the painting *Portrait of Christopher D. Fisher, Fourth Reich Skinhead* (1995) in the collection of the Detroit Institute of Arts is a great example of Williams at his best – rather, he seems to have allowed his personal narrative into his paintings to great effect. In the painting *A Walk in Windsor Hills* (2011), he incorporates elements of Post-Impressionism, Ensor, and Klee-like explorations of human form, mixing styles with a delight in paint that his earlier works tried to hold at bay.

In *The Unmasking* (2011) we get something of a self-portrait, in a bright, carnival style reminiscent of Picasso. Fear and fantasy are interwoven, and the artist confronts his own identity—that of a black, middle-aged male. Psychological states are conflated with the physicality of his body (Williams lost a leg in a car accident at an early age), and the results are painted with sweeping, dance-like gestures.

This is not to say that there aren't still shadows left to explore, and Williams does poke around a bit in the darker recesses of the soul. *Blow* (2010) gives us a ghostly, haunted canvas of a figure in a chalk-stripe suit, peering out of the shadows. There is something of Gorky in this piece, with its outlined figures and transparent arabesques, but there is enough of Walt Disney, with big cartoony eyes and heads, to keep the horror away.

The funny thing about growing old is that life doesn't really become more complicated. In fact, it kinda becomes simpler. Most days everything can be summed up with one of two questions: How bad will it hurt? How much will it cost? It comes as no surprise, really, that most Late Works (Matisse's cut-outs, for example) bring this reductive philosophy to visual form. But in Williams's works, we also see something more. Émile Zola called for "an Art of flesh and blood": "What I look for in a picture before anything else is the man." Williams gives us this, and more, in these works.

Thunderball

Jonathan Meese: *Hot Earl Green Sausage Tea Barbie (First Flush)*; Bortolami Gallery, New York.
Published November 21, 2011; *CultureCatch*.

Meese continues to explore depictions of power, specifically our fascination with historically abusive authority figures. In the past his work has focused on Hitler, Mussolini, James Bond's Blofeld, and Humpty Dumpty, among others. In this exhibition Meese presents a clutter-filled room of oversized painted plywood furnishings for world domination (desks, control panels, lecterns)—except everything is a little rough-hewn and oversized. And the propaganda strewn throughout, a little wacky. He seems to be on a pogrom against 1. "My Pretty Pony," 2. Martin Heidegger, 3. Scarlett Johansson, 4. Walt Disney, 5. . . . well, you get the idea. Piles of such cultural detritus have been swept into a giant pile waiting for immolation, under a hand-lettered sign that reads "DIKTATUR DER KUNST." It could be easily taken for an adolescent statement about "The Man," as it were, had this *mise-en-scène* not borne such a striking resemblance to Zuccotti Park. Indeed, we are even reminded of Joseph Beuys's propagandistic statements, such as "Art is Capital" and "Every Human Being is an Artist"—somewhat disingenuous platitudes passed off as philosophical aphorisms. Meese addresses the viewer on a less lofty and more genuine level, with placards and posters that state "Art is Total Beauty," "Art is Toysoldierism," or "Art is Total Lolita." His conflation of surrealistic aesthetics and abuse-of-power histories would seem just plain silly if it didn't keep pointing back to how often art and power have crossed paths historically. Think of the painter/dictator Adolph Hitler, the writer/watercolorist/Prime Minister Churchill, or the landscapist/General/President Eisenhower, for example.

Where the work really goes deeper is in the four self-portrait paintings in the second room. All are in very traditional oil on linen, sketched rapidly in a very Late Picasso style, and incorporate such "signature" Meese-ian elements as Iron Crosses, Adidas stripe logos, and elements of text. All of them have paragraph-long titles. They harken back to a period in German painting after World War I when painting itself was a highly politicized act, particularly when depicting the human form. In France many called for a "return to order," for an art that celebrated the physical integrity of the body—the body made whole again after the ravages of the war, and later, the industrialization of society. For the first time since the Industrial Age began, populations were more urban than rural, labor was becoming more intellectual than physical, and technology and greater freedom of travel were shaping a society that was gradually detaching itself from the land. Artists began to celebrate the "heroic" human form, suggesting the "ideal" body, as derived from Classical and Renaissance models. Even artists such as Braque and Picasso, who had so recently been committed to Cubism, began to paint in older, more traditional styles. The German Expressionists took a more "primitive," rough approach to painting, focusing on gesture, primary colors, and bold handling in their work. Meese clearly draws on these sources and combines figurative distortions, such as flattened, mask-like faces with snout-like noses, black eyes, and graffiti phalluses; he mixes dramatic paint handling and dramatic tonal contrasts with paramilitary symbols and goofy medals. His work calls to mind Picasso's musketeer paintings, with silly generals parading around in made-up costumes—silly until we compare them to real-life characters, such as Gaddafi in his Michael Jackson uniforms.

Whether Meese would approve such a reading of these works is questionable. Seriousness doesn't seem to rank high on his list of what Kunst should be. We might be thankful for that, because if he were serious it would be kinda scary.

Atrocity Exhibition

Maurizio Cattelan: *All*; Solomon R. Guggenheim Museum, New York.
Published November 27, 2011; *CultureCatch*.

The waiting list to get a table at Cana, the new Mario Batali restaurant, is more than three months and very exclusive. You probably couldn't get one. The menus are hand-printed to resemble medieval incunabula. The servers wear Catholic schoolgirl uniforms; the tonsured sommelier wears sandals and a monk's robe. At our table we are drinking Virgin Marys. Philip Seymour Hoffman is devouring a second tray of appetizers: caviar, and dollops of sour cream on small wafers. My assistant, Juliet, who is drunk, has fucked off to the toilet, leaving me to deal with the pile of bound drafts of my screenplay *Mutant Pussy*.

The famous African American director (*Uncle Tom's Cabin-Boy, Jenny Does Da Block*) attached to the project is having the lamb. He spears a string bean in garlic sauce and mutters, "Very interesting." I am not sure if he means the script or the string bean in garlic sauce. He seems less than enthusiastic. Salvation eventually comes in the form of the dessert cart. We are handed small menus that read "Last Temptations." I order angel food cake with passion fruit sorbet for Juliet (who still has not returned). The famous African American director lights a joint.

The ironic thing about blasphemy is that, in order for there to be any cathartic meaning for the blasphemer, he must first *believe* in the subject or object he is debasing. Like, *really* believe in it. De Sade's endless accounts of nun rapes and shooting loads into the Eucharist would hold little interest, in their own right, if we were not so intrigued by how *devout* a believer he truly was. Maurizio Cattelan intrigues us for similar reasons, but to lesser effect. For all his posturing, à la Marcel Duchamp, he constantly returns to themes of a religious nature that belie his crueler intentions. His draped, marble figures suggest both Lazarus and Beuys's *I Like America and America Likes Me* (1974). A horse hangs below a hand-lettered sign that reads "INRI" (Iesvs Nazarenvs Rex Ivdaeorvm), a donkey carries a TV set, and Pope John Paul II is felled by a giant meteorite (*The Ninth Hour*, 1999). His recurring use of taxidermy gives us animals resurrected, and a small, penitent Adolph Hitler (*Him*, 2001) depicts the dictator seeking redemption.

Cattelan has, for most of his career, worked against having a career. His first solo show, in 1989, consisted of a closed gallery with a sign hanging in front that read "Be Back Soon." Early contributions to group shows held gems like a rope of knotted bed sheets dangling Rapunzel-like from a window (*A Sunday in Rivara*, 1992) or a billboard presented at the Venice Biennial promoting a new perfume (*Working is a Bad Job*, 1993). His working-class background and "born this way" bad-boy attitude pretty much marked out the path that his works eventually took: delinquent, schoolboy antics that tried hard to be anti-authoritarian and somewhat perversely blasphemous, while managing to be ingratiating enough to appear in major museum shows and exhibitions. His retrospective, *All*, at the Guggenheim, proves no exception.

The entire exhibition, meant to be an exercise in juvenile hilarity, is hung from the museum's oculus, "strung up," Cattelan explains, "like the family cat." Maybe. However, as we trudge upward, winding our way on Frank Lloyd Wright's ramp, we experience Cattelan's history as a sad Golgotha. Possibly despairing at his own productions, Cattelan has announced that this retrospective marks his retirement from the worldly creation of art making. Paul, in his letter to the Galatians, wrote, "For whatsoever a man soweth, that shall he also reap."

Cattelan's best efforts, and indeed this is a major visual spectacle, have left the audience mere gleaners. We might hope, after burying this work in the ash yard of art history, that Cattelan might resurrect himself, or his career at least, and atone somehow for these minor transgressions of art.

Snow Blind

Paul McCarthy: *The Dwarves, The Forests*; Hauser and Wirth, New York.
Published December 8, 2011; *CultureCatch*.

Once upon a time, as a queen sat sewing at her window, she pricked her finger, and three drops of blood fell on the snow gathered on the ebony windowsill. As she looked at the blood she said, "Oh, how I wish I had a daughter who had skin as white as snow, lips as red as blood, and hair black as ebony." Soon the queen gave birth to a baby girl whose skin was as white as snow, lips as red as blood, and hair as black as ebony. She named her Snow White. *The Dwarves, The Forests* is the first exhibition of sculptures to come from Paul McCarthy's recent exploration of the classic nineteenth-century German folk tale *Snow White* (*Schneewittchen*) and of the modern reinterpretation, Disney's 1937 animated *Snow White and the Seven Dwarfs*.

Bronze sculptures of Disney-like dwarves comprise most of the show—mutant ones, though, with gouged-out eyes, giant phallic noses, and bodies punctured with extra anuses and vaginas. These fractured-fairytale characters straddle the line between funny and obscene but somehow come off tinged with pathos. Constructed first from clay and found objects before being cast in bronze, traces of the preliminary creative efforts are left strewn about the pedestals: accumulated broken tools and such, connoting the effects of time. Including the blades, brushes, knives, and chisels—the tools of the trade—in the compositions reveals a layer of added meaning.

Not allowing for any afterthought, a sculptor of marble can create his work *sine cera*; with no unfortunate stroke of the hammer and chisel having to be hidden with little daubs of wax and marble dust. These perfect works were called "sincere." McCarthy plays with this concept in these works by first fucking up some of our culture's most beloved and perfect icons and then redeeming them through the abstraction of bronze. For McCarthy, the dark material and patina suggests Kazimir Malevich, Ad Reinhardt, Alberto Burri, and others who struggled to break through to pure abstraction. On the one hand we might consider McCarthy somewhat arrogant to think that these enlarged toys might sit in the same box with Malevich's *Black Squares*, but on closer examination of *White Snow Dwarf Head 5* (2011) and *White Snow Dwarf 6* (2010–2011), we see the themes of transience, death, and contingency that also weave their way through Malevich's Suprematist compositions. Like the Russian Constructivists, McCarthy is stuck in a non-believing world, one motivated by war and failing economies, and he is simply trying to create metaphors for escape.

He does achieve actual beauty in *White Snow and Dopey, Wood* (2011), a piece carved in black walnut. Here, an avatar of innocence familiar from a million cheap collectible figurines is resurrected as a giant, sexually transcendent saint. The exquisite carving, and the sculpture's expressive posture and ecstatic facial expression, are reminiscent of Italian Baroque masterworks—in particular Gian Lorenzo Bernini's orgasmic *Transverberation of Saint Teresa* (1647–52), as well as the German artist Tilman Riemenschneider's later manneristic works, the limewood figures. The organic qualities of the wood suggest something of the story line of the original Snow White story, with her triple-deaths and resurrections and ultimate initiation into womanhood. Far from being a simple riff on the horrors of pop culture, here McCarthy takes us a little deeper into the darker woods of the soul.

Naked

Edgar Degas: *Degas and the Nude*; Museum of Fine Arts, Boston.
Published December 14, 2011; *CultureCatch*.

Of all the artists who came to be known as Impressionists, with their emphasis on the effects of light and color—*plein air* painting—and focus on outdoor *motifs*, it was Edgar Degas who held on to the tradition of the figure as both subject and inspiration. In this aspect of his work he was, in some ways, the last artist of his generation to incorporate the long-standing belief that the depiction of people, whether heroic, iconic, or merely quotidian, was the noblest achievement of a painter.

When asked why he painted the ballet, Degas said, "Because it is all that is left us of the combined movement of the Greeks." This justification is what one would expect, based on his unwavering interest in the subject of the figure. Degas could see a Venus or Nike adjusting a sandal in the ballerina fixing a slipper (*Dancer Looking at the Sole of her Right Foot*, 1896–1911). Similarly, in 1856 he saw the Parthenon figures and Attic vase painting and translated those into images of the dancer Eugénie Fiocre. Like the Greeks, he believed in the primacy of the human form as the wellspring of art. His *Scene of War in the Middle Ages* (1863–65) and *Young Spartans Exercising* (1860–62) drew their compositions from Greek histories.

Degas's painting methods embraced some of the exacting disciplines of the ballet; he often mimicked the movements and positions of his models in the studio as he worked, as if rehearsing for a performance himself. The impact of his work may be diminished with the passing of time (not to mention the countless museum gift shop calendar reproductions), and the modern viewer may miss some important details, having become too familiar with the pictures. At the time he was making them, however, reviews mentioned his "extraordinary alertness to common and unidealized fact" and his "vulgar awkwardness about some of the pink legs . . . scantily endowed with beauty." In *After the Bath (Woman Drying Herself)* (1896) with its suggestion of Rubens's *Diana* or Rembrandt's *Bathsheba*, Degas updated the genre of the bather by painting working-class women (read dancers and prostitutes), not mythological or Biblical figures. With their backs turned to the viewer as they bathe, comb their hair, and so on, they are oblivious to being observed, or, as Degas wrote, "It is as though you were looking through a keyhole."

Degas's failing eyesight may have resulted in more simplified compositions, especially in his pastels. The influence of van Gogh, Gauguin, and others may have led him to brighter colors, more expressionist gesture, and simplified compositions. In his later work he especially captured the figure in movement (for example, *The Tub* [1886]), which the advent of photography was making obsolete. It is arguably fair to say that Degas, a nineteenth-century artist who lived well into the twentieth century, brought to the portrayal of the nude some of the same seismic changes that Cézanne did to landscape. Degas's influence in that respect was incalculably important; Picasso, Matisse, de Kooning, and Bacon would continue these explorations. Even today, painters, whether consciously or not, still draw new meanings from his constant searching of the figure for inspiration. Vincent van Gogh, in a letter to Gaugin, wrote that the "calm and modeled nudes of Degas have a kind of perfection that, like *coitus*, can make the infinite tangible for us."

Red Sails

Howard Hodgkin: Gagosian Gallery, New York.
Published December 19, 2011; *CultureCatch*.

James Lord once wrote of Proust that "he realized, if ever anybody did, how the recapture of time gone by can create an infinite future." This pursuit of memory, both vivid and buried, has been depicted by painters quite often in the form of the sea. Jackson Pollock's *Full Fathom Five* (1947), with its skeins of watery paint covering the detritus of the studio (keys, coins, cigarettes, and so on) like buried ocean treasure, stands as one of the prime examples of such work. Howard Hodgkin's recent paintings extend this "search of memory" further.

Hodgkin paints deceptively simple oceanscapes—two or three swaths of color separating water from sky and surrounded by plank-like pieces of wood, rough-hewn, like pieces of sunken ships. In his seascapes he presents allusive fragments of scenes remembered, experienced long ago, and partially obscured by time. *Egypt* (2007–08), *Wine-Dark Sea* (2010), and *After Whistler* (2010) present simplified, painterly strokes done with little hesitation, though with much aforethought, which suggest, rather than accurately describe, specific times and places where the artist has traveled. Rather than working "from life," Hodgkin spends a great deal of time in preparation for his encounters with his found supports (plywood, driftwood, vintage tabletops, and so on) and then attacks them with color, in great, sweeping strokes. He has remarked of his work, "I don't think you can lightly paint a picture. It's an activity I take very seriously." This, in essence, is the heart of the work. Though he may spend years in preparation, contemplating a painting, his concise gesture makes the final work look deceptively simple. His maximalist gestures, saturated palette, gestural stroke, and theatrical framing create scenes that both suggest his experience and trigger our own memories.

Remembrance is, in principle, inexhaustible; the key to such a process in a work of art is not inscribed on the surface of things but is found, instead, in the intersections where the materials and the artist's gestures affect our own histories. The Impressionists created such pictures in their own manner, as did Giacometti, Pollock, and Johns. Hodgkin continues this tradition, generating impressions of places that vary with subsequent events and viewings. His inclusion of the frame into the picture plane has the effect of drawing us further into his imaginary world. The tangible surfaces—aged, weathered, and patinated with use—supply further material that he uses as a form of collage.

In the largest work in this exhibition, *Where Seldom Is Heard a Discouraging Word* (2007–2008), a bright green "sky" suggests an inverted landscape. The mottled paint handling says "grass," as well as "sunset." Hodgkin playfully alludes to how things may be distorted in our memories over time, some things being obfuscated, whereas others are clarified. On a deeper level, though, the painting has a more universal theme. On an atomic scale, everything is connected. Each particle in a human body was once part of a star, itself a residue of the Big Bang. On a subatomic level, everything is guided by four essential forces (the strong force that binds particles together, the weak force that disintegrates them, gravity, and electromagnetism). In essence, we are composed of a universal pool of elements. When viewed from far away (in time, or space, or memory), things get very confusing. It is the dual role of the artist to invent new ways of seeing and to record the past—exploring the lost horizons of memory.

Take a Look Around

Lola Montes Schnabel: *Love Before Intimacy*; The Hole, New York.
Published January 8, 2012; *CultureCatch*.

These five works, created over the past year, which incorporate an impressive range of materials (asphalt, oil, Plaster-Weld, and copper-plating solution), comprise an allegorical group of figurative works that tell the story of androgynous youths on a remote Greek island. Schnabel states, "They depict a time of love before sexuality, with the nude youths, occasionally shrouded in sheepskins, romping playfully . . . in the landscape." Schnabel constructs these figures systematically, painting with a highly intuitive, though limited, five-color palette similar to the five-color Ko Kutani school of Japanese ceramics. The expressionist gesture of her brush is subtle, allowing for the mixed media, which have been thinned, to bleed and pool, like calligraphic brush painting. Schnabel allows the pigments to form together in layers, emolliated by the Plaster-Weld, combining the old-school pigments with the modern construction material.

Two works merit particular note. In *Albatross* (2011), a figure drags an albatross across a teal expanse of canvas, maybe an inside allusion to the burden of dragging art-historical baggage as an artist. In *Fox* (2011), the last work in the series, two figures ultimately come together in ecstasy, leaving behind this idyllic world for something else. We see elements of van Gogh, Edvard Munch, and Alice Neel jumbled together—not just in the obvious surface comparisons, but in those artists' pursuit of pulling contemporary stories out of older allegorical themes. René Ricard, one of the most perceptive critics of the 1970s and '80s, wrote, "Invention isn't important; it's the patent, the transition from the public sector into the private, the monopolizing personal usurpation of a public utility, of prior art; no matter who owned it before . . . Artists have a responsibility to their work to raise it above the vernacular." As an artist who was born at around the same time that Ricard was writing these words, Schnabel seems to have absorbed their meaning or content through some form of osmosis. Putting her own stamp on concepts seems to be exactly what these works are all about.

Schnabel appears to be exploring, with a sense of economy of means and gesture, aspects of her own life that are both personal and, through art history and literature, universal. Far from being simple remixes or pastiches of other artists' styles and techniques, Schnabel melds together these disparate elements and creates something paradoxically timeless and radical.

Violent Femmes

Sanja Iveković: *Sweet Violence*; Museum of Modern Art, New York.
Published January 13, 2012; *CultureCatch*.

From my window on the 69th floor of the Temperance Building, I can see the monument to Rosa Luxemburg that Chancellor Nirenberg erected in Zapruder Park after President Manson resigned and The Bund took control of the city. The first thing they did was to tell everyone that we no longer had to worry about The Flu; the virus had mutated and was now known as The Plague. Infection was spread through physical contact, most often rape (Katya and I had a good laugh at that), and the resulting zombies it produced were now wandering the city.

Posters of women in sunglasses are plastered on walls. They warn what's left of the panicked population that one side effect of the zombification is dilation of the pupils, until the whole eye turns black. Zombies look for the whites of the eyes. Sunglasses, the posters tell us, are a fashion-must this season.

I am staring at the sculpture in the square, the golden lady atop a tall obelisk. I know that it says "kunst" on the side facing me. I can't remember what it says on the other three sides. I have only been outside once since they put it in the square. Just once, when the Neroin ran out and I had to get more. There was a full clip in the Glock before I went out, but now there are just two rounds left: one for Katya and one for me. Ha Ha. Katya's breathing is slow and ragged. She is starving to death. So am I. I don't get my period anymore, but I have cramps all the time. They distract me from the hunger. Without more Neroin we aren't going to make it much longer. And, besides, I want to see what the other words on the sculpture are before I die. The red handbills, crumpled like leaves, flutter in the wind around the square. They inform us that there are now Red States and Blue States. Red States are for the zombies. We now live in a Red State.

I go over to Katya, who is lying on the bed. She hasn't slept in six days. Her eyes barely open. "I'm going out," I say. She whispers, "Under the moonlight? The serious moonlight?" "Oh, baby," I say, "Just you shut your mouth. I have something to help you sleep." She smiles, turns her head away for a moment. The shell casing makes no sound as it hits the carpet. I lock the door carefully as I am leaving, but not before I pile extra blankets on top of Katya to keep her safe and warm. I am going to be ravenous when I get home.

Sanja Iveković, feminist, activist, artist, and video pioneer, makes art that blurs the boundaries between the reality that we know and the realities that we can imagine. Her retrospective at The Museum of Modern Art covers four decades of her career and includes seminal works, such as *Sweet Violence* (1974), *Personal Cuts* (1982), and the monumental sculptural installation *Lady Rosa of Luxembourg* (2001).

Rosa is impressively installed in the museum's lobby. The gilded figure of a pregnant woman atop a 34-foot-tall obelisk, with words such as "kunst," "kitsch," "la justice," and "bitch" inscribed at the base, creates a recontextualized, feminist take on the phallocentric Barnett Newman sculpture, which often occupies the same space. Made for a temporary public art project in Luxembourg, *Rosa* is a full-scale replica of that city's *Gëlle Fra (Golden Lady)* war memorial, except that the original figure is the Greek goddess Nike, and the pedestal is inscribed with quotations celebrating national, male, war heroes.

Her series *Women's House* includes a set of poster-sized photographs appropriated from ads for high-end sunglasses, each depicting a model hiding behind a pair of Foster Grants. The ad copy is obscured by the story of an abused woman, upending the image by suggesting the glasses hide black eyes and broken noses. Unlike her contemporary Marina Abramović, who last year was encamped in MoMA, sitting eight hours a day staring at the visitors, Iveković creates art that intervenes between the viewer and a potentially hostile world—works of art that hurl themselves in front of us, both as interrogations of our contemporary cultural assumptions and warnings of things to come.

Temptation

Damien Hirst: *The Complete Spot Paintings 1986–2011*; Gagosian Gallery: New York,
London, Paris, Beverly Hills, Rome, Athens, Geneva, and Hong Kong.
Published January 27, 2012; *CultureCatch*.

The philosopher Andy Warhol once wrote that Modernity was all about making choices.
Making choices and liking things. Campbell's soup, tuna fish, movie stars, transvestites, drugs,
and male hustlers were all bound together. Choose the one you like best. Individually, or in
endless combinations. Damien Hirst's art, and in particular his *Spot Paintings*, realize this
philosophy and, in fact, may be the end-game of painting that the artist Andy Warhol strove
to achieve. *The Complete Spot Paintings* are presented at all eleven of Gagosian's locations
simultaneously and feature more than 300 individual works, from the first spot on a board that
Hirst created in 1986 to the most recent work (painted by a huge team of assistants) in 2011.
We are given a survey of spots in myriad sizes, from the smallest *Spot Painting* comprising half
a spot and measuring 1 x 1 1/2 inches (1996), to a work of monumental spottiness comprised
of only four spots, each 60 inches in diameter. The most recent painting (the one completed in
2011) contains 25,781 spots that are each 1 millimeter in diameter—with no single color ever
repeated. This fact must be taken on trust, as such chromatic analysis is impossible *in situ*.

Unusual for exhibitions, gift shops are located within the Gagosian's 24th Street
and Madison Avenue galleries. Whether meant to take the piss or not, it is both a witty
commentary on "moving merch" by the former iconoclast from Leeds and a way of making
additional, and seemingly endless, *Spot Paintings*. Spot key chains. Spot wallets. Spot cuff links.
Spot handbags. Spot clocks. Spot coffee cups. Stick-on spots . . .

As much of a visual and technical achievement as the exhibition is, there is one
Spot Painting missing—perhaps Hirst's most ambitious. The Beagle 2 was a British space
project that formed part of the Mars Express mission in 2003. On board the landing vehicle
was a *Spot Painting*. In an effort to publicize the project, its designers sought and received
the endorsement and participation of several British artists. Damon Albarn and the band
Blur composed the call sign. Hirst's gold-plated *Spot Painting* was to double as the "test
card" (calibration target plate) intended for color calibrating the Beagle 2's cameras and
spectrophotometers once it was placed on the Mars surface. Although the Beagle 2 craft was
successfully deployed from the Mars Express "mothership" on December 25, confirmation of a
successful landing was not received. In the days following, the Lovell Telescope at Jodrell Bank
also failed to pick up a signal from Beagle 2. Attempts to locate the lander continued through
February 2004, using the Mars Express transmissions. Although regular calls continued
to be made, they went unanswered. The possibility of connecting to the lander rested on
February 2, the date when the Beagle 2 was pre-programmed to expect the Mars Express
probe to fly overhead and revert to Autotransmit, the last communication back-up mode.
No communication was established with Beagle 2. The Beagle 2 was officially declared lost on
February 6, 2004. All hope for interplanetary *Spot Paintings* ended.

Dark Christmas

Various artists: *Dark Christmas*; Leo Koenig, Inc., New York.
Published February 1, 2012; *Brooklyn Rail*.

Dark Christmas, at Leo Koenig, gives us an alternative view of the holiday—something like *The Grinch Who Stole Christmas* meets *Caligula*. Andres Serrano's *Piss Christ* (1987) comes off looking greeting-card friendly—when placed in the context of Cindy Sherman's *Untitled #122* (1983), a Mommy Dearest-looking, bleached-blonde, and slightly eggnoggy-drenched self-portrait. Hans Bellmer's photographs of broken toy dolls from the 1930s and '40s add a poignant but creepy touch. Paul McCarthy's *Hot Dog* (1974), a series of photographs of an early performance, is both fascinating and repulsive—though something from his Santa Claus series would have been a better fit. Of particular note in this lively grouping are several examples of outstanding painting, including Georg Baselitz's seminal *The Big Night Down the Drain* (1962–63) and Nicola Tyson's *Self-Portrait with Friend* (2011), a radiant double portrait in cheerful hues. The latter is reminiscent of Matisse's *The Conversation* (1908–12), in which Matisse depicts his wife Amélie in a black and green housecoat, seated in a throne-like armchair, while he wears his signature striped pajamas. Tyson simplifies her background into two flat planes of color—yellow for the walls and blue for the ground. In an exhibition dominated by darkly-themed works, Tyson's *Self-Portrait with Friend* is a welcome gift, indeed.

Bat Out of Hell

Joyce Pensato: *Batman Returns*; Friedrich Petzel Gallery, New York.
Published February 5, 2012; *CultureCatch*.

In the 1970s, The Joker, Batman's greatest nemesis, had his own nine-issue comic book series, in which he faces off against a variety of both superheroes and supervillains. Because of the restrictive "comic books code," "good" ultimately had to triumph over "evil" in every storyline. This led to some creative writing strategies—that is, how to make one of the most morally unhinged villains in superhero lore appear to do something "good" every third issue. In the fourth and fifth issue, this problem is solved by The Joker's kidnapping of a Charles Schultz-like character and keeping him a prisoner in the HaHaHacienda. Although The Joker demands a huge ransom for the return of Gotham's beloved cartoonist, he also derives great, sadistic pleasure from forcing the artist to write cartoons in which the Charlie Brown character is drowned, beaten up, has his puppy killed . . . In the end, although The Joker eludes Batman, it is the cartoonist who has revenge. He refuses to leave even after the ransom is paid. "Now I'm gonna draw myself kicking the little brat!" he says. "Leave? You can't make me leave! I'm having too much fun! I'm NEVER going to LEAVE! Ha. Ha ha! HaHaHa. HAHAHAHA . . ." Schultz, himself a longtime proponent of Modern and Conceptual Art, applauded the humor of the story.

Joyce Pensato uses Batman as the predominant subject and inspiration for this exhibition. The Batman motif first appeared in her drawings in the mid-'70s and was only used periodically since then—her mainstay subjects being animated television characters, such as Bart Simpson, Homer, Mickey Mouse, and Cartman. Although these characters allow Pensato the opportunity to juxtapose her heroic, muscular gestural painting technique with the graphic lines of the animated figure, it is in these images of The Bat that she elevates her work to a deeper, psychological level.

In *Batman I*, *Batman II*, and *Batman III* (all 2011), we see the cowled face of Batman being reduced to a cipher. Through violent spattered strokes, she creates an image that resembles the Bat Signal—the image that Commissioner Gordon shines on the clouds to call the hero when Gotham is in trouble. The psychology of Pensato excavating the Batman image in this way calls to mind Freud's theory of The Return of the Repressed. The Return of the Repressed is the process whereby repressed elements, preserved in the unconscious, tend to reappear in consciousness or in behavior in the shape of secondary and more or less unrecognizable "derivatives of the unconscious." Parapraxes—bungled or symptomatic actions—are examples of such derivatives. Beginning with *The Interpretation of Dreams* (1900), Freud emphasized the "indestructible" nature of unconscious material as the irreducible character of memory traces. If we have no memories of events during the first years of life, this is because of the repression that affects them. In a sense, one could say memories are retained, their recollection depending solely on the way in which they are (or are not) invested with libidinal energy. In these paintings we see Pensato mining childhood images for hidden, internal meanings and significance, uncovering something personal in the universal visual language of pop graphic icons.

In the installation pieces included in the exhibition, *Fuggetabout It I* (2012) and *Fuggetabout It II* (2012), we are given a plethora of studio ephemera: photos of James Dean, Marlon Brando (from *The Godfather*), Hallowe'en masks, Larry Clark pin-up hustlers, and *Sopranos* publicity pictures. All of this source material is splattered with silver and black paint, like a crime scene might appear in a black-and-white police photo. Here Pensato elaborates on the creation of her imagery, allowing us into the recreated studio where her heroes—and villains—are made. While the installations themselves are interesting (they are reminiscent of Paul McCarthy), she runs the risk of allowing the viewer too deep into her lair. We may never want to leave. Ha. Ha ha. HaHaHaHa. HAHAHAHAHA . . .

Bulls on Parade

Jean Dubuffet: *The Last Two Years*; Pace Gallery, New York.
Published February 9, 2012; *CultureCatch*.

Jean Dubuffet (1901–1985) was born in Le Havre and moved to Paris where he was briefly enrolled at the Académie Julian. Leaving the school in 1918, he began to follow his own path in painting, and, after a brief sojourn in wine dealing (the family business), spent the rest of his artistic life seeking an authentic art based on the work of prisoners, the insane, the naïve, and other marginal outsiders. The style he developed, and which ultimately became its own school, is now called Art Brut.

Dubuffet often presented himself as outside the "art world," but this is mildly disingenuous. He was a close friend of both André Masson and Antonin Artaud. His copious writings on art were gathered in the seminal book *Asphyxiating Culture*—almost a bible for art students following the wave of Neo Expressionism and the Transavangardia in the late seventies and eighties. Jean-Michel Basquiat, Terry Winters, Brice Marden, to name a few, made work that would have been nearly impossible without Dubuffet's trailblazing *Hourloupe* works in the sixties.

In *The Last Two Years*, we are given examples of two series of paintings Dubuffet did in the eighties: *Mires* (Test Patterns) and *Non-Lieux* (No-Grounds, a legal term meaning neither guilty nor innocent). These high-energy, reductive, free-form works compress many of the themes and effects that Dubuffet often sought into concise, thoughtful paintings that belie the age of the artist. (These are his final works, much like Matisse's *Cut-Outs*.) At the time they were shown, Daniel Abadie wrote that the works demonstrated Dubuffet's "ambition to create a meta-language of visual art with its own rules and syntax free of any habitual mind-set, thereby eluding both the sneaky subliminal conditioning of the culture and established social norms, in which the painter discerns the same reductive power, the same refusal of any independent adventure . . ."

Adventure was and is the keyword to approaching Dubuffet's paintings. In *Mire G 96 (Kowloon) June 22, 1983*, Dubuffet's graffiti lines and simplified red-yellow-blue palette remind us of Keith Haring's large-scale works and describe a Chinese peninsula—one that Dubuffet wanted to visit but never did (or would). In some ways he used limited means to suggest greater stories, like his compatriot Jean-Luc Godard (with *Alphaville*). He created worlds that both existed in reality and were shaped by his own vision of reality. *Mire G 67 (Boléro) May 11, 1983* alludes to the bolero, a form of Spanish dance, as well as the waistcoat worn by bullfighters. The speed of execution and the mastery of the paint handling remind us of Picasso's late works; Dubuffet also finished a painting a day toward the end, proudly inscribing the dates and times on the back of the canvases. (Fragonard was known to do this too.) The reference to the bullfight is significant. Picasso identified with it; it was almost his signature theme. In these paintings Dubuffet is in the ring, so to speak, with Picasso.

Dubuffet wrote about these final efforts to his dealer, Arne Glimcher: "These paintings were intended to challenge the objective nature of being. The notion of being is presented here as relative rather than irrefutable: it is merely a projection of our minds, a whim of our thinking. The mind has the right to establish being wherever it cares to and for as long as it likes. There is no intrinsic difference between being and fantasy; being is an attribute that the mind assigns to fantasy. One could apply the term 'nihilism' to this challenge of being, but it is reverse nihilism, since it confers the power of being on any fantasy whatsoever, given that being is a secretion of our minds . . . being and thinking are one and the same."

Gigantic

Rachel Kneebone: *Regarding Rodin*; Brooklyn Museum, Brooklyn.
Published February 14, 2012; *CultureCatch*.

Vitruvius, in *The Ten Books on Architecture*, proposed that the perfected form of the human body could be diagrammed by being placed inside both a circle and a square. Though he himself did not provide illustrations, Leonardo da Vinci made a drawing demonstrating this proposition to illustrate Paciolio's *On Divine Proportion* (1509). This was more than a geometric exercise, as Vitruvius imbued the square and the circle with divine attributes: the circle represented the cosmos and the square, those things secular. In the Middle Ages artists painted the crucifixion, both as a representation of Christ's divinity as well as his incarnation as an earthly being. Five hundred years later, August Rodin upended many of these concepts regarding the proportion and deportment of the figure in sculpture with his monumental *The Gates of Hell* and *Monument to Balzac*.

The British sculptor Rachel Kneebone, making her museum debut at the Brooklyn Museum, creates a dialog between her porcelain sculpture and Rodin's bronzes. Rainer Maria Rilke wrote of Rodin's work, "No part of the body was insignificant or trivial, for even the smallest of them was alive. Life, which appeared on faces with the clarity of a dial, easily read and full of signs of the times, was greater and more diffuse . . . more eternal." Rodin twisted and torqued bronze into a simulation of muscle in action. His studies of individual parts of the body, arms, legs, and so on were subsets of larger equations, yet worlds unto themselves. Kneebone adopts his strategies and then expands on them, like a fractal mathematical equation—endlessly multiplying limbs and torsos, piling them up, and rearranging them.

In *Eyes that look close at wounds themselves are wounded* (2010), a figure sits atop a round plinth. Brambles of fingers, ivy, and roses creep up the base, while a hooded figure, its cowl pulled back, seems to scream from a vulva-like orifice. Its Alien-like body, all knuckles and cunts, is arched, dragging a third set of labia along the ground like a snail. Somehow Kneebone imbues this wretched creature with enough pathos to balance out the sci-fi horror by taking a page from Rodin's book. He wrote, "Why am I blamed? Why is the head allowed and not [other] portions of the body? Every part of the human figure is expressive." Kneebone produces some of the same effects as Rodin's *Burghers of Calais* (1884–1889) with a visceral connection to the body that Rodin sought. Human emotions such as grief and despair are expressed through gesture—though fragmented, we connect them, through viewing, into a story.

Rodin's *Burghers* was controversial in its time for showing struggle rather than achievement. It tried to recreate an event rather than depict the outcome. In Kneebone's work the shrouded figure is both Lazarus and Michelangelo's Pietà—its amorphousness allows us to project ourselves on it too. A mass of teeming viscera and vag—it presents vulnerability rather than talks about it.

Kneebone combines and subverts two conventions of sculpture, the triumphal monument and the historical representation of heroes. By working in porcelain, she is bringing a feminist twist to the very idea of "monumental" artwork. Her large-scale *The Paradise of Despair* (2011) usurps the concept of the triumphal column, a classical monument of military victory that dates back to Vitruvius. She slyly intertwines parody into the mix; in place of a noble or heroic figure, she gives us five headless bodies, upside down. Smaller figures crawl up the base to form piles of victims, or participants in a mutant orgy. Whether a paean to war victims or tribute to de Sade, Kneebone, like Rodin, creates a cosmos big enough for both.

On Some Faraway Beach

Liz Markus: *The Look of Love*; Zieher Smith, New York.
Published February 21, 2012; *CultureCatch*.

Color, like scent, is one of the most powerful triggers of memory. The smell of cinnamon or nutmeg brings us back to our childhood kitchens, sweetly reminiscent; like something Mother used to bake. Or a signature perfume reminds us of a first fuck. Liz Markus uses color to tap into our collective memories, evoking the hues of time—period colors: seventies Polaroids, eighties adverts, and the lurid tints of souvenir postcards. In the past her work used color as a weapon—a blunt, punk-rockers attempt at identity. The paintings in *The Look of Love* show Markus all grown-up, referencing a complex history of Modernism and Color Field painting.

In *Leaving My Best Friend* (2012), dark palm trees sway, backlit, as if viewed from a beach chair in Margaritaville. Roy G. Biv rainbows of color are washed across the scene, reminding us that we are gazing at a work of fiction. Meta-painting on one level; a nod to how contingent our grasp on nature has become on another. These beaches may be scenes from Paradise, or one of the oil-slicked beaches of the BP gulf. Vivid purples and oranges dominate, but it is the deftly jotted palms that hold our attention—almost *Sumi-e*-like in their execution. What at first glance may appear to be *A rebours* (à la Huysmans) is in fact more in keeping with Jackson Pollock's statement "I am Nature."

I Say a Little Prayer for You (2012) and *When You're Shattered* (2012) are paintings of a different order altogether. These stained, washy, earth-toned landscapes show Markus reclaiming the territory once held by the late Helen Frankenthaler. These works drop some of the reserve of her more ironic past and show her taking on the styles of her artistic heroes (such as Morris Louis or Jules Olitski) head-on. Her style, bold and forthright, evokes something of van Gogh, who created landscapes that were also imbued with a sense of passion. His shifting perspectives and slashing brushstrokes, like Markus's splashy puddles of pigment, privileged expression over representation. In a letter to his brother Theo, van Gogh wrote, "A painter does better to start from the colors on his palette than to start from Nature . . . you must set it down at once and then leave it alone . . . paint in one rush, as much as possible, in one rush . . . the ideal is to paint '*comme le lion qui dévore le morceau*.'" Markus brings a lived sense of place to these works, despite their improbable sources. She injects poetry back into paint.

In an 1872 essay on contemporary poetry, the philosopher Hyppolyte Taine might have been describing these watery works: "Trust the spirit, as Nature does, to make the form; for otherwise we only imprison the spirit, and not embody it. Inward evermore to outward—so in life, and so in art, which is still life . . . Poetry, thus conceived, has only one protagonist, the soul and mind of the poet; and only one style—a suffering and triumphant cry from the heart."

Celebrity Skin

Eric Fischl: *Portraits*; Mary Boone Gallery, New York.
Published February 27, 2012; *CultureCatch*.

We are eating lunch at La Mer. Fish tacos, something called bichon frisé ceviche, and churros y sea urchins chocolat. There are seven empty bottles of a 1983 Dom Perignon on the table, along with several empty phials of what I thought was cocaine but wasn't. Spike Lee, David Salle, Winona Ryder, and Trent Reznor are trying to discuss a new Julian Schnabel film, but I can't hear them as Oleander, a model/actress, and my date, keeps interrupting. Alba Clemente (sans Francesco), Gwyneth Paltrow, and Dave Navarro are discussing the new Coldplay CD. There is silver glitter everywhere, and it keeps blowing into my glass. Outside, past the dry-ice machine, a limo is waiting to pick us up. My screenplay (*Mutant Pussy*) has mysteriously disappeared, but a PA has gone to fetch another copy. Juliet, my assistant, is, as usual, in the toilet, this time with Ron Jeremy, who will be playing the part of a "whimsical nanny" in the film.

[Jump cut]

The location changes to the gallery and: Several extras are standing around smoking, and the set dressers are pouring sand over the floor to create a "beachy feel." The paintings in the set are bright—lots of celebrity portraits. A large one, *Simon and Anh* (2003) of Simon Cowell and his girlfriend (nude, sprawled out over him, with something resembling a . . . furry chinchilla in her lap), is taken down, then put back up again when the director changes his mind. Silver glitter from the restaurant has made its way into the gallery. The cinematographer is apoplectic and orders its removal immediately. I am wearing a black Prada pullover turtleneck, Levi's, and custom-made shoes (by someone named Dieter in Berlin) that resemble hooves. Oleander is now talking to Jay Leno's Adderall dealer and has also apparently found a new supply of champagne.

Burned into the opening sequence of the film: Dating from 1992 to 2011, the works in the exhibition range from sketched portraits cropped to the face, to commanding single figures, to complex arrangements of couples, families, or groups. As in the fraught suburban scenes for which he first rose to prominence, with each approach to portraiture Fischl demonstrates his mastery of conjuring form and light from paint to communicate the psychological bearing of his subjects.

In front of a large painting called *Joan and John* (2002) of a couple wearing what looks like Abercrombie & Fitch, or maybe Ralph Lauren, and the woman resembling Anna Wintour, the actual couple is talking to Lorne Michaels. "I open restaurants," Joan says as Lorne tries to escape. "The last one I opened was in West Hollywood. Maybe you have been to it. It is neo-classic Californian cuisine . . ." Lorne backs away slowly, saying, "Um, I've never been to *West* Hollywood . . . though I'm, uh, sure I would love it . . ." He goes and stands in front of his portrait, *Lorne* (2006) and begins to chat with Amy Poehler. Lars Ulrich and Sting are looking at *The Clemente Family* (2005).

[Scene deleted]

Richard Price, who is writing the screenplay, enters, tripping over some cable left near the door. Smoke from the fog machine is filling up the gallery, and everybody is waving it away, trying to find their marks. Richard's girlfriend, Teddy (a female, female impersonator), sees *The Prices: Richard, Judy, Annie, and Gen* (2008) and storms out. Cindy Sherman shoots pictures of the mini-drama on her iPhone. Colored gels—lavender, fuchsia, puce, and something called forsythia—are tried out and discarded as various lead actors complain about how they make them look "wan." Finally, the art director chooses a large beach scene (*The Gang* [2006]) and arranges the principal actors in front of it for the first shot: Mara Rooney arguing with Kate Winslet about bull markets on Wall Street affecting their relationship. Later in the film, Kate will adopt a Somali baby, after Mara's character finds out she had aborted their co-partnered, turkey-baster fetus. A scenic artist is quickly painting a portrait of Winslet into the beach scene, as she was a last-minute replacement for Keira Knightley, who has entered rehab at an "undisclosed location" in Malibu. Steve Martin, who plays Rooney's father, a ruthless businessman with Alzheimer's, stands nearby, rehearsing his lines, which will eventually be cut. Someone spills a drink on Bill Pullman's jacket, and a new one is quickly produced.

The director calls action, people begin milling around, the Steadicam moving in on the scene, the special effects guy starts the snow machine, and Skrillex begins playing in the background.

Small Faces

Various artists: *The Renaissance Portrait from Donatello to Bellini*; Metropolitan Museum of Art, New York.
Published February 28, 2012; *CultureCatch*.

The Metropolitan Museum of Art in New York, in conjunction with the Bode-Museum, Berlin, has gathered over 150 fifteenth-century portraits: sculptures, drawings, paintings, and bronzes. Unlike most Renaissance portrait exhibitions, this one limits its purview to Italian artists and focuses specifically on the courts of Florence and Venice, as well as the princely courts of Ferrara, Milan, and Naples. This approach wisely narrows our view of this seminal moment in history, one that literally defined the way that "the portrait" would be viewed for centuries to come.

The exhibition is divided into several rooms, giving examples of portraits of women, portraits of men, and pictures depicting the new ruling classes, such as the Medicis. The show opens with works by Donatello and by Fra Angelico. Here we see the birth of the portrait: a series of four profiles of men with turban-like headcloths, a codified form of portraiture—what the Dutch later called *troines*, or types. Paolo Uccello's *Profile of a Man* (1430–40) and Masaccio's *Profile of a Man* (1426–27) are spectacular examples of the artist wringing out of this genre the personalities of the individual while still maintaining one foot in the past; we see them taking a tentative step in the direction of what we would consider today to be a portrait. In *The Civilization of the Renaissance in Italy* (1860), Jacob Burckhardt wrote, with regard to the changing face of the portrait, "Man previously was conscious of himself only as a member of a race, people, . . . family . . . In Italy this veil first melted . . . An *objective* treatment and consideration became possible. The *subjective* side at the same time asserted itself . . . Man became a spiritual *individual* and was recognized as such."

The second room, showing portraits of women, represents the greatest shift in thinking—not just in portraiture, but in suitable subjects for a portrait. A mere century before, Giovanni Boccaccio had written, "The female is an imperfect animal, stirred by a thousand passions both unpleasant and abominable even to think of, let alone to consider: if men looked upon women as they should they would take care to steer away." In Florence, though, Botticelli brought the portrayal of women to a high order of painting. Artists had begun to see female portraiture as, first and foremost, a tribute to idealized beauty. Paintings were documents of a betrothal or a celebration of a marriage; the idealization of the subject was, in effect, a testament to her spiritual worth. One contemporary motto ran, *Virtutem Forma Decorat* (Beauty Adorns Virtue). With his *Ideal Portrait of a Lady (Simonetta Vespucci)* (1475–80), Botticelli was less interested in mimesis, wanting to display his artful portrayal of the subject in order to render her more virtuous and worthy. In contrast, Lorenzo di Credi's *Portrait of a Young Woman* (late 1490s) is an otherworldly study in the sacrament of marriage. Ginevra di Giovanni di Niccolò, the daughter of a Florentine merchant, holds an engagement ring, her features blurred by the *sfumato* so highly prized in da Vinci's paintings, and she is surrounded by juniper bushes (her namesake).

Botticelli's *Giuliano de' Medici* (1478–80) is more of an homage than an actual portrait. Painted after his assassination, Botticelli worked from de' Medici's death mask (also on view). We are perhaps more accustomed to this kind of Renaissance portrait—the strong patricians, their families, their wives—presented for display in the family house. These served to promote the idea of their worthiness; many Florentines believed that their nobility must be earned through striving and success. Indeed, with courtly intrigues and assassinations, sometimes a direct lineage was impossible to maintain.

Another aspect, though, to these more familiar images is Domenico Ghirlandaio's *Portrait of an Old Man and a Boy* (1490). Ghirlandaio renders, in tempera's lush hues, ugliness—not of character, but of visage (the old man probably suffered from rhinophyma)—tempered by a sensitive portrayal of familial love through his grandson. Aristotle's *Poetics* speaks of the possibility of creating beauty through a masterful portrayal of what is ugly, in order to describe what is good. Ghirlandaio brings this to life by showing us the scarred face of the grandfather seen through the adoring eyes of the child.

Side by side, Andrea Mantegna's *Francesco Gonzaga* (n.d.) and Pisanello's *Leonello d'Este* (1444) show us just how little has changed in six centuries. Mantegna's delicate tempera painting, with its pinks and blues, might remind us of Picasso's *The Actor* (1904) from his Rose Period (in the Met's collection). Pisanello's portrait combines a rich brocade tunic, a whorly head of stylish hair, and a sinewy rose bush climbing behind the profile of d'Este. It relates to nothing so much as van Gogh's *La Berceuse (Woman Rocking a Cradle; Augustine-Alix Pellicot Roulin, 1851–1930)* (1889) (also at the Met). No, really—go compare the two.

Isabella d'Este wrote to the Countess of Acerra in 1493, with regard to a recent gift of a portrait, "Now that we have your image both on paper and in wax, we shall hold it very dear and look at it often." We still are.

Tripping Daisy

Terry Winters: *Cricket Music, Tessellation Figures, & Notebook*; Matthew Marks Gallery, New York.
Published March 3, 2012; *CultureCatch*.

Abstraction, particularly in painting, is difficult to write about. You are often stuck with banalities like, "That white area should be a little bit more to the left," or "That blue reminds me of this one day when I was surfing Zuma . . ." Andy Warhol, whenever he wanted to avoid a subject of discussion—like death—would fob off the topic by saying, "Gee, that's so . . . abstract." The bane of writing about art, this abstraction is.

Terry Winters, one of the few artists in the New Abstraction movement in the eighties (along with Ross Bleckner, certain Gerhard Richters, Christopher Wool) made it somewhat easier; he dealt in abstraction of things: plants, pigment structures seen under a microscope, flora and fauna—something we could get a handle on. In the last decade he has broadened his range, creating allover works, Baroque labyrinths, architectural paint structures, which, while not traveling far from his original territory, seemed to open up possibilities in his painterly project.

His recent show, *Cricket Music, Tessellation Figures, & Notebook*, takes these ideas and brings them further into the realm of conceptual abstraction. He has introduced digital space and optic processes into the new work, creating an often dazzling, though sometimes oblique, sense of space. Winters depicts forms inspired by mathematical concepts, such as tessellations and knot theory, as well as shapes drawn from the natural and scientific world. His kaleidoscopic compositions of overlapping grids and patterns create complex pictorial spaces, and his recent use of transparent glazes (as opposed to his previous dense, hand-ground pigments) allow the viewer to see, as he says, "all the events that went into the making of the painting." "Tessellation Figures" in the title refers to the process of creating a two-dimensional plane through the repetition of a geometric shape.

Winters, a highly articulate artist, speaks about the influence of digital technologies in his painting. In a recent discussion he said, "The back and forth between media you're describing is part of what I was saying about changes in rhythm and shifts of scale. . . . Bringing in a wide range of reference materials along with other processes, techniques, and physical approaches to the way the paintings are constructed, are ways of expanding the work into new territories. . . . I think computers fundamentally change the way people approach information and visualization. Space is generated through thought, and that has some relationship to new technologies."

Indeed, *Tessellation Figures (1)* (2011) presents a layered, fractal-like kaleidoscope, something like Alice down the rabbit hole. Its handmade facture, though, reminds us of early CGI images in movies, or of sixties experimental film. *Tessellation Figures* (2011) morphs Winters's earlier, earthy ground and biomorphic figures into a mash-up with a puzzle-like rectilinear form. Next to the completed form, three shapes, like the extra parts we end up with when we take apart a car engine or build an IKEA bookshelf, hover to the right. Forms in search of a host. *Tessellation Figures (4)* (2011) is the show's standout—the biological, flowery forms balance the composition, layers of triangular shapes strike a trippy note, and the washy blue ground is reminiscent of Matisse's still lifes. The organic and the synthetic mesh in harmony.

Notebooks, presented in a second gallery, explain the thinking process from which these paintings developed. Layered computer printouts, children's drawings, texts from science books are all grist for Winters's mill. While it is a common complaint that an artist should do his homework, just not show it in a gallery, Winters's noodlings are of interest here. He is a smart artist doing smart work. It is a bonus, and our good fortune, that they happen to be beautiful paintings as well.

Halber Mensch

Georg Baselitz: Gagosian Gallery, New York.
Published March 6, 2012; *CultureCatch*.

> Art demands fanaticism.
> — Adolf Hitler, 1915

Georg Baselitz's (born 1938, Deutschbaselitz, Saxony, Germany) recent work at Gagosian, paintings on a monumental scale, present the artist as a still-vital explorer, using both his personal history as well as myriad art historical references in a search for a unified, iconic image. Enormous canvases, measuring over twelve feet high, combine elements from his early works, such as *Die grosse Nacht im Eimer* (1962–63) and *A Modern Painter* (1966), remixed in a gambit designed to distance himself still further from the nearly thirty-year span of his signature, inverted, pseudo-Ab Ex work. A sense of nostalgia and reflection is evident here, as well as an undiminished appetite for new forms and styles.

Of these pieces, Baselitz says, "I don't want to create a monster; I want to make something which is new, exceptional, something that only I do . . . something that references tradition but is still new." Tradition is key here; *Melancholic Design* (2011–12), *Ending* (2011), and *The Flugelhornist Gracie Irlam* (2012) reference Antonin Artaud's peyote drawings, Jackson Pollock's *Portrait and a Dream* (1953), Jean-Michel Basquiat, and Jean Dubuffet. *Enddesign* (2011) is a nod to Albrecht Dürer's *Melencolia I* (1514). We also get, more overtly, Richard Diebenkorn and Lester Johnson in the utterly forgettable *Beginning* (2011) and *Nobody was at home in London?* (2011). In all these pictures, which are horizontally bisected à la Rothko or an Exquisite Corpse drawing, gestural brushwork in pale greens, pinks, and terra-cottas riff on the early cartoon paintings of Philip Guston—a nice twist, as Guston stole a whole lot back in the early sixties from Baselitz's *Pandemonium* period. Like in his 2007 exhibition *Remixes*, which were brilliant reduxes of his back catalog, Baselitz continues to obsessively pour over, and distill, his earlier periods, trying to find new ways of creating paintings—as well as attempting to reassemble the heroic figures he shattered and turned turvey-topsy in the late sixties. From a vantage of maturity, he seems to say, it is time to put Humpty Dumpty back together again.

This makes sense, as Baselitz himself—coming from East to West Germany as a youth and having lived in Germany through the reunification of the nineties—seems to reenact in paint much of his autobiography. The disintegrating figures of his "Heroic Type," Artists, Soldiers, Hunters, and so on, presented his characters as fragments—fragments of the history that Walter Benjamin described. Seen from our point of view, they represented his attempt at a psychological archeological dig. Donald Kuspit wrote of Baselitz in the late eighties that his was "an openly German art, in style and theme . . . haunted by the question of its relationship to the Nazi past . . . using [his] work as a touchstone to frame questions of German Neo-Expressionism in terms of Freud's distinction between mourning and melancholy: is it more a matter of mourning for the German disaster of World War II or of melancholy attachment to a mythically heroic Germany—a bygone "prelapsarian" Germany? Inherent in the German sense of self is the sense of being a damaged subject, always on the verge of disintegration." In these paintings, to an even larger degree than the works to which Kuspit was referring, we see Baselitz attempting to stitch together all the elements (styles, histories, stories) of his past, and, contrary to his explanations of the work, create something like a Frankenstein's Monster of painting.

We might see his "mash-ups" of styles and symbols as an older artist taking stock, trying to figure out his sense of place in history. We might also see these paintings as history lessons for a newer generation—one not raised in "Post-War Germany." They are indexes of history, both art and personal, which might best be read as a primer of painting—a cut-and-paste scrapbook, or the notes of a painter for the future.

When Darkness Doubles

David Lynch: Tilton Gallery, New York.
Published March 20, 2012; *CultureCatch*.

Let's begin with this, from *Les fleurs du mal*: "Everything, even the color black / Seemed refurbished, bright, iridescent / The liquid encased in its glory / In the crystallized ray . . ."

Although better known as a filmmaker, David Lynch, who is exhibiting is paintings, collages and photographs at Tilton Gallery, has for years walked the fine line between art and entertainment. Like Julian Schnabel, though, Lynch's paintings occupy a separate terrain, and offer a rare opportunity to see into the psyche of a very private artist who also happens to be a very public figure. Lynch has stated that "all my paintings are organic, violent comedies. They have to be violently done and primitive and crude, and to achieve that I try to let nature paint more than I paint. I wouldn't know what to do with color . . . to me is too real. It's limiting. It doesn't allow too much of a dream. The more you throw black into [it] the more dreamy it gets . . . Black has depth. It's like a little egress; you can go into it, and because it keeps on continuing to be dark, the mind kicks in, and a lot of things that are going on in there become manifest. And you start seeing what you're afraid of. You start seeing what you love, and it becomes like a dream."

Lynch's films, from *Eraserhead* to *The Elephant Man* to *Twin Peaks*, have contained dream-sequences which unite both the internal narrative of the story, as well as link together his movies through their use of this trope. In much the same way Lynch's paintings function as windows into a dream world. Stark, primitive images, like those of Forrest Bess, are tied together with surrealist text, or found objects, creating Exquisite Corpse compositions. He explains: "The words in the paintings are sometimes important to make you start thinking about what else is going on in there. And a lot of times, the words excite me as shapes, and something'll grow out of that. I used to cut these little letters out and glue them on. They just look good all lined up like teeth . . . sometimes they become the title of the painting."

Going to Visit UR House (2008-09), a watercolor, gives us the rows of text teeth, narrating a non-story, of sorts, of a figure gazing out into an empty landscape. *Boy Lights Fire* (2011), mines a similar vein in a surreal, collage like structure. A figure, with extruded arms holds little lights, like a strand from a Christmas tree. The picture is composed of three panels, with the text tying the composition together. We don't get resolution, but rather, as in his films, bits of a story which we finish in our own minds. The more recent works, like *Truck Lifts Rock by Tower* (2012) and *All I Want for Christmas is My Two Front Teeth* (2012) reduce the pictorial structure down to a sparse, childlike scrawl. In the hands of a lesser artist this might seem a coy ploy for authenticity; in Lynch's capable hands, though, the creep factor just rises.

Night Dark Night

Mira Schor: *Voice and Speech*; Marvelli Gallery, New York.
Published April 4, 2012; *CultureCatch*.

"From the Muses of Helicon, let us begin our singing, haunt Helicon's great and lofty mountain, and dance on soft feet around the altar of the mighty son of Kronos." From Hesiod's *Theogony*: "Night bore hateful Doom and dark Fate and Death, She bore Sleep, and she bore the Tribe of Dreams . . ."

"We live as we dream," wrote Joseph Conrad, "alone." Mira Schor's recent exhibition at Marvelli, *Voice and Speech*, makes a compelling argument against Conrad's existentialist notions, in paintings that are interrogations of thinking, speaking, writing and, of course, the act of painting. In this exhibition of recent paintings, Schor explores the concepts of "voice" and "speech" in contemporary politics and art theory, inspired by an idea put forward in Michel de Certeau's *The Practice of Everyday Life*. De Certeau's theme is that there exists a knowledge that precedes theory and which retains "voice" even when "speech" attempts to subsume it. It is the knowledge that causes the city dweller to inscribe living patterns of usage onto the fixed grid of the planned city; it's the knowledge of the folkloric, of craft. He writes, "In turn, 'the voice' will also insinuate itself into the text as a mark or a trace, an effect of a metonymy of the body . . . a transitory figure, an indiscreet ghost, a 'pagan' or 'wild' reminiscence in the scriptural economy, a disturbing sound from a different tradition, and a pre-text for interminable interpretive productions."

Schor's recent works, like *Voice and Speech* (2011), *Here/Then* (2011), *Conditions of Practice* (2011), and *The Space Where Painting Used to Be* (2010) are philosophical meditations on the place of painting in contemporary culture, on the visual artist as a thinking being, and on painting as a sensual space for visualizing thought. These paintings have a pastoral setting: in each work a figure walks or reclines under a flanged, tree-like diagrammatical structure, in a garden of sorts, reading, writing or simply existing in space. The moment of the activity caught in an intensely worked surface, in washes of malachite greens and lead whites, suggesting nature without describing it. *Here/Now, There/Now* depicts Schor's thoughts upon reading a book entitled *What is Contemporary Art?*, which she extrapolated on to ask "Where is contemporary art?" and determined that the contemporary, the now, is not here, where she is—in the West, in the tradition of painting, but there, in a global world of new media. She felt that the Western traditions of painting and, in particular, the New York School style of art she emerged from, are part of a "then" and that the elusive, desired "now" is always going to be somewhere "out there." Her little avatar-like figure can only return to, in Voltaire's words from *Candide*, *"il faut cultiver notre jardin"* and paint the space she herself occupies.

A grouping of four new canvases *The Dreams of All of Us* (2012), *Negative of the Positive* (2012), *The Darkest Part of the Night* (2012) and *This is the Future* (2012) present variations on a theme of the reading/sleeping/dreaming avatar, surrounded by rectilinear shapes, or compartments, which contain the words "the dreams of us all." In *Night* and *Future* the words have been redacted, as if lost or faded, like a dream upon wakening. The reading figure in *Dreams* becomes a reclining sleeper in *Negative*—the black on black composition of this work brings to mind Malevich, and the rebus composition evokes that surreal dreamer Magritte. *Negative* stands out from the series, mostly by its stark geometries and funereal tone—suggesting nothing so much as a meditation on the difference between death and sleep. In contrast to the more earthly "gardens," Schor depicts that moment of falling asleep, where the body is left behind, and we wander off, all of us, perhaps into some vaster collective unconscious; to dream—all alone together.

Black and Blue

Ron Gorchov: Cheim & Read, New York.
Published April 9, 2012; *CultureCatch*.

Endurance is a character trait often overlooked in an artist, as it often is in an athlete. Ron Gorchov, who is exhibiting new paintings at Cheim & Read, is definitely a marathoner in the art world, and one to whom more attention should be given.

Born in 1930, Gorchov has lived and worked in New York since the early '50s, where he had his first solo show in 1960, was included in the Whitney's *Thirty American Painters Under Thirty-Six*, and was friends with Willem de Kooning and Mark Rothko. His most recent museum exhibition, in 2006, at PS1 garnered the attention and support of Vito Schnabel and *The Brooklyn Rail* publisher Phong Bui, who curated this current exhibit.

Part of the continued interest in Gorchov's work can be attributed to his signature canvas constructions, where the canvas is stretched and roughly stapled over a precisely crafted wooden armature in a shield or saddle-like shape. Linen or canvas is stretched tenuously around the frame's edges, drawing attention to the artifice of the painting, and creating tension between the works surface the usually unseen construction of the stretcher bars. The viewer is drawn to look at the revealed sides and support of the frame, like a magician performing an elaborate card trick, then telling you how it was done. Gorchov draws us in with his sensual yet severe abstraction—then reminds us that painting is just an illusion after all.

It is this duality of image and structure that is the basis of Gorchov's painterly project. Responding to the predetermined structure of the canvas, he delicately layers and abrades the surface, creating a rich, pentimenti ground. Over this he deploys a two-handed technique to paint ovoid, amoeba-like shapes, which often resembled bruises on the surface of the bowed paintings. In his past works these shapes were often mirror images, the shape on the left was painted with his left hand, the right one with the right hand. *Artemesia* (2011) with two blue lozenges is a prime example of Gorchov Classic. *Adonis* (2010) and *Thersites Chastened* (2012) are Gorchov 2.0: the first, a shield shaped canvas with two ochre shapes, which bring to mind kouros sculpture, stately yet obliquely balanced; the second, a saddle-type canvas, with a roughly textured impasto ground, show him expanding upon the parameters of his formula.

Two other works in the show explore the possibilities of the shaped canvas: *Pegasi* (2012) and *Tan Seti* (2012). Stacked six panels high, in an overlapping, scalloped tower, these two works bear passing resemblance to a spine, or planetary rings, or some other lines of geometric structure. In *Pegasi*, the colored panels are white/black/red/blue/yellow/green. We might be tempted to read them as the colors of the chakras—reinforcing our notion of a spine-themed reading of the work. *Tan Seti's* ochre/teal/rust/evergreen/light blue/pink is more of a geological core sample, or read horizontally, light reflecting off of lapping waves. In either case, it really matters little if we miss the mark—Gorchov's work is all about careful planning and OG painterly painting. He is building spaces for our imaginations to wander around in.

The Van Gogh Boat

Keith Haring: *1978–1982*; Brooklyn Museum, Brooklyn.
Published May 5, 2012; *ArtSlant.*

Not since Andy Warhol has an artist been as driven to achieve both popular and critical success simultaneously as Keith Haring. Although his trademark images of radiant babies, anthropomorphized televisions, barking dogs, and UFOs caught the attention of the NYC subway-riding masses, and his Pop Shop products rivaled Warhol's Factory output, Haring received little museum attention during his lifetime. René Ricard, in 1981, wrote about Haring with great prescience: "Everyone wants to get on the Van Gogh Boat. There is no trip so horrible that someone won't take it. Nobody wants to miss the Van Gogh Boat. The idea of the unrecognized genius slaving away in a garret is a deliciously foolish one. We must credit the life of Vincent Van Gogh for really sending that myth into orbit. How many pictures did he sell? One. He couldn't give them away . . . We're so ashamed of his life that the rest of art history will be retribution for Van Gogh's neglect. No one wants to be part of a generation that ignores another Van Gogh."

Haring, who was born in Reading, Pennsylvania, (and would have been 54 this week), went to school at the School of Visual Arts where he studied painting, performance, and installation. Evidence of his early interests are apparent in the Brooklyn Museum show, which is packed with his notebook drawings, his videos, and videos documenting Haring's installation and performance pieces. Comparisons to van Gogh do hold up when one encounters such unbridled Catholic tastes when it comes to art forms, as well as a shared propensity to document his life and working process through journals and letters. These texts, amply displayed, allow us to see into Haring's working process—and his calligraphic sketches are wonderful background material when seen next to his large-scale ink drawings. His ability to transform words into images and back again would eventually give way to a purely image-based art, but his early posters for shows, parties, and nightclubs are both witty and sophisticated graphic design.

Highlights of the exhibition include some of Haring's early video pieces. *Painting Myself into a Corner* (1979) shows him doing just that, creating a black and white floor mural, backing himself into a (literal) corner. But it is ultimately Haring's drawings from this period, which catapulted him into the realm of instant brand recognition, that steal the show. Drawings on subway posters, in chalk on the blacked-out enamel paint used to obliterate outdated ads, take up several rooms. Their by-now familiar iconography in no way diminishes Haring's graphic power. A small drawing, *Untitled* (1980) in ink on florescent orange sign paper, of a pig's head emerging over a horizon reminds us of Goya's dog; Haring's strong art historical grounding gives both the image, as well as his larger mural-sized pieces, a resonance that we might only now begin to appreciate fully. It is the strength of the exhibition that it focuses on the period of Haring's work when he had not yet fully settled into the museum-ready style that he eventually obtained.

The works here—the best of them still look edgy, a little rough—show a young Haring daring his audience to like him, while at the same time courting the acclaim he was so desperate for and didn't quite achieve before his death. These works, and Haring, might finally be seen as, if not great art, at least as Art, now that the hype has dissipated. With Haring, nobody has missed the Van Gogh Boat.

Cuts You Up

Robert Yoder: Platform Gallery, Seattle.
Published May 9, 2012; *CultureCatch*.

Van Gogh wrote, "Ah, portraiture, portraiture with the thought, the soul of the model in it, that is what I think must come . . . It is one's duty to paint the rich and magnificent aspects of nature . . . Do I make myself understood? I am just trying to make you see this simple great truth: one can paint all of humanity by the simple means of portraiture." Robert Yoder, in his current show at Platform Gallery, seems to exemplify van Gogh's credo. Unlike van Gogh, however, Yoder uses the portrait not to paint all of humanity, but rather, to get inside the subject, using painting to examine each individual, well, individually.

All of Yoder's works have elements of collage, and it seems the act of collage, of cutting up, has led him to a form of portrait painting that resembles dissection almost as much as documentation. From his earlier works, which were made from castaway road signs, children's building blocks, hazard tape, and magazines, he has moved into a method of painting where he begins with elements of drawing—body parts, features, gestures, etc.—that begin as random pictographs on the canvas; then he stiches them back together, golem fashion, through an allover abstracted painterly method. His final image, in effect, is imageless; we end with a synecdoche of a person. The canvas, with its bumps and blemishes, is a stand-in for the person depicted; an excellent example is *Untitled (Ian Again)* (2011).

Like Willem de Kooning, Yoder employs oil paint for its wet sensuality. By beginning with representational drawing, then abstracting images, he is, in effect, recreating a brief history of twentieth-century painting in these works, as well. The process involves a leap of faith on our parts—what we see isn't actually what we see. Yoder's works are more about his relationship to the subject, and our trust in him must be implicit for any reading of the work to be gauged successful. Details, emerging and fading through the picture's surface, ultimately give us the clues that we need to read the paintings as something drawn from nature, not aesthetic caprice, and our patience is rewarded. What at first appears random ultimately comes together to form a resonant image.

His works on paper, such as *Teenage Donna (Released)* (2012), follow a similar logic. Like his earlier works, which resembled aerial views or maps of topographical settings, these pieces incorporate diagrammatic elements, large areas of graphite drawing, and a cut-and-paste method that borders on kink. Yoder in fact says as much: "I have recently introduced large amounts of black into the paintings. The density of these works creates a roughness and adds a punk/S/M aesthetic to the overall effect . . . they are graphic, hard, and unapologetic with their subject matter and intention. They are coming from an untapped place within me, a place that struggles with addiction and shame and socially unacceptable fantasies." In less capable hands this might become art-as-therapy projects, but with Yoder we are in the realm of *The Girl with the Dragon Tattoo*—smart, hardcore, and stylish. Beautiful—not pretty.

Blister in the Sun

Dana Schutz: *Piano in the Rain*; Friedrich Petzel Gallery, New York.
Published May 15, 2012; *CultureCatch*.

The sitcom, or situation comedy, is a television show format that usually features a family scenario (for example, a husband and wife, like in *The Honeymooners*), or a larger, extended family (*The Cosby Show*), or some kind of surrogate family (*Barney Miller*, *Cheers*). Into this weekly formula a mini-crisis or drama ensues, threatening to unravel the delicate fabric of the familial tranquility. Historically, theatrical comedies have often dealt with the concerns of human activities and conditions in ways that drama can't, cloaking tragedy with humor. Shakespeare, for example, often used his comedies to deal with subject matter that might have been problematic to present as drama; the entirety of Restoration theatre was based on the use of satire as a form of social and political critique.

Dana Schutz appropriates the familiar forms and styles of Munch, Ensor, and Guston, taking in equal measures their darkly humorous figuration, theatrical settings, and often simple narrative structure. Into these motifs, which resemble the sitcom setting and storyline, Schutz weaves tales featuring a lead protagonist (like Guston's Nixon), and she incorporates herself into the act as the narrator of the stories (Baselitz often did something similar in his works of the early 1960s). In her first one-person show in 2002, Schutz used a character called Frank, "the last man on earth," an aging hippy, straight out of casting; Frank even resembled the comedian Chris Elliot.

In this exhibition of new paintings, Schutz's characters seek to overcome what might at first seem impossible, dysfunctional, or potentially hilarious situations. The show's title, *Piano in the Rain*, suggests that these obstacles, though offering the potential for slapstick, hint at a darker, romantic allegory shrouded in humor. In *Hop* (2012), a man wearing a woolly Cliff Huxtable turtleneck sweater and brown corduroys is confronted by a large angry bunny. And shooting *Heroin in the Wind* (2012), like playing the piano in the rain, is, at best, a dicey proposition.

In *Small Apartment* (2012), Schutz lowers the level of Chaplinesque funniness, instead creating a scene that is more *Sleepless in Seattle*—a couple sits across from each other over a wadded-tissue-strewn table in a breakfast nook. Although they hold hands, they seem disconnected; the male protagonist looks toward us, while the female lead stares blankly at the table. Like all of Schutz's work, the drama is secondary to the act of painting, and *Small Apartment* employs an array of techniques. Her slashes and squiggles, applied with brush, scraper, oil stick, and squeegee, ultimately upstage the action. *Small Apartment* might bring to mind Matisse's *Conversation* (1908–12) in which he depicted his wife Amélie in a black and green housecoat, and himself in his signature striped pajamas, facing each other across a balcony in which the word "*non*" was written in scrolled letters. *Small Apartment* suggests that, although Schutz explores the possibilities of a humorous approach to painting, she is still very much aware of its power to convey genuine emotional depth.

Karma Chameleon

Francesco Clemente: *Nostalgia/Utopia*; Mary Boone Gallery, New York.
Published May 18, 2012; *CultureCatch*.

In both his work and his life, Francesco Clemente has made a career of breaking down boundaries. His multimedia approach to art—through painting, sculpture, photography, and bookmaking—and his peripatetic, nomad-like lifestyle share a common theme of restlessness and ambiguity. In his recent exhibition at Mary Boone, he has created a suite of paintings that reinforce our impression of him, painting works that run through Colonial Baroque, Afro-Brazilian, Indian, and Modernist iconographies. The strategies employed here, drawing on a variety of sources and influences, seek to present some commonality of experience, of shared ideas.

Here Clemente stays within the lines of paint and objects fixed to canvases, while allowing his stylistic noodlings to free-range, combining his imagery with a poetic grace. Although individual motifs in Clemente's pictures can be linked to his change-of-address living arrangements (homes in New York, India, Italy), the precise reading of any work remains elusive. In one painting, *Untitled* (2011–12), an African mask attached to a painting of a radiant sunflower drips two strands of pearls, which coil on the floor like puddles. Another painting, *Untitled* (2011–12), depicts a horizontally bisected diptych with pieces of rainbow-hued barbed wire stretched across the top panel and fragments of body parts and a blindfolded head occupying the lower half. The top panel features a painted quilt or tile pattern that, combined with the razor wire, seems to juxtapose the homey feel of the quilt pattern with the alternately protective/repellent barbs.

Trungpa (2011–2012) is a straightforward painting of a Catherine wheel, or mandala, filled with little bird-shaped rocks. The picture refers to the Tibetan Buddhist teacher Chögyam Trungpa Rinpoche (1939–1987), who was trained in the Nyingma tradition of Buddhism, the oldest school, and was an adherent of the *rimay* or "non-sectarian" movement within Tibetan Buddhism. The *rimay* movement aspired to bring together and make available all the valuable teachings of the different schools, free of sectarian rivalry. Throughout his life, and through his teaching, Trungpa Rinpoche sought to bring the teachings he had received to the largest possible audience. Clemente's painting includes a still life at the center of the wheel—a vanitas of skull, candle, red bird, and artist's palette. The reference to the Buddhist teacher might be seen as a stand-in for Clemente, who seeks to enlighten through his art by bringing seemingly disparate styles and methods together.

A large painting of a woman leaning against a lectern, her finger in a small book marking a page or passage, is titled *Temperance* (2011–12). Painted in warm sepia against a bright yellow background, which resembles a Pompeian fresco, the Mannerist distortions of the figure suggest the Italian style and reference Manet's *Woman with a Parrot* (1866) (in the Metropolitan Museum of Art). Two pitchers are attached to the top corners of the painting, their emptiness suggesting moderation. While the heavy-handed title, like the pitchers, is a little empty, the work itself is quite beautiful. As with much of Clemente's work, it isn't the final destination where we arrive that is the reward for looking; it is the journey we take with him.

This Wreckage I Call Me

Martin Kippenberger: *The Raft of the Medusa*; Carolina Nitsch Project Room, New York. Published June 11, 2012; *CultureCatch*.

Call me Ishmael.

Martin Kippenberger completed *The Raft of the Medusa* portfolio in 1996, one year before his untimely death at the age of 44. *Martin Kippenberger: The Raft of the Medusa* at Carolina

Nitsch Project Room comprises the complete portfolio of fourteen lithographs, as well as a selection of drawings and collages related to the portfolio.

There is something inherently message-in-a-bottle-like about the printmaking process. Making imagery in multiples speaks to the frailty of art: it is the hope of the collector of a print that attrition in the edition will result in one's ultimately owning the last extant one, turning the multiple into a unique work of art. Printmaking, more than any other artistic discipline, recognizes the impermanence of objects and the transitory nature of art.

In these prints Kippenberger casts himself as the various figures in the famous painting *The Raft of the Medusa* (1818–1819) by Théodore Géricault. The massive canvas, completed in 1819, is an icon of French Romanticism and depicts the tragedy that took place in 1816 when a French Royal Navy frigate ran aground off the west coast of Africa. Due to the shortage of lifeboats, 150 of the ship's less well-off passengers hastily built a raft measuring 20 x 60 feet and were set adrift for twelve days. When they were rescued, only fifteen remained; the others died of starvation, were killed or thrown overboard, or threw themselves into the sea in despair. Géricault conducted extensive research on his subject by interviewing survivors, making preparatory sketches from subjects at a morgue, and creating a scale model of the raft.

Similarly, Kippenberger enlisted his wife and photographer Elfie Semotan to document him posing as the tortured subjects in Géricault's painting, which he used as reference for the lithographs and paintings. One of the prints illustrates a segment of the raft, and Kippenberger even had a carpet woven with a diagram of the raft. Kippenberger's project is, in some way, an homage to Géricault and the nineteenth-century studio practice, but also an irreverent parody.

Werner Büttner, a painter and friend, called Kippenberger "a virtuoso at giving offense." In two of the prints Kippenberger is reenacting the role of the pinnacle character in Géricault's painting who is waving a cloth to get the attention of a ship in the distance. However, Kippenberger depicts himself in the same pose in front of a background of appropriated alcohol labels, vying for the attention of an audience. Kippenberger's body, atrophied and bloated through years of struggle with alcoholism, is in stark contrast to the emaciated, dying victims in Géricault's painting. Many of the prints, though, appear to be sincerely reverent to Géricault's subjects, alluding to and psychologically embodying their harrowing ordeal and suffering.

Kippenberger was fond of skewed aphorisms. The title of his last poem, written shortly before his death, perhaps best encapsulates his life and *The Raft of the Medusa* in particular: "Never give up before it's too late."

Slow Burn

Rodney Dickson: *Painting*; Klemens Gasser & Tanja Grunert, Inc., New York.
Published June 24, 2012; *ArtSlant*.

To call Rodney Dickson a painter's painter does him something of a disservice, implying that his work speaks only to the few and initiated. In fact, both Dickson and his paintings strive for a more communal, universal language—one that collectively might understand the search that he undertakes with each painting. In an age that has seen the deconstruction, reconstruction, and post-reconstruction of painting, Dickson reaches back to an era that saw the act of painterly engagement as, first and foremost, an attempt at expression. His recent works at Gasser & Grunert show him at the peak of his career.

Barnett Newman wrote of his own work that he sought:

> . . . an art of impact and enigma, an art of feeling, as van Gogh wrote of his own painting, "Heartbroken and therefore heartbreaking . . . I use color to express myself forcibly . . . that's it as far as theory goes now. Stroke can be interwoven with feeling . . . from the pain of impasto to the exhilaration of stippling; from the serenity of smooth paint (like porcelain) to the sublimity of radiating strokes." He spoke of reducing imagery in favor of strengthening the feeling behind the work, of "leaving out some trees" or "some shrubs that are not in character" to get at that character in the painting, the fundamental truth of it.

These recent paintings—abstract, though tempered with references both to art history as well as an engagement with nature—are large, enveloping the viewer, much like the work of Newman or Pollock. Color is used as a descriptive element, suggesting van Gogh's wheat fields or sunflowers, in works such as *Untitled (R.D.7)* (2012), or as pure form, with a nod to Julian Schnabel or Bradley Walker Tomlin, in *Untitled (R.D.14)* (2012). With these recent works, Dickson paints on a black ground, and his muscular strokes and expressive handling do indeed evoke the same awkward, hard-earned struggle that the best of Schnabel's black velvet paintings have. Dickson, though, is no Neo-Expressionist. His paintings evolve out of a genuine effort—one that he has spoken of as leaving him exhausted by the process. His paintings wear their hearts on their sleeves, his attempts to make the next work better than the last strike us as genuine—such a simple goal, so seldom seen in other painter's efforts.

It is tempting to list the art and artists whose work bears resemblance to Dickson's, both in subject and spirit—painting heroes such as Milton Resnick, Leon Kossoff, or Frank Auerbach. These artists' works are valid touchstones to apprehend such pieces as *Untitled (R.D.8)* (2012) or *Untitled (R.D.6)* (2012). Both the sensual handling, as well as the umbers and acid yellows, bring to mind the School of London. But Dickson travels far and wide to collect the impressions that he processes through paint. Inspired by an artist residency last year in the Xu Cun Mountains of Shanxi Province, China, the surreal environment, and its diffused light from the misty clouds that obscured the lush landscape inspired Dickson and influenced his Western paint handling with an Eastern sense of lightness. It is also tempting to see the thick impasto of these paintings as concealing, or burying, his imagery, but that might be a mistake. In the 1950s, Bruno Alfieri argued for Jackson Pollock's work in *L'Arte Moderna* in a statement that bears reading as an argument for the relevance of Dickson's work today: "Each one of his pictures is a part of himself . . . They will show Pollock to me—pieces of Pollock. That is, I start from the picture, and discover the man."

Rubberband Man

Richard Prince: *14 Paintings*; 303 Gallery, New York.
Published June 13, 2012; *CultureCatch*.

In a 1927 article on fetishism Sigmund Freud allowed that a person who erotically fixated on an inanimate object had found a substitute for their perceived missing phallus. He gave as an example a young male patient who had fetishized the "shine on the nose" of a woman. In fixating on this elusive phenomenon, the patient had chosen as his erotic object a condition that characterized eroticized elements in general; that is, they cannot actually be possessed and therefore are eternally elusive. The desired thing is ultimately ungraspable.

In some ways the work of Richard Prince has been an investigation into the American fetish object for decades. His car hood sculptures, reproduced images of Brooke Shields and Hollywood movie star promo pictures, and silk-screened paintings of jokes and cartoons from those ultimate fetish-culture publications *Playboy* and *The New Yorker* have all been about aesthetic depictions of things that he perceived our post-modern culture to be in pursuit of, though never obtaining. Even his *Hoods* series of wall relief sculptures, with their shiny surfaces referring to 1960s L.A. Finish Fetish artists, such as Robert Irwin or John McCracken, follows Freud's theorization as a prescribed methodology.

Prince's recent exhibition *14 Paintings* might be seen as either an extension of this investigation or an attempt to obviate his previous works. Following a simple, consistent method, Prince stretches black rubber bands, staples them into geometric, many-sided figures over a newspaper ground painted a mottled white, à la Jasper Johns. This programmatic approach, which emphasizes the "reveal" of his process, gives a nod to sculptors such as Richard Tuttle, as well as geometric abstraction paintings like those of Al Held at the same time. Pieces such as *Untitled* (2011) or *Untitled* (2011) [pictured above] are uniform equivalents. In fact, taken as a whole, this series comes across as more of a diagrammatic study of architecture or geometry than painterly studies. Where Prince does allow his usual sardonic humor to slip through is in his statement/press release. He writes, possibly giving us an entry into the thinking behind the work:

> Some people see leaves falling from a tree and see it as, leaves falling from
> a tree. Others see it as an inexhaustible mystery of the signified from the
> mundane closed-off simulation of a world sign.
>
> The world is intolerably dreary. You escape it by seeing and naming what
> had heretofore been unspeakable.
>
> The best images have sensations of unreality, illimitable vastness, brilliant
> light, and the gloss and smoothness of material things.

In essence, Prince is presenting us with something like a Rorschach Test of Minimalist painting. It is an aestheticized, fetish object—but only if we see it that way. In 1938, Theodor Adorno analyzed the phantasmagorical effects of Richard Wagner's theory of *Gesamtkunstwerk,* as developed in the Ring cycle of operas, arguing that the dreamlike escape from everyday life, which sought to envelope the spectator in an all-encompassing aesthetic experience of music, words, and images, relied on astounding arrays of effects and infinitely repeated musical motifs. Adorno called this "an atomization of the material—which breaks it down into the smallest possible components," and he compares it to modern industrial labor processes, or modern architecture, with its emphasis on quotidian materials and ugly functionality.

The hostility of such works to the physical, sensuous body can be compared with a phenomenon described by Walter Benjamin in his essay "The Work of Art in the Age of Mechanical Reproduction." Benjamin writes that modern aesthetic techniques, such as film and photography (which we could expand to include digital media), has broken down the "cult value" or "aura" of the art object—its "personality" so to speak. It has been rendered democratized, the aesthetic equivalent of Wonder Bread. In some ways this speaks directly to what Prince is doing in these paintings. He has created objects that mock the fetishization of his earlier works, yet in the process of debasing his concept through these manufactured, mundane works, he has come up with something that can best be described as abject fetishism. To paraphrase Marie Antoinette, Prince is having the best of both worlds, eating his Wonder Bread and having it too.

Sign of the Times

Various artists: *Signs & Symbols*; Whitney Museum of American Art, New York. Published July 5, 2012; *CultureCatch*.

Saturday I woke up early, went for a run in Central Park, had breakfast at The Carlyle, and at 10 went over to the Whitney Museum to meet the artist and director Michael Lee Nirenberg (I just finished an interview with him on his new performance documentary *Redacted*), the actor James Franco who Nirenberg was meeting to discuss doing the voice-over narrative for another doc, and Nirenberg's assistant Lana (who also works in the film industry, mostly punching up scripts for comedies) to catch the new exhibit *Signs & Symbols*, featuring the work of Adolph Gottlieb, Mark Tobey, Will Barnet, Forrest Bess, and others.

Drawn from the permanent collection, the works in the show represent a strain of graphic expressionism that was largely overshadowed in the fifties by more painterly works, such as Jackson Pollock's spattered canvases, or Mark Rothko's stained, atmospheric takes on Veronica's Veil.

One of the first pieces we see is a sculpture by David Smith called *Hudson River* (1951). It's comprised of welded steel, bent and twisted into small punctuation-like forms. As we take it in, Lana points out that the title of the show was the name of a Nabokov short story that was published as both "Signs and Symbols" and "Symbols and Signs." "I think that the ambiguity that Nobokov had toward that story relates to the uncertainty of the artworks here," she says. "These guys were coming up with their own kind of language."

Franco agrees, and Nirenberg wanders into another gallery, stopping before two Pollock ink drawings (both *Untitled* [1939–42] and [1944]). He points out how the calligraphy in these smaller pieces is like a letter, or poem, when compared to the larger works that he would become known for. I stop in front of an Adolph Gottlieb, *Frozen Sounds #1* (1951), a masterpiece, in my opinion, and remark that he always seemed to be under-recognized historically as an important painter—the series of *Imaginary Landcapes* being very important. "Too Jewy," piped in Lana. Nirenberg's eyes roll back, and he groans, "Here we go again, Lana . . . your anti-Semitism is *so* predictable." Franco and I laugh at their little in-joke. (Lana is half-Jewish on her mother's side; her father is Japanese.) "I kind of agree with Lana," I say, "if she is maybe referring to some parallels between Gottlieb's compositions and Hebraic writing." Franco picks up on this immediately.

He says, "I can see the parallels. Hebraic writing, unlike ours, is regulated vertically. Latin characters are firmly planted on a baseline. Hebraic letters cling to an upper register . . ." I point out how Gottlieb's colored shapes float above a horizon line, all the action taking place above ground level. Franco continues, " . . . as if suspended from an inverse gravity, like rays of light or something. You are reading the letters as if they are coming over a horizon. Anything above the register line is the Absolute, below is the domain of writing, or mankind. Only one letter traditionally breaks this demarcated line: *Lamed*, which refers to the word *lamad*, meaning to learn or to teach and is the root of the word *Talmud*." I point out how Gottlieb is using paint, something traditionally outside the realm of language, to create a new language based on shape and color. "Still too Jewy," Lana says, smiling.

As we wander around the show, we stop in front of Forrest Bess's painting *Letters*. Bess had been included in the last Whitney Biennial with six paintings, documentation of his writings, and photographs of his attempts at self-transformative surgery. Franco muses out loud, "Bess was a Texas fisherman whose colorfully stark paintings were largely intended to be symbolic keys to a personal theory about the essential hermaphroditism of humans. The paintings alone are profound, but the accompanying texts he left behind, mostly excerpts from letters to the critic Meyer Shapiro, give a crucial, additional understanding of his work. Some might think Bess was insane, and considering that he performed self-surgery on his penis to help prove his theories of hermaphroditism, there are at least grounds for this. Bess spent his life isolated on the Gulf, seventy miles outside of Houston, making a scant living from fishing and his paintings. He started showing in New York at the same time as the Abstract Expressionists but didn't enjoy the same turn of acceptance that they did in the sixties. As with Pollock and some of the others, his early work derived from the Mexican muralists—like David Alfaro Siqueiros and Diego Rivera—and ideas of infusing myths into the artwork. Van Gogh's landscapes and still lifes were also influential to Bess, as was his example as a letter writer. There was ostensibly a master book, now lost, that Bess called his 'thesis' in which he detailed his ideas of the liberation of humankind through hermaphroditism. He had hoped to show these theories alongside the paintings, but Betty Parsons—who also showed Pollock and Rothko—refused."

"She did show his paintings, though," Lana, always keen on business details, interjects, "and did sell a few." The Whitney accompanied the paintings with his letters to Shapiro, Carl Jung, and others whom he trusted with his psychosexual explorations. The most crucial and disturbing of these accounts details the fistula he made on the underside of his penis to transform himself into a hermaphrodite, of sorts.

At noon we go into the bookstore. Lana buys some postcards, the new biography of Martin Kippenberger, and a scarf printed with a Roy Lichtenstein design. Nirenberg buys a book of photographs of silly dogs dressed up in funny costumes and in hilarious poses, by William Wegman. He says, "My son is going to love this! Oliver really likes dogs!" Franco kids Nirenberg that he was using Oliver as an excuse to buy the book. Then we go to the café to buy large coffees and go outside to smoke.

We have to leave early to make a two-o'clock matinee of the Pulitzer Prize-winning play *Clybourne Park*. As we walk down Madison from 75th to 48th Street, we continue discussing Forrest Bess. Nirenberg muses aloud, "When I went to the Biennial, I almost got sick reading the descriptions of what he did to himself. And the photos! [Bess took pictures of his body before and after the operations.] He was insane, wasn't he? I mean if he hadn't been a painter, would we consider him to be a genius or just crazy for what he did?"

As we continue walking, the park is to our right, and the coffee we bought from the museum café is good. Lana jumps into the dialog, "He is kind of like a more fucked-up version of van Gogh. Instead of cutting off his ear, he almost cut off his *dick*! I think it makes his work even more interesting—I mean, how many artists are *that* committed to their fucked-up ideas?"

Franco responds, "You're right, but that's because his ideas are interesting as ideas, whether he was medically right or not about how hermaphroditism might lead to utopia. Immortality is not important when he is using such ideas for his art. In the conceptual realm of art, his ideas only need to open questions and create nodes for new discussion. But when he started practicing these ideas on his own body, he added the pressure of actually being medically correct about his theories, instead of just theoretically provocative." I agree, and Franco continues, "The self-surgery was where the line between sanity and instability became ambiguous, but I suppose that was the point, and that was why it was important to have the writings alongside the paintings. For Bess, the paintings were gestures as concrete as the self-surgery. They were symbols intended to unlock the Jungian collective unconscious in all of us." Even though school is out, Franco still talks like he is writing a paper for some art theory class.

Later, as we hurried down Broadway trying to catch a cab to that new restaurant Cana, in Tribeca, the marquee lights started coming on, signs of a different sort.

Station to Station

Alighiero Boetti: *Game Plan*; Museum of Modern Art, New York.
Published July 30, 2012; *CultureCatch*.

The ride downtown to Cana, the new restaurant in Tribeca, was slow—traffic all the way. Lana called to confirm the reservations she had made earlier in the week. We finally arrived, only to find out that a wedding rehearsal dinner party (an Upper East Side couple who appear frequently on Page Six) had booked the place last-minute, filling up most of the good tables. Fortunately we were escorted to a large banquette in the back, which afforded us some privacy, at least. We were meeting some friends, including writer Alissa Bennett and the Norwegian artist Bjarne Melgaard, who had just come back from the Venice Biennial. There were several people I didn't recognize immediately, but I was quickly introduced to reality television show hosts Jerry Saltz and China Chow (who were there doing a tech scout for their new Bravo network TV show: *Stars of the 2012 Venice Biennial—Where Are They Now?*).

Both Saltz and Chow are excited and effusive—Saltz enthusiastically examining a large drawing Melgaard is making on the tablecloth of a funny, large-nosed manatee lapping at a giant ejaculating phallus, with the words "HIV Nazi Fuckboi" scrawled underneath, as well as something in Norwegian that I can't quite make out. Skrillex's mashup of Liturgy's cover of "The Boys of Summer" plays in the background. Chow is talking to Stella Schnabel and Lee Rinaldo. Mario Batali comes out of the kitchen to welcome Franco, the two hugging, backslapping. Franco introduces Nirenberg and Lana. Bennett and Melgaard are having an animated discussion, annoyingly cute, punctuated with inside-joke nicknames, like "Whore Pig" and "Cunt." Chow, sensing a break in the various conversations, pipes in, "Does anybody want to see my tits?"

Bennett and Melgaard are discussing the Boetti retrospective at MoMA. The retrospective, organized in collaboration with the Museo Reina Sofía in Madrid and the Tate Modern in London, is the largest presentation to date outside of Italy of works by Italian artist Alighiero Boetti (1940–1994). Working in his hometown of Turin in the early 1960s amidst a close community of artists that included Luciano Fabro, Mario Merz, Giulio Paolini, and Michelangelo Pistoletto, Boetti established himself as one of the leading artists of the *Arte Povera* movement, the particularly Italian style of minimalism that flourished in the sixties.

"I think that Boetti, like Pasolini, was interested in creating mythologies around the artist more than in creating an artwork," says Bennett. Melgaard, no stranger to mythologizing, agrees.

Bennett continues, "His mythical travels, the importance in times and dates, and his use of material as metaphor were all a part of his contribution to the myth of artist as some kind of mystical figure or martyr. Look at how artists like Clemente and Cucci followed along after him—like disciples! His aphorisms about making art, the nature of time, and identity were conveyed through his work like parables—he was a very shamanistic or messianic artist, like Beuys." "Very true," I say, "I think that his journey as an artist was more imaginary than actualized—he presented a model for a way of working that played with ideas of what both art and reality were . . . If you believed in what he was doing, if you went along for the ride, your experience of his work was richer than if you just look at his objects. He exhorts you to believe in his work, in spite of what he says . . . I mean, what are all those rugs he made in Afghanistan if not prayer mats?"

Organized chronologically, the exhibition spans Boetti's entire career, beginning with a large reproduction of a self-portrait—an altered photograph that makes him appear as a set of identical twins (*Gemelli*, 1968). This bit of fiction sets the tone for the exhibition—he would refer to himself as a "double" throughout his career, adding "*e*" (and) to his name: Alighiero e Boetti. Boetti said of this doubling, "Often when I draw I use both of my hands. Normally I am right-handed. When I draw with my left hand it is a kind of conversation with myself exploring the positive and the negative, the ego and alter ego, the order and disorder and mounting it on paper. It is as if on one hand there is Alighiero and on the other, Boetti."

"Art is a big fucking lie," says Melgaard, paraphrasing Picasso, "which reveals the truth." Boetti's sculptural works, or objects as he preferred to call them, comprised of everyday materials including wood, cardboard, and aluminum, are brought together and installed in a dense configuration inspired by their original clustered presentations. These early works convey the material experiments of the period, as well as notions of measurement and chance that Boetti played with and revised throughout his career. In 1969 Boetti began exploring notions of duality and multiplicity, order and disorder, travel and geography, and he initiated postal and map works, imagining distant places. For the work *Viaggi Postali*, begun the summer of 1969, Boetti sent envelopes to friends, family, and fellow artists but used imaginary addresses, forwarding each returned envelope to yet another non-existent place. Boetti thus created imaginary journeys for the people he admired. "He was a forerunner to the *Transavanguardia* movement in the '80s," Melgaard interjects. "What he played with in terms of imaginary geographies, artists like Clemente lived out in their works. Kippenberger created a museum in Greece—Boetti opened a hotel in Afghanistan." (The One Hotel, which existed from 1971 until the Soviet invasion in 1979). I add, "During that period, Boetti began working with local artisans to produce embroideries such as the *Mappas* (maps), *Arazzi* (word squares), and *Tuttos* (literally, "Everything").

An important aspect of Boetti's oeuvre is drawing, which runs as a constant throughout his work. Drawing was both an activity and a moment of transformation to Boetti. He wrote, "I had been going in one direction . . . Then I began to doubt this direction. In the spring of 1969 I left the studio in Turin. It had become a depot for materials. I left all of this as it was and began again from zero with a pencil and a sheet of paper." In a sense, Boetti began to use the act of drawing to map out all his future actions as an artist. One piece in the exhibit, *Scrittura graffita (Scraped Writing)* (1968), two concrete tablets scratched into while still wet, resemble nothing so much as a humble Ten Commandments. A monumental ball-point-pen drawing from 1973, spelling out the title "*Mettere a mondo il mondo (Bringing the world into the world)*" points to some of Boetti's ideas about art making that were fundamental to his practice: that the artist, rather than inventing, simply brings what already exists in the world into the work; and that everything in the world is potentially useful for the artist.

The headwaiter, a tall, dark-haired woman named Mary, approaches the table to deliver a couple of bottles of complimentary champagne, Laurent-Perrier Grand Siècle La Cuvée, to Franco, who was seated at the center of the banquette. The arrival of the champagne interrupts his conversation with Darren Aronofsky on the performance artist Marina Abramović, when Mary whispers to him that there is a call for him on the house phone—"Your Father," she explains. "Not now," he murmurs. "What does He expect from me? Tell Him it is not yet my Hour."

Deborah Kass arrives with Lena Dunham. We crowd closer into the banquette. Kass brushes away silver confetti to better see Melgaard's drawing, which now fills most of the tablecloth. Melgaard is sketching Mickey Mouse sodomizing a ball-gagged Bugs Bunny. "Oh, Cunty," giggles Bennett, "you spelled 'fuckhole' wrong!" Conversations are interwoven, a tapestry of sound. The heat is stifling; the air conditioner is broken, Batalli explains. The air smells of saffron, camel shit, incense. "The Berliner Banhof, in 1945 . . ." Saltz says, recounting a recent trip to Germany, "Now *that* was the station where the *stations* stopped."

Chow removes her top, saying, "See?" and Mary, having gone to relay Franco's message, returns, this time quietly whispering to him that the wine for the wedding party in the front of the restaurant has run out. Franco asks, "What is a wedding without the Divine Benediction? Mary, bring me water." She quickly orders a server to bring water to the table, six glasses of clear water in small, Philippe Starck-designed bowls. Franco lowers his head, his eyes heavy-lidded and faraway. The water transformed into wine. He speaks softly now, the table growing quiet to catch his words. "Whoever thirsts may come to me," he promises, "and whoever believes in me shall drink his fill." It was a sign, the first of many, witnessed by the twelve of us seated around the table. Franco continues, "If there were no signs, you would not come to me, but because you have faith, my words will cure, my hand will heal . . . to understand that which you don't know, you must first pass through *where* you do not know . . ."

L'Age d'Or

Edouard Vuillard: *A Painter and His Muses, 1890–1940*; The Jewish Museum, New York. Published August 27, 2012; *Artslant.*

As a young painter in the 1890s, Vuillard became a member of the Parisian group of avant-garde artists known as the Nabis ("prophets" in Hebrew and Arabic). Taking their inspiration from the Post-Impressionist Paul Gauguin (who was 20 years Vuillard's senior) as well as Toulouse-Lautrec (who was just four years older), the Nabis used simplified form and planes of pure color to create decorative, subtly emotive pictures, with a somewhat spiritual bent. During his Nabi period, which lasted through most of the last decade of the century, Vuillard produced some of his best-known works: paintings of friends and family (mostly his mother and sister) in closed interior spaces filled with patterned wallpapers, carpets, drapery, and clothing. His mother's apartment, which she used as a workshop (she was a seamstress), figured prominently.

The Drawer (1892) shows Vuillard's interest in creating psychologically resonant images within the confines of the domestic interior. His mother's workspace is presented through an arrangement of contrasting lights and shadows, patterned wallpaper, and draped fabrics, against solid passages of dark wood paneling. A dresser (loosely sketched in) has one drawer open, with a dress and sash spilling out, like a spectral, ectoplasmic figure. The sepia-toned passages of the painting refer perhaps to the photographic tableaus that Vuillard arranged and used as preparatory sketches and studies for his paintings. The spotted red/black/white/gray dot pattern of the wallpaper foreshadows Edvard Munch's similar use of such a color motif in his later work *Between the Clock and the Bed* (1940–43). In *The Reader* (1897–99), a portrait of Romain Coolus, Vuillard flattens the planes of color, compressing the space of the picture, to focus all the attention on the young man's absorption in his book.

In another portrait, *Aurélien Lugné-Poë* (1891), Vuillard reveals something of his interest in contemporary theater. The actor and theater impresario Lugné-Poë shared a tiny studio on the Rue Pigalle with Vuillard and fellow Nabi Pierre Bonnard. Experimental drama flourished in Paris at the end of the nineteenth century. Vuillard was not only an avid theater attendee, but, as evidenced in the lithographic broadsheets and playbills on display (for Henrik Ibsen's *Rosmersholm* and *An Enemy of the People*, both from the 1893 season), he also had a keen interest in graphic arts. He would later contribute set designs, lighting effects, and programs for plays by Ibsen, Maeterlinck, and Strindberg to the Théâtre de l'Oeuvre.

"I don't paint portraits," Vuillard once remarked, "I paint people in their surroundings." Vuillard's early interest in developing a psychological narrative in his interiors, as well as his work in theatrical productions, would ultimately be synthesized in later works such as *David David-Weill* (1925), an urbane and witty picture of an art patron ensconced within his trove of gilt-framed paintings (including Chardin and Guiard), stands as a sort of masterpiece of this later, mature style. Vuillard's art, as it reached maturity, has been compared to the writing of Marcel Proust. For both artists, the meaning of the work was an accumulation of layers of lush visual detail, closely observed—at once capturing moments of time, and through their art, transcending it.

Be Here Now

Angela Dufresne: *Parlors and Pastorals*; Monya Rowe Gallery, New York; CRG Gallery, New York.
Published September 8, 2012; *CultureCatch*.

Things fall apart . . . at least in the recent paintings of Angela Dufresne, whose works are in a two-gallery exhibition at Monya Rowe and CRG entitled *Parlors and Pastorals*. That is the impression at first glance: nominal landscapes and scenes of bourgeois interiors, these paintings, awash with color and executed with an impressive arsenal of painterly paint handling, are slipping glimpses into scenes both real and imagined, caught in a state of permanent contingency.

Alphaville Sublime (2012) and *Putting Out in the Parlor of King Alexander* (2012) are a good starting point in the immersive world that Dufresne has created, which was ostensibly inspired by Buster Keaton's *The Playhouse* (1921), a play-within-a-play-within-a-play *tour de force* of early filmmaking. Dufresne applies the same methodology of stripping away illusions of reality and notions of continuity, and, like Keaton, uses physicality (in all its humorous aspects) to present something like paintings of pictures of paintings being painted. With references to *Alphaville* (1965), Godard's inversion of the science fiction genre, and the ornate stage-managed theatrics of Regency French painting, these large canvases play with a lexicon of styles and handling that incorporates elements of Giacometti, Mathieu, Hartigan, and Richter, with paint slathered, washed, scraped, jotted, scumbled, and wiped away as she works—layering image over image until finally arriving at, or rather, walking away from, a picture of suspended gesture. In *Lady David-Rosemary Angeles in a Golden Swamp* (2012), the artist inverts the gender of Bernini's David, combining portraits of her mother and herself into a hybrid figure in a landscape inspired by Albert Bierstadt of trees in the Hudson Valley. An exploration of Tiepolo's *The Banquet of Cleopatra* (1743–44) is mashed-up into *Banquette Concerto with Head* (2012): the balustrade in the original Baroque painting becomes a rope bridge, the table centerpiece a severed head.

Dufresne resurrects the old-fashioned notion of the painterly "sketch"—something we have perhaps forgotten after a century of Modernism. We used to distinguish between the working sketch or *étude* (study)—a notational, almost mnemonic, device—and the full sketch, or *ébauche*—a true canvas, usually monochrome, which recorded the artist's raw, *alla prima* impressions. Tiepolo, Velázquez, and Tintoretto were masters of the sketch; Delacroix, in spite of his pissing on about "finished" masterpieces, was its last great practitioner. In our time, with information flowing faster than ever, breathing new life into this painterly genre seems more relevant than retro.

There is something sweetly sincere about *Hanna Schygulla Again Because There Can't Be Too Much of Her* (2012). This tiny study of Rainer Werner Fassbinder's favorite muse calls to mind Fassbinder's penchant for making movies about making movies. It also slows Dufresne's brush, limits her field of play, and allows the paint to coalesce and build. It provides a nice counterpoint to the larger pieces, a moment of quiet against the high theater of the larger works. Its intimate scale allows us a closer look at Dufresne's method and reveals more of the painter. Barnett Newman wrote, "Painting should give one a sense of place: that one knows he's there, aware of himself. In that sense he relates to me when I made the painting, because in that sense I was there . . . To me that sense of place has not only a mystery, but has that sense of metaphysical face. I hope my painting has the impact of giving someone, as it did to me, that feeling . . . of connection to others." Yeah, a lot to pin on a portrait of a German B-movie actress, but Dufresne somehow manages to do it. And in the room the women come and go, talking of Michelangelo . . .

Almost Famous

Richard Phillips: Gagosian Gallery, New York.
Published September 21, 2012; *CultureCatch*.

I am running late, so I park the Ducati on the sidewalk and toss the keys to an eager production assistant. It is incredibly hot and crowded as I push my way through a crowd of background actors to the location, which has been carefully designed to look like a gallery. Wardrobe has given me an antique Ramones t-shirt (which actually has some of Debbie Harry's vintage blood on the sleeve) and a period Hugo Boss Nazi SS uniform jacket with five firing-squad bullet holes through the left lapel (vintage blood carefully removed). Also, store-torn Alexander McQueen jeans (a gift from an Olsen twin, I think) and flip-flops, which are decorated with pictures of colorful monkeys. I stop to talk to Rachel Weisz, who seems to remember me from her chemistry reading for the part of a "kindly doctor" in *Stasi Sluts II* but suddenly excuses herself, gesturing excitedly to Philip Glass, who is wiping *tapenade* off his black Prada turtleneck. Everything else—the cramped perspective of the gallery, Lars von Trier and Lena Dunham talking to Christopher Nolan, the noise—all form a vague penumbra; the unsatisfactory footage of this shoot will later be edited out in the final film. The director, Michael Lee Nirenberg, storms through the set barking orders for paintings to be taken down, removed, or rehung on different walls.

The gallery is packed with beautiful celebrities. Blake Lively, Keira Knightley (who replaced Natalie Portman at the last minute), Heath Ledger, and Willem Dafoe are casually chatting in front of *Adriana III* (2012), a picture of someone called Adriana Lima. Since nobody knows who she is, subtitles will be burned in later, reading:

> Phillips has collaborated with Brazilian supermodel Adriana Lima to
> create a new series of paintings that depict her against backdrops of iconic
> Brazilian landmarks, such as Oscar Niemeyer's Catedral de Brasília, the
> patterned sidewalks of Copa Cabana, and the *favelas* of Rio. In these scenes,
> such as *Adriana I* (2012), in which Lima poses seductively across the roof
> of the cathedral, the impact of her preternatural beauty and the aura she
> commands as a supermodel is conflated, and thus equated with, national
> icons of economic and political culture.

Ryan Reynolds, who is playing the role of the painter and filmmaker Richard Phillips, is walking about the gallery and talking to Cindy Sherman, who is shooting a segment for TMZ on her iPhone. "I was approached by a lot of people who saw my videos and said, 'You know, I really am so bored and don't like video art at all, but I loved your film,'" he is saying to Cindy, impressively hitting his marks. "I mean, a lot of video art that's made takes for granted what people are willing to put up with and see." He stops walking and continues speaking, dramatically: "I have embarked on a new phase of work that hinges on the self-awareness of real-life subjects. *Lindsay Lohan* (2011) and *Sasha Grey* (2011) made their debut at the *Commercial Break* film project at the 2011 Biennale di Venezia. In these 'motion portraits' the actresses pose erotically—Grey in a modernist John Lautner home and Lohan in an aquamarine infinity pool. Both actresses project self-conscious recognition in their performances and, in turn, point toward the transformative potential of narrative action, framed by their compelling beauty. My third film, *First Point* (2012), is my second collaboration with Lohan and third collaboration with legendary surf filmmaker Taylor Steele. A contemporary *film noir*, *First Point* juxtaposes haunting nocturnal imagery with surf sequences by the female pro-surfer Kassia Meador, who is Lindsay's stunt double."

After his antics at the restaurant (and refusing to pay a corkage fee), James Franco is mercifully nowhere to be found. Bjarne Melgaard has fucked off to the toilet with Tyler Perry, which is a little disconcerting, as the only drugs I am aware of are in Perry's giant Louis Vuitton makeup bag. A large group of people has clustered in front of a giant painting of Lohan wearing yellow sunglasses, *First Point* (2012). Lohan herself, out on bail after being charged with shoplifting, or breaking and entering, or maybe drunk driving—I really can't remember—is standing in front of the painting, wearing a yellow Top Shop pullover and an ankle tracking bracelet, which measures her blood alcohol level. Michael Stipe, who is wearing something resembling cargo pants, is trying to get her to set it off by offering her his drink. Skrillex's mix of Pussy Riot's cover of the Go-Go's "Our Lips are Sealed" is playing, very loudly, in the background.

Someone brings Reynolds a revised copy of the script, and he continues, "Each of the individuals I collaborated with are known for image production on an extremely high level throughout the world. In this work, their iconic status is being used not just to comment about the power of beauty or whatever, but it's actually being used to explore different psychological states—transformative moments in the actors' lives themselves, or the models' relationship to culture." Melgaard returns, carefully dabbing at what appears to be blood on his sleeve, and is immediately cornered by Stipe. "Have you seen my newest sculptures?" Stipe gushes, "They are the berries!" Melgaard replies, slightly less enthusiastically, "I haven't, but they must be incredible . . . I was always a big fucking fan of yours when you were in Green Day."

Jessica Biel and Victoria Beckham are studying a large painting of Lindsay Lohan, *Lindsay II* (2012), where she is reclining on a beach set wearing a white top. "It's a Michael Kors *swimsuit* . . ." says Biel. Beckham interrupts, "No, I think it's Victoria's Secret *underwear* . . . it is a commentary on a post-feminist auto-critique of the queer gaze." It *is* a beautiful painting; gauzy and atmospheric. Chuck Close and Vito Schnabel are looking at *Sasha III* (2012), a painting of Sasha Grey. "This reminds me of your portraits. Just a head—simple, concise, direct," Schnabel says to Close. "My work is more about the making of an image, not celebrity," responds Close. "My paintings are all of friends, many of them I have painted for 30 years or more. I can't help it if they became famous!" Close makes a valid point. In spite of the similarities that *Sasha III* has to certain paintings by Gerhard Richter of the Baader-Meinhof terrorists (*Baader-Meinhof October 18, 1977*, [1988]), particularly the triptych of the murdered Ulrike Meinhof, those comparisons become overshadowed by references in Phillips's painting to Grey in films like *Spring Break Gangbang VII* and *The Spurt Locker*. Probably the most disconcerting thing about Grey is how uncomfortable she looks wearing clothes.

Reynolds continues reading, "When we can't determine what art is—when we get to that point where we're not sure, that's the strongest likelihood that we're actually experiencing something great. That's what the art world is most afraid of because we don't know how to assign value, whether it's cultural or otherwise. In a way, the films were meant to be a destabilizing artwork. They exist in another area, a zone where we were free to work." It is pretty clear that these paintings are about big ideas. You can see that in *Black Water* (2012).

An eerie, nighttime seascape of roiling waves, with no celebrities at all lounging on the beach or even surfing, it is obviously referencing the tragic Hollywood death of Natalie Wood. Christopher Walken, who will appear in a cameo later in the film, happens to walk past.

Five Easy Pieces

Jackson Pollock and Tony Smith: *Sculpture: An Exhibition on the Centennial of their Births*; Matthew Marks Gallery, New York.
Tony Smith: *Source*; Matthew Marks Gallery, New York.
Published October 5, 2012; *Artslant*.

Nominally a show of sculpture, Matthew Marks is presenting something more like relics of art world myth, or a romanticized artist-buddy story (think *Lust for Life* or Schnabel's *Basquiat*). It seems an odd pairing at first glance—Pollock, whose paintings consist of poured or dripped skeins of paint are the archetype of Ab Ex passion, and Tony Smith, whose Buckminster Fuller-like geodesic monuments ushered in an Age of Cool. This show presents the remains of a day, one spent at Smith's New Jersey home, when Smith tried to coax out of the fallow (and soon-to-be-dead) Pollock a few last attempts at making art and ended up becoming a sculptor himself.

This five-work show is essentially a teaser for the uber-Minimal show, *Source*, at Marks's larger space on 24th Street. Although Smith produced relatively few actual objects (hence his early claim to a Conceptual artist title) during his brief career as a sculptor (he began as a successful architect), he managed to leave behind a body of work that vigorously explored both an orthodox form of Minimalism as well as working in a vein of seemingly antithetical investigation into relational figuration (for example, *Die* [1962]) and illusionism. His *Source* (1967), first exhibited at *Documenta IV* in Kassel, Germany (1967), weighs in at over six tons and refers to Gustave Courbet's 1864 painting *The Source of the Loue*. Smith, speaking about *Source* in 1971, said, "It would take many lines to explain why I consider Courbet's *Source of the Loue* to be so uniquely related to Ab Ex painting, but I do associate it with the work of many of my late friends. Anyhow, when I saw my sculpture [Smith usually sent or telephoned instructions, measurements, and materials lists to industrial fabricators], I thought of this great flood gushing from the rock face." With its hint of splayed limbs, one might also "see into" *Source* Courbet's other great painting, *Origin of the World* (1866).

It is quite fascinating, after seeing the work of the mature Smith, to see his literal artistic birth in the Pollock/Smith sideshow. *Untitled* (1956), a cob-job of carpentry, presents insight into the psychology of creating sculpture—that most hands-on of art forms—in such a detached manner. Two-by-four boards, which are already a standardized unit of material, are roughly nailed together. Their joining is less important than the jutting angles and forms they produce. In another *Untitled* (1956), we see the embryonic core of all of Smith's later works: an egg carton, cast in concrete, covered in sand, resembling some sort of placenta or slime left behind from an emerging sea creature. Egg cartons, like two-by-fours, serve as a pre-determined grid. Like Smith's early graph paper drawings, honeycomb paintings, or pod paintings (see *Untitled* [1962], hung next to *Source* with its colored bars of flat, straight-out-of-the-tube colors), all share the same concept of his mature works—that of geometric, modular composite forms.

If Smith's sculptures represent the Alpha of this exhibit, Pollock's are the Omega. By the time of their Jersey weekend, Pollock had all but ceased producing work. Following an earlier intervention with Barnett Newman, who, along with Smith jumpstarted Pollock with the seeds of paint that became *Blue Poles* (1952), Smith again played art therapist, presenting Pollock with materials and objects for him to press into service as sculpture. The less said about the results here, the better. There is little that can be added to the cairn of Pollock lore that would shed any light on his already monumental achievements, and to dwell on his faltering end smacks too much of the gleeful necrophilia usually reserved for Marilyn Monroe, Jack Kennedy, or Elvis. Instead, let's leave today's story on a hopeful note, however false it may be.

Pollock excavated large, glacial boulders from behind the Springs, New York, house he shared with the painter Lee Krasner, piling them up for some unrealized future project. At one point he had told Krasner that he might even carve into them. "One of these days," he told her, "I'll get back to sculpture."

50 Shades of Gray

Pablo Picasso: *Picasso Black and White*; Guggenheim Museum, New York.
Published November 12, 2012; *Artslant.*

Claiming once that color weakened his work, being merely an addition to an already finished canvas, Picasso eliminated it from his palette during many phases of his well-documented career. If one wanted to make the case that the haunting blue period and the sugary rose period were the painterly equivalents of tinted photos, then there might be a case to be made for it being a lifelong practice with which Picasso demonstrated the supremacy of drawing above all else in his work. Clearly the Guggenheim, in this well-curated exhibition, makes a strong argument for this position—bringing nearly 150 paintings, many of which have never been seen before in New York, as well as some that have never been exhibited publicly, to its Frank Lloyd Wright temple of Modernism.

Although nominally a show of black-and-white works, the show offers a number of plays on what constituted this reduced palette for Picasso—in works where sepia tones replace strict blacks, showing the influence that photography had for the painter, and in other areas, including sculpture, a dark medium when it is patinated bronze. One encounters this immediately in *Woman with Vase* (1933), a primordial creature holding the titular vessel in an outstretched paw. In 1937 a cement version was placed outside of the Spanish Pavilion at the Paris World's Fair, where *Guernica* (1937) (the last word in black and white painting) was first displayed. Picasso had arrived at a notational physiognomy of Marie-Thérèse Walter, which he captures in three dimensions in this work, while also alluding to the Iberian sculpture about which he was so passionate throughout his lifetime. Climbing the ramps at the museum, one encounters *Woman Ironing* (1904), a blue-hued painting, with its references to Degas's charcoal and pastel drawings, and *Head of a Man* (1906), a cubist, roughly hewn drawing of a head with gouged out, or hollowed, eyes. The violence and despair that Picasso wrings from these simple works is immense yet does not compare to the pre-surrealism of *Female Nude with a Guitar* (1909), a geometric study in chalk on canvas of his mistress, replete with two sets of tits and a smile carved into her neck (50 years before de Kooning's *Woman* paintings) like a tracheotomy scar.

There are endless confectionary portraits of Olga Khokhlova, his first wife; *The Artist's Wife* (1920), *Seated Nude* (1922–23), and *Portrait of Olga in a Fur Collar* (1923) show Picasso returning to the neo-classicism of both style and subject. But we already see his interest in this type of work waning, through the mere repetitiveness of these drawings, and are rewarded for our patience with what is the heart of this exhibition, the works of the 1930s and 1940s, primarily inspired by both Surrealism and Marie-Thérèse Walter. With its graphic, stylized, and distorted forms, *The Milliner's Workshop* (1926) paved the road for *Guernica*, with its sensual arabesques creating a hallucinatory feel for the cramped space of the shop where Walter's mother worked. Here we see Picasso departing from the strict, angular planes of Cubism and creating a new pictorial vocabulary based on her athletic physicality; he creates a population of biomorphic female mutants, balloon-limbed and pliable, yet sturdy and resilient. *Arabesque Woman* (1931) seems to be a schematic for his future creatures, and *The Kiss* (1930), a surreal sketch of spiked-tongued lovers, is a notation for the larger version with which this exhibit concludes (*The Kiss* [1969]).

Although there is no *Guernica*, its counterpart, *The Kitchen* (1948), alludes to the horrors of the war and its effect on a frightened, hungry civilian population. Other post-

Guernica works feature skulls, still lifes, and monstrous, snouted women with claw-like hands, alluding to both Dora Maar and his favorite Afghan dog. It is in these works that his style is clarified and condensed, with his signature lopsided eyes and bisected heads. The rest of the show is comprised of more expressionist versions or variations on these paintings—with additional elements of Manet, Delacroix, and Matisse appropriated. Although writing about his early Cubist pictures, Gertrude Stein could have been describing any one of these works when she said, "There is infinite variety of color in these pictures, and by the vitality of painting, the grays really become color."

Master of Puppets

Bjarne Melgaard: *A New Novel by Bjarne Melgaard*; Luxembourg & Dayan, New York. Published November 25, 2012; *CultureCatch*.

I open one eye. Sunlight pours in through my Zaha Hadid-designed venetian blinds, casting horizontal shadows on the walls, turning the room into a recumbent prison cell. I was supposed to meet James Franco (who is still a little sore at me for beating him out of the part of Cocktimus Prime in Sue de Beer's hardcore version of *Transformers: Revenge of the Fallen*) in Central Park an hour ago, but my Philippe Starck alarm clock (which I fully believe is haunted) failed to wake me. I open both eyes, decide that it is probably safe, and dress quickly: black crinolined Brioni smoking jacket, Hello Kitty t-shirt, baby seal-skin pants, and boots hand carved in Brazilian rosewood (by some guy in Tokyo, whose name is comprised entirely of consonants and who has a nine-year waiting list) which resemble small cats, with inlaid Madagascar ebony eyes. I creep softly out of the bedroom, the Yohji Yamamoto espresso machine, also possibly haunted, seems to glare at me as I cross through the kitchen. I whistle softly (a few bars of the new Coldplay song) as I walk by. My head is pounding: last night we went to the new Eric Ripert joint *Si Vous Plate*, drinks at 1 Oak, dancing at Cisboi with Stavros Niarchos III, Lars Ulrich, Heath Ledger, Lindsay Lohan, and an Olsen twin (Brittany, the smart one, who may or may not still be somewhere in my apartment), and finally, I'm pretty sure, an exorcism in Bushwick. No Olsen in sight, I bolt for the door.

Franco is waiting for me by the 86th street entrance to the park. "Hey man," he says and, seeing my condition, takes pity and empties his pockets: a crumpled cigarette (check), three children's Tylenol (creepy), weaponized morphine (pass), and a new Japanese synthetic called Meow Meow (a mild psychotropic shaped like Flintstones vitamins). I take a Betty Rubble and a Dino. We had made plans to run and then look at art—Franco suggests Picasso at the Guggenheim or maybe Gagosian. We settle on Bjarne Melgaard's show at Luxembourg & Dayan.

Melgaard has transformed the gallery into a three-dimensional, meta version of his most recent novel. For those who are unfamiliar with his work, Melgaard is a prolific, profane, and much-admired polymath. In addition to creating paintings, drawings, films, furniture, and objects, he has written over a dozen novels. These exploded accretions of words and ideas, with their fevers of graphic violence, explicit sadomasochistic sex, and unexpected poignancy, do not adhere to the conventions of dignified narrative. For Melgaard, the novel is a site where ideas, both good and bad, can proliferate freely and where attention follows the upended logic of what actually takes place instead of what ideally should happen. Melgaard steadfastly refuses to locate the frontier between reality and fantasy. "I am more interested in telling a good story than a boring truth," he has said.

Franco, feeling left out again (I am beginning to regret actually *getting* the Cocktimus Prime part; maybe I can convince de Beer to give him the role of Mudflap, a tiny dildo with no lines), starts talking about *his* new book: "*My* first chapbook came out, *Strongest of the Litter*, but people seem to be more interested in who I'm dating than poetry. Oh yeah, I got nominated for a National Entertainment Journalism award for writing Huffington Post blogs, but no other outlet is going to run that story, right? Hahaha—why would *Gawker* or the *New York Post* want to publicize that an actor-slash-Yale doctoral candidate is nominated for an award for something that they are doing themselves? I'm pretty proud of it, but I can see why they must hate me." *I* hate you, I think to myself.

The exhibition *A New Novel by Bjarne Melgaard* coincides with the publication of the artist's latest novel, his first ever to be published commercially in English. Working closely with a group of leading designers and craftspeople, Melgaard transformed the gallery's Upper East Side townhouse into a completely immersive environment that uses his new novel's story—its protagonist's tortured infatuation with a doorman and the willing degradations of a surrounding cast of characters—as a point of departure to plumb further the through-line of his entire practice: an exploration of the ways in which sex and violence dovetail with love and loneliness. Franco is ebullient, "This is fantastic! He is an artist, playing a writer, who is playing an artist! How brilliant! How Meta! It reminds me of what Pablo Picasso said: 'Art is a lie that reveals the Truth.'"

The first floor, a wallpapered living room, the walls aged, water-stained, and peeling, is filled with surreal furniture, handmade dolls, Pink Panther drawings, ephemera (the Pink Panther, Britt Ekland, and Peter Sellers serve as surrogates for characters from both his novel and the larger pantheon of recurring figures in his overall body of work), and homages to Savannah, the porn actress who committed suicide at the age of 24 after a disfiguring car accident. We stumble over stacks of Melgaard's novel, placed like vertical Carl Andre's throughout the room. Poetry Concrete.

Climbing to the second floor we encounter more tableaux: dioramas of dolls smoking crack, or performing needless surgeries on each other, and a stop-motion BDSM doll-snuff film. More than 150 dolls of different sizes were made for the show by JoJo Baby, Gabe Bartalos, Colleen Rochette, and Jessica Scott. These odd figurines wear couture clothing made by Lazaro Hernandez and Jack McCollough of Proenza Schouler in collaboration with Melgaard. The rooms where the dolls appear are furnished with rugs and layers of patterned wallpaper of his own design, along with furniture created in collaboration with Billy Cotton and upholstered in vintage Ozzie Clark dresses, textiles made by Proenza Schouler, and a jacquard fabric based on the paintings Melgaard created for the exhibition.

Alissa Bennett, a writer and director of the gallery, emerges, resplendent in a forsythia-colored vintage Prada dress and eel-skin and anaconda Manolos. "I am so glad you stopped by! Bjarne will be here any minute!" Seeing Franco's befuddlement at the seeming morass of the installation, Bennett takes us up to the third floor. "The centerpiece!" she says, enthusiastically. Thirteen new paintings—lush, lavishly colored, and visually seductive pictures of tigers presented within the tableaux rooms of the house. Their ropey skeins of intense color evoke viscera, offering a beautiful interpretation of the violence depicted in Melgaard's book. Like the cartoon animals depicted elsewhere in his oeuvre, these tigers serve as stand-ins for the artist, charismatic and camouflaged, constantly negotiating between the dual impulses of predation and love. Melgaard began making the tiger paintings while preparing for a major exhibition at the Institute of Contemporary Arts in London. He collaborated with Bellevue Survivors, a group of disabled people in recovery from mental or emotional challenge including political torture. The lawlessness of the mind and its ultimate unsuitability for strict codes, as well as shifting boundaries between reality and fantasy worlds, serve as powerful subtexts for Melgaard's canvases. He is both a Rimbaud and a Proust. The canvases are hinged to the wall; Bennett explains, "Bjarne has written extra chapters to the novel on the back of each one. He is combining all of the work into one large meta-work—image and object and language all fused together."

I am reminded of something that James Joyce's psychiatrist, who also treated his schizophrenic daughter, said to him regarding his oblique, autistic writing. She remarked that the only difference between his explorations and his daughter's illness was that he dove into the darker realms of psychology, whereas his daughter sank. It is a difficult balancing act, presenting chaos without succumbing to it. Melgaard mines ever-deeper depths in his work; he is an intrepid sub-mariner of the psyche—his writing our diving bell, his paintings, fragile rafts.

Call Me Ishmael

Barnaby Furnas: *If Wishes Were Fishes . . .*; Marianne Boesky Gallery, New York.
Published December 11, 2012; *Artslant*.

> Once, while Jesus was walking by the Sea of Galilee, he saw two brothers,
> Simon, and his brother Andrew, casting a net into the sea, for they were
> fishermen.
> And he said unto them, follow me, and I will make you fishers of men.
> And they immediately left their nets and followed him.
> —(Matthew 4:18–20)

Barnaby Furnas has always had a penchant for drama in paint. From images of heavy metal bands to giant veils of crashing, velvety, blood-red seas. Here Furnas has taken as his starting point Herman Melville's *Moby Dick*, and elements from the story of Jonah and the Whale. As ambitious as it might seem, to cast such a large net, he has managed to bring in, through an eclectic amalgam of styles and technique, a fine catch. Furnas described his enterprise: "What interested me about whaling in the first place was that they (the whales) gave us light—their fat allowed us to bring God's light into the darkness of the night so we could see our fingers and maybe read after the sun went down."

Furnas is not the first painter to be drawn to the whaling/painting analogy—van Gogh compared the two oily arts, Frank Stella monotonously tried to illustrate Melville's manuscript chapter by chapter, and Sean Landers recently set sail with paintings of clown captains. Furnas draws from some of these sources, as well as a whole history of modernist painting, and cobbles together something entirely his own here. In these paintings the emphasis is on the painting's ground, into which washes of pigment are stained, ground, or spattered; areas are masked or taped loosely, allowing the liquidity of the paint to flow under the hard edges. His seemingly controlled approach to painting is belied by gravity's effects; nature has the upper hand here. Though anticipated, its effects surprise.

There are numerous small panels of whalers: the flensers, the portioners, and one of an Abraham Lincoln-y looking Ahab in a stove-pipe hat. (*The Flenser #3* [2012], *The Portioner* [2012], *Ahab #1* [2012]). These small "character studies," spattered with whale blood, go about their jobs, their deft speed connoted by multiple, Cubo-Futurist-style arms, carving away—a metaphor for the painter at work, as well as the Calvinist references that Furnas aims for: many hands make light work, Benjamin Franklin wrote. A vertical figure standing in front of an arched whale's tail becomes a tale of a different sort (*Johah and the Whale #4* [2012]), with its waterfall surface creating a Veronica's Veil in paint.

The largest painting, *The Whalers* (2012), is reminiscent of John Singleton Copley's *Watson and the Shark* (1778), both for its large-scale theatrics and for the way in which narrative is conveyed through the gestures of the figures—as well as the painter's gestures through his materials. Here the whale is mortally wounded; a plume of blood gushes and spatters, and perfect droplets of blood and something rectangular and white, like confetti, emerge from the blowhole. Seagulls flap in all directions. The figures are rigid with the strain of the killing and possibly frozen with fear. The sea roils. In a painterly gesture of great mastery, Furnas has sketched in, in pencil, the whale's upper row of teeth yet left them unpainted. Perhaps telegraphing the whale's ultimate fate, Achilles-like. Here we are truly reminded of Melville and his Ahab's end—but we, the viewers of this spectacle, are lucky Ishmael, left standing. "The drama's done. Why then here does any one step forth? Because one did survive the wreck . . . I floated on a soft and dirge-like main. The unharming sharks, they glided by as if with padlocks on their mouths; the savage sea-hawks sailed with sheathed beaks."

Luxe, Calme, et Volupté

Henri Matisse: *In Search of True Painting*; Metropolitan Museum of Art, New York.
Published February 19, 2013; *Artslant*.

The prospect of seeing forty-nine of Matisse's finest works should be enticement enough, however, the Metropolitan Museum of Art has upped the ante by arranging this somewhat thematic exhibition in groupings, which show the painter refining his personal explorations in modernist paintings through endless, subtle variations. Although the pedagogical aspects of this might seem a little staid at first flush, upon close study one becomes entranced by the intricate, reductive logic that lay at the heart of all of Matisse's works.

From the start Matisse was an equal-opportunity gatherer and collector of other artists' styles and sensibilities: Giotto, Moreau, Cézanne, and van Gogh, to name a few. This is apparent right from the start of the show. Two paintings, *Still Life with Compote and Fruit* (1899) and *Still Life with Compote, Apples and Oranges* (1899), show Matisse moving already toward a reductive approach to paint. The former is all Seurat-inspired semaphoric dots and dashes, whereas the second anticipates Morandi's minimalist *nature mortes*. In the next gallery we see something similar with *Seated Nude* (1909) and *Nude with a White Scarf* (1909). *White Scarf*, with its thick, muscular strokes and black outlining speaks to German Expressionism, particularly Max Beckmann. *Seated Nude*, apparently done after *Scarf* as a sort of souvenir, partakes of something like Picasso's perverse personal Surrealism, in spirit. Here the model is lightly sketched in, with amputee arms, BTK legs, and missing breasts. Unlike the refined *Scarf*, *Nude* reveals her bare snoopie, creating a frisson of peep show action—something that seldom happens in Matisse's work from models.

In a 1912 interview Matisse said about his working method, "I never retouch a sketch: I take a canvas the same size, as I may change the composition somewhat. But I always strive to give the same feeling while carrying it a little further . . ." This is true in the three variations of *Le Luxe* (1907–08) where we get to compare and contrast the original, a revised version, and a charcoal sketch (made for his personal consumption). In the several paintings of the model Laurette (particularly *Laurette in a Green Robe, Black Background* [1916]), Matisse begins to play with black—what would become a lifelong fascination. In *Green Robe*, blacks define background, the delineation of the armchair, and the figure—subtle, and revealed only by patient gazing. In a later series of works, studies of the beach at Étretat, where Monet and Courbet had already created programmatic, methodological groups of works depicting the beach and distinctive seaside cliffs, Matisse combines subject and style seamlessly. In simplified studies of a beach clambake, he reduces both the naturalistic detail, and metaphorically, the beach snacks: from a seaweed-wrapped chowder of fish, skate, and clams, to (in the final variation) a solitary eel. Only a boat's sail, emerging along the waterline in the background, like a shark's tooth, provides a steady, metronomic beat to these fugue studies.

One of the big problems in making such sweeping statements like "I never retouch a sketch . . ." is that eventually one will probably end up doing exactly the opposite. By the time we get to *The Dream* (1940), Matisse had begun to seriously rework every canvas he painted. His assistant, Lydia Delectorskaya, had taken on the role of chief documenter of his progress, having each day's work photographed. Beginning with *The Large Blue Dress* (1937), showing the progress between February 26 and April 3, we see how he winnowed down the composition, from something approaching naturalism to the final, highly stylized, cut-out masterpiece. With *The Dream*, which tackles a theme that Picasso was wrestling with in serialized fashion, we get the whole process. In his 1945 Galerie Maeght exhibition, *The Dream* was hung surrounded by large black-and-white photos of its creation (faithfully recreated at the Metropolitan). He insisted to Maeght that the purpose of such a novel hanging was pedagogical; showing the development of the work through its various respective states toward a definitive conclusion clarified his intent. What might have seemed a silly, and possibly pretentious, idea at the time turns out to have been prescient. Looking back at Matisse's work a century later, we sometimes forget just how far he took painting into a new visual language. The man who was chided as being a "wild beast" at the beginning of his career, was, in fact, a painter of great perception, refinement, and delicacy, in the end.

Family Affair

Dieter Roth. Björn Roth; Hauser & Wirth, New York.
Published February 8, 2013; *CultureCatch*.

Bruno Alfieri, one of the most outspoken writers on Jackson Pollock's work, was not so impressed by an exhibition of Pollock's poured paintings. To Alfieri, the artwork seemed to be thrown together randomly, with little thought. In 1950, *Time Magazine*'s article "Chaos, Damn It!" quoted Alfieri on Pollock's work: There is "nothing but uncontrolled impulse . . . It is easy to detect the following things in all of his paintings: chaos; absolute lack of harmony; complete lack of structural organization; total absence of technique, however rudimentary; once again, chaos." A cursory appraisal of the work of Dieter Roth, and his son Björn Roth, might initially elicit the same response. This three-decade-long meditation on what Robert Rauschenberg called the "gap between art and life" is a collection of candy, clothes, and old workbenches (*Grosse Tischruine* [*Large Table Ruin*] [1978–1998]), as well as paintings, videos of the artist at work and on the can (*Solo Scenes* [1997–1998]), and lastly, and most impressively, a towering monolithic sculpture, which is, in fact, a studio floor cut in half and upended (*The Floor I: Studio-floor from Mosfellsbaer, Iceland* [1973–1992] and *The Floor II: Studio-floor from Mosfellsbaer, Iceland* [1977–1998]).

The centerpiece of the show, however, is a performance/installation by Roth's son, Björn—a rebuilding of the original Dieter Roth sugar kitchen located at the Dieter Roth Foundation's Schimmelmuseum in Germany. A makeshift galley has been fashioned, complete with a stove, upon which sugar and E. Guittard chocolate are melted and poured into rough, foot-tall molds that resemble a dog, a lion, or a portrait of *Père* Roth (depending on whom you ask—in Roth's work, specificity is not a long suit), which are then stacked into two, ceiling-high towers of shelves. Björn Roth describes them as an *homage* to the New York skyline—the oblique reference to the World Trade Center, remaining Roth-esquely oblique; they might just as well evoke Tolkien's *The Two Towers*, with their rainbow-colored candy animal figures and wizened, wizard-like visage of Roth.

The real art at the heart of this piece is Dieter Roth's 20-year-long collaboration with his son Björn. Here, Björn rebuilds the installation with the help of his own sons, Oddur and Einar, working each day to fashion a chocolate tower, *Selbstturm (Self Tower)* (1994–2013), and a *Zuckerturm (Sugar Tower)* (1994–2013), a piece that collapsed under its own weight in 1994—masterpieces ceaselessly in the making. What at first glance might seem to be chaos and caprice (Roth's first American exhibition consisted of thirty-six suitcases filled with rotting cheese, after all), might, with the proper amount of time and distance, be viewed as one great meta-work. Here is an artist who was not content to merely paint and sculpt, but, rather, used everything, including his progeny, in a total work of art. Whether this vision was *ad hoc* or not is probably irrelevant; the result of the experiment is the same. While Joseph Beuys proposed that "every man is an artist," Roth posits some next-level shit—that, indeed, artists are born.

Daydream Nation

Various artists: *NYC 1993: Experimental Jet Set, Trash and No Star*; The New Museum, New York.
Julian Schnabel: *1978–1981*; Oko, New York.
Published February 16, 2013; *MAINTENANT 9*.

> One must turn to the past to move forward.
> –Akan proverb

We are sitting around a banquette at Nell's, well sorted, and I am overwhelmed with a vague sadness all of a sudden—the conversations around the table, a sonic penumbra: who has new tits (girls with names like Coriander and Chloe), who is in rehab ("she has a *nasal* addiction"), who fucked whom with what (don't ask), and possibly, for the first time in recent memory, I no longer care what I am wearing (Comme des Garçons leather jacket over a vintage Led Zeppelin t-shirt, *imitation* of Imitation of Christ store-torn jeans, Prada driving shoes, with no socks, as my awesome new ankle tattoo—neo-tribal—is still too fresh and bandaged with Saran Wrap). Someone comes to take orders, and Damien, who has drawn eyes on the head of his cock with a Sharpie, stands up, takes it out (a Camel Light dangling from his urethra), wags it, and says, ventriloquist-like, "Three Black and Tans and two E's, please." The table dissolves into laughter. I think that a piece of uneaten tofu on the plate in front of me is whispering something important. It is definitely time to leave.

Outside, Jeff Koons jokingly offers a homeless guy his AmEx card, pulling it away at the last moment and laughing; and Johnny Depp, embarrassed, hangs back, writing him a check. There are suggestions of better places to go in Soho, with names like Spy or Toy or Goy. Gwyneth Paltrow suggests we go to a club called HIV, but we end up tagging along with Ashley Bickerton, Jay MacInerny, Larry Clark, and Kate Moss to someone's loft, which has been decorated with silver helium balloons and glitter and a 15-foot rail of blow on a long mirror on the floor to celebrate either someone's opening or a new record or possibly a cure for AIDS or Sean Landers's new novel. The Julian Schnabel show at Oko, which features just *one* painting (*St. Sebastian*, 1979), has drawn a huge crowd, and some of the runoff has spilled in. Leonardo DiCaprio is on the floor hoovering from the enormous line with River Phoenix, and Jack Pierson is snapping Polaroids and muttering things like "fagulous." There is a suite of new Cindy Sherman C-prints on the wall where she is dressed up to look like various members of an SS Death Squad.

Someone who is definitely *not* a DJ is playing Oasis, and Damon Albarn throws a Guinness bottle through a window. Thurston Moore takes over at the turntables and starts playing the Beatle's *White Album* at half-speed. People start dancing again. Wolfgang Tillmans sees me standing in the kitchen, which was done by Andrea Zittel—the tables fold into the walls, and the cabinets double for growing hydroponic weed—and asks me if I want to meet some girls. "They are really beautiful," he says. "I mean, they *are* 16, but they look like they're 14." I pass and wander aimlessly around the loft, wishing I had done more Ketamine before we left. I remember that I had come with a date, but since I can't remember her name (ironic, since she only has one, like Moby), it seems a little pointless to ask if anyone has seen her.

There is a small painting of Kurt Cobain or Liam Gallagher that seems to stare at me from the wall in the bathroom as I piss into what I am hoping is a toilet. Someone has scrawled "I Fucked Tracey Emin" on the mirror in Hard Candy Black-Cherry-Bomb lipstick.

Sadie Benning is making a Pixelvision movie in one of the bedrooms starring Matthew Barney and Kristin Oppenheim. They have pulled all the 1,000-thread-count Egyptian cotton sheets off the Frank Gehry Eager Beaver cardboard bed and are pretending to be ghosts. Barney is holding two silver ass plugs over his sheet-covered head, pretending to be a bull-ghost, and starts to mount the Oppenheim ghost, who is alternately saying "boo" and "moo." I melt into the wall and pretend along with them for a while. Someone has written "I smell the blood of les tricoteuses" in orange spray paint on one of the walls, and, feeling a little creeped out, I slip back to the party.

Stavros Niarchos II, René Ricard, John Currin, and Alex Bag are drinking champagne from a bottle in the hallway. As I pass between them, one of them says, "No, she is a *female* female impersonator. I hear she is in the new Nirvana video . . ." I find a sealed tin of Beluga from Dean & DeLuca on a Philippe Starck princess coffee table and pick it up. I push aside a clutter of untouched Chinese take-out containers and little bottles of Evian. I sit down on the Droog Design couch, cradling the tin, tears welling up uncontrollably, and lean back, marveling at the perfection of it all.

Public Image, Ltd.

Jean-Michel Basquiat: Gagosian Gallery, New York.
Published February 23, 2013; *CultureCatch*.

> Life is a dark chain of events.
> –Frederick Nietzsche

> Pay for Soup.
> Build a Fort.
> Set that on Fire.
> –SAMO (Jean Michel Basquiat)

Jean-Michel Basquiat was a unique and prodigious artistic talent who fused drawing and painting, pop culture and music, with history and poetry to produce an artistic language and content that was entirely his own. Combining the tools of graffiti (Sharpie markers, spray enamel, and chalk) with those of fine art (oil and acrylic paint, collage, and oil stick), his best paintings maintain a powerful tension between opposing aesthetic forces—thought and expression; control and spontaneity; wit, urbanity, and primitivism—while providing acerbic commentary on the harsher realities of race, culture, and society in the early 1980s New York social landscape. In vividly colored canvases, forceful, schematic figures and menacing, mask-like faces are inscribed against fields jostling with images, signs, symbols, and words used like brushstrokes. The frenetic, all-over quality of many of the large works suggests a drive toward a sort of disjunctive mapping, rather than the building of a classically unified composition, where seemingly unrelated marks suddenly coalesce in syncopated rhythms; comparisons were made of his work to boxing and the cool jazz of Miles Davis.

In retrospect, judging from the carefully curated selection of Basquiat's best paintings here, it might have been a little too easy to place his work in the category of Neo Expressionism, with its bombast and emphasis on direct, experiential painting—as closer looks reveal that his process (no doubt influenced by his working relationship with Warhol) didn't quite fit so neatly into the same camp as Schnabel and Clemente, but walked a fine line between high and low culture. In his essay "The Culture Industry: Enlightenment as Mass Deception," the art theorist and social critic Theodor Adorno attempted to analyze the transformation of the cultural sphere in industrialized capitalist society. Adorno argued that as a result of the increasing rationalization of life in a technological society, the cultural sphere becomes one of the areas through which the dominant economic norms are inserted. He posited that this commodification of culture leads inevitably to the conflation of the avant-garde—or high culture—and those lower forms of popular entertainment or spectacle. For Adorno the end result of this mash-up is Kitsch. Perhaps no artist in the twentieth century since Warhol understood how to commodify kitsch into a believable art form as much as Basquiat.

We can see in such pictures as *In Italian* (1983), with its layers of images of currency, reproduced and repeated underdrawings (Basquiat used the copy machine in much the same way that Warhol used the silkscreen), and the use of cheap, castaway wood and tarp for canvas support. *Untitled (Julius Caesar on Gold)* (1981) also makes reference to the currency of *kunst* (imitation gold paint), power (Caesar holding a cartoonishly large sword), and primitive, imagistic markings, which add a sense of street cred (via graffiti). Basquiat proves a canny manipulator of those Post-Colonial theorists in the eighties who were seeking authentic examples of "authentic" African American art; later artists such as Glen Ligon and Ellen Gallagher would be enlisted toward the same ends. But Basquiat ultimately proves a different kind of painter—one who managed to keep (most) of his authentic early reputation as a product of the street graffiti movement, while also working the burgeoning gallery scene of Boone, Nosei, and Bischofberger. In analyzing the paintings of Courbet, T.J. Clark writes, "The critics did not object to the exploitation of popular art; on the contrary, it was already accepted as a source of imagery and inspiration, as one way to revive the exhausted forms of 'high art.'" But to adopt the procedures and even the values of popular art, that was subversive. He exploited high art—its techniques, its size, and something of its sophistication—in order to revive popular art. His art, like any other, would in the end be assimilated. But for the moment, for a few years, the attempt troubled the public. One critic, in an attempt at categorization, resorted to the value-free description of the paintings as a "menagerie of bipeds." How better to describe Basquiat's *Untitled* (1981) or *La Hara* (1981)? In *Eyes and Eggs* (1987), he achieves an iconic image (Joe the fry cook holding a pan of eggs—whose shape echoes his goofy eyes—painted on a canvas tarp covered with footprints; we deduce that the tarp was once laid horizontal, creating an "arena" or "boxing ring" for the painter's work), but this image was ready-made for the posters, coffee cups, and t-shirts it now ubiquitously adorns. This is not a painter who did not think in the long term of how his images would be reproduced but, rather, understood very deeply that when his carefully crafted public image would fade away, the pictures would live on to carry quite different, generally acceptable meanings to the public.

This is not to say that Basquiat's work is a series of calculated stratagems—in fact, Warhol was drawn to the idea of working with him because he saw in his drawing style, his hand, something reminiscent of his own early painting attempts (before the graphic designer in him banished scribbly drawing). There still remains, in the best of his paintings, such as *Gold Griot* (1984), a powerful, draughtsman-like intensity. Pliny the Elder, in his *Natural History*, spent a great deal of attention focusing on the origin of painting. In Book 35, called *An Account of Painting and Colors*, he writes, "We have no certain knowledge as to the birth of the art of painting, nor does this enquiry fall under our consideration. The Egyptians assent that it was invented by themselves . . . the Greeks . . . claim it was invented at Sicyon . . . or Corinth; but they all agree that it originated in the tracing of lines . . ." To which we might add, " . . . and continued in New York, on Great Jones Street."

Voodoo Problems

Peter Williams: Foxy Production, New York.
Published March 7, 2013; *CultureCatch*.

> Art should *not* have to be a certain way.
> —Willem de Kooning

For Peter Williams's first solo exhibition at Foxy Production, he is showing work from two distinct but interconnected bodies of work: large figurative paintings depict fanciful, fractured narratives that mix cultural and personal histories with fields of pattern and color; and a set of smaller paintings that distil and intensify visual moments from the larger works, magnifying and expanding them. Williams's paintings tell entropic tales, with figures caught in moments that show their fragility—scenes of everyday life, both seen and imagined.

Williams's painting process begins with drawing. He focuses first on shape and then color to create depth and volume in seemingly flat spaces. Contrasting with the fields of the background, the figures he paints engage in surreal, humorous, and disturbing relationships. His open-ended visual stories combine a wide range of references: from photographs of lynchings and the death of Trayvon Martin, to Diego Velázquez, Robert Colescott, Andy Warhol, and Walt Disney. With the painting *Untitled* (2013) we might also add Pierre Matisse and Nicola Tyson; Williams depicts three figures against a sharply delineated ground of pure color. A man, wearing flowery pajamas, swoops down Chagall-style with a bouquet of flowers, perhaps presenting them to the two nude (except for stockings) female creatures who are wearing something akin to an Elizabethan collar/shield/helmet combination. Their faces bear a protruding snout or nozzle; one seems to be wearing strap-on tits, and the other either pisses or menstruates out of a purple-hued snoopie. In this painting, Williams manages to pull off an amazing amount in the parameters within which he works—the beautiful color doesn't fight against the weirdness, it melds with it; Matisse pulls off something similar in *Le Luxe* (1907–08).

Idyllic fantasies, nightmares, and the human comedy all have a place in Williams's fantastic narratives. In *Untitled* (2012), a tree creature is lifting up a boy in red-and-white checkered overalls, with its branches in the center of the painting. The boy wears pale makeup à la Pierrot and seems resigned or relaxed and limp, despite the towering presence of the much larger creature. The two characters are in an ocher field, with abstract green foliage in the distance. Crosshatch marks bring to mind Munch's *Self-Portrait: Between the Clock and the Bed* (1943) or Jasper Johns's paintings of the seventies. All around them are variously shaped fanciful beings, staring at this strange ritual. A woman smiles, revealing the word "geeez" carved into her front teeth. Others surround the little vignette, eating Doritos, carrying an "Obama 2012" sign; one, who also has a trunk with "gasoline" painted on it, watches intently, while another, more Cubist-inspired with a bifurcated face, stares out at us with the *mirada fuerte* (strong glance) found in many Picasso portraits.

Though Williams handles crowd scenes with the skill of a Cecil B. DeMille, he can also do small, haunted, and claustrophobic like Samuel Beckett. In *Untitled* (2013), which has a deep red ground, a naked pink figure with an oversized yellow head carries two guns, one with the word "soap" scratched into the paint; one of his legs is a wood two-by-four. He looks over his shoulder, his face a mask of fear or surprise. He is glancing up at an enormous pink head with turquoise nostrils, peering down from the painting's top edge. Whether this is a benevolent god or malevolent giant is neither indicated nor even seems important, as, with Williams's best work, it isn't the conclusions we draw that are important, it is the questions that it raises. Like Courbet, Picasso, or Bacon, he presents the body as both fact and fiction— the body as a vehicle, an object whose physicality is often forgotten as we experience it through moments of excitement, fear, pleasure, pain, or dreaming.

Funtime

Various artists: *Gutai: Splendid Playground*; Solomon R. Guggenheim, New York. Published April 23, 2013; *CultureCatch*.

> Discarding the frame, getting off the walls, shifting from immobile time to lived time, we aspire to create a new painting.
> —Suburō Murakami, Osaka, 1957

> Kick out the jams, motherfuckers!
> —MC5, Detroit, 1968

The Guggenheim Museum's *Gutai: Splendid Playground* presents the work of Japan's most influential avant-garde collective of the postwar era. Founded by the visionary artist Jirō Yoshihara in 1954, the Gutai group was legendary in its own time. Its young members explored new art forms, combining performance, painting, and interactive environments, and realized an "international common ground" of experimental art through the worldwide reach of their exhibition and publication activities.

The Gutai Art Association (active 1954–72) originated in Ashiya, near Osaka, in western Japan. Spanning two generations, the group totaled fifty-nine Japanese artists over its eighteen-year history. The name "Gutai" literally means "concreteness" and captures the direct engagement with materials its members were experimenting with around the time of its founding in 1954. From its earliest festival-like events, Gutai artists sought to break down the barriers between art, the ordinary public, and everyday life. They continuously took on new artistic challenges using the body in direct action with materials, time and space, and nature and technology. Charting Gutai's creation of visual, conceptual, and theoretical terrains, this exhibition is organized throughout the museum in chronological and thematic sections: Play, Network, Concept, the Concrete, Performance Painting, and Environment Art.

Interestingly, it is this first concept, "play," that united their work to both the art and philosophy of the Western world where they were trying to make inroads via their programs and objects. Like Rousseau (France), Maria Montessori (Italy), or John Dewey (the United States), Gutai artists introduced children to the work at extremely young ages, in the context of free play, with sincere hopes that it might change and mold them. Even Foucault and Freire agreed in some measure to the validity of this approach, though in a more limited, academic way.

The outdoor exhibitions of 1955 and 1956 set the stage for the group's artistic strategies. Held in a pine grove park in Ashiya, these events brought art outside and released it from its confines, for example Sadamasa Motonaga's magisterial *Work (Water)* (1956/2011). The Guggenheim commissioned the artist to recreate this work for the rotunda, where he hangs common, polyethylene tubes of varying widths filled with brightly colored water between the rotunda levels, making giant brushstrokes out of catenaries in the open air that catch the sunlight.

Moving from what Yoshihara decried as "fraudulent appearances" to lived reality, Gutai artists invented ways to go beyond contemporary styles of abstract painting into concrete pictures, blurring representational significance by incorporating raw matter, as well as time and space, as the stuff of art. Atsuko Tanaka's *Work (Bell)* (1955/1993) reimagines an artwork as an acoustic composition of living sound through a sequential ringing of electric alarm bells.

Her interests in schematic and technical representation, wiring systems, lights, and the human form reached a pinnacle in her best-known work, *Electric Dress* (1956). The artist wore this spectacular costume made of flashing incandescent light bulbs painted in bright yellow, green, red, and blue.

Like *Art Informel* and the New Realists, Gutai rejected psychic automatism for acts of corporeal materiality in the real world. Yoshihara's involvement with the revitalization of Japanese traditional arts, specifically Japanese calligraphy, also informed his idea of art making as an unmediated experiential encounter between artist, gesture, and material. Kazuo Shiraga's *Untitled* (1957), made by the artist painting on the floor with his bare feet, or Saburō Murakami's *Passage* (1956), a performance of the artist flinging himself through taut paper screens, both demonstrate Gutai's call to release the "scream of matter itself." Gutai artists extended their objectives to theater, music, and film. For example, the *Gutai Card Box* (1962/2013) transforms the act of viewing paintings into an interaction; at the Guggenheim, visitors can insert $1 into the box, purchasing a small, original piece of art from someone hidden inside the vending machine. The box has two-way mirrors, so the person in the box selecting which card to dispense can see the visitor, but the visitor cannot see the person in the box.

As the global pioneers of environmental art, Gutai's participatory environments take the form of organic or geometric abstract sculptures incorporating kinetic, light, and sound art, turning exhibition spaces into chaotic dens of screeching, pulsing, machine-like organisms. Minoru Yoshida's erotic machine-sculpture *Bisexual Flower* (1969) mines the psychedelic effects of this approach. With its garish Plexiglas, black lights, and visible, low-tech machinery, it is an update on Duchamp's *Bride Stripped Bare by Her Bachelors, Even* (1915–21), 1960s style. Gutai environments drew from contemporary architecture, technology, and urban design to promote a futuristic, space-age aesthetic. This can be seen in Senkichirō Nasaka's giant armature composed of aluminum plumbing pipes punctured with holes, broadcasting a music composition as it zigzags its way up the exhibition space. This site of creativity is what Shiraga called "a splendid playground" and what Yoshihara sought as a "free site that can contribute to the progress of humanity."

Nights Without Armor

Karen Heagle: *Battle Armor*; Churner and Churner, New York.
Published June 11, 2013; *Artslant*.

Heraclitus wrote, "Nothing is constant but change," illustrating succinctly his philosophy of the nature of the universe; with her current exhibit *Battle Armor*, Karen Heagle illustrates this adage, with paintings that show that old motifs can have new life breathed into them, in the right hands. In the past, Karen Heagle has made reference to heroic figures in her paintings: the Incredible Hulk and Zena the Warrior princess, for example; in her recent show of paintings on paper at Churner and Churner in New York, she revisits some of the same themes, and sense of the heroic, through her choice of subject matter, primarily medieval armor, and combines it with a painterly style that draws from great *nature morte* and *vanitas* artists like Hals, Chardin, and Soutine.

When asked how she would describe her recent work and its progression, Heagle replied, "I am developing imagery that reflects autobiographical symbolism . . . For several years I worked with oil paint on wood panels, but six years ago I began working exclusively on paper. I've started using collage, gold leaf, and copper leaf, preferring to work on a larger scale. I engage my mediums with a blunt yet expressive physicality." Heagle treats paper as if it were canvas; her figures and objects rendered life-sized and the application of the various leafing sheets give the work an otherworldly light, such that they call to mind Russian icons or the Northern European devotional triptychs of van Eyck.

It is clear from the start of the show, with *Prodigal Daughter* (2013), that Heagle is not just mimicking past masters, but is carving out her own niche in painting. *Prodigal Daughter* depicts a rapid, muscular sketch of a motorcycle leaning against a golden wall of paint and leaf. It announces, slyly, that we are on *her* trip through this show, the empty seat of the bike beckoning us to come along. *Prodigal Daughter* serves as a strange cypher when placed in the context of the antique images that comprise the rest of the exhibition. When asked about this, Heagle addressed the idea of melding the contemporary with the past:

"It was a painting that was in my graduate thesis show at Pratt in the fall of 1994. In my current exhibition, this version of *Prodigal Daughter* is revisiting the themes and ideas it addressed. In essence, it's a type of self-portrait. When I made the original, I was just coming out as gay. So I wanted to make the painting again, almost twenty years later. I wanted to look at how far gay culture has come, related to how far I had come as a gay person. With the increased acceptance of queer culture, I was seeking to explore what queer imagery is in our contemporary culture."

When viewed from Heagle's perspective, we might see the armor also as a self-portrait. Coming out in the early nineties, the era of Bush I and Jesse Helms, must have taken on aspects of a battle for acknowledgement and equality in society—the same things, one might also add, that painters generally strive for.

The real heart of this exhibit, though, is the still lifes of armor that Heagle has culled mostly from the large collection of the Metropolitan Museum of Art. Depiction of armor, knights, and the like has held its place in the history of painting. Rembrandt and Hals jump to mind immediately, as well as tapestry cycles, such as the Unicorn Tapestries. The small helmet said to be worn by Joan of Arc, which is in the collection of the Met, as well as other examples of women's armor, seem to inspire the story Heagle tells in these works. In *Battle Armor with Codpiece* (2012), she faithfully renders the suit of metal, with its spiky shoulder plates and other accoutrements. She pays special attention to the shiny metal codpiece, which she admits to enhancing a bit, turning the hard-on into another lance, of sorts, perhaps slyly mocking the sense of narcissistic, peacock-like vanity that the suits lend themselves to so easily. One imagines a further line of study where she might morph the animal with the human, perhaps painting suits of armor designed for horses—metal that both protects the animals and, more often, drowns them at river crossings. As a sidenote, Heagle presents two small portraits of actors, *Untitled (Isabella Rossellini)* (2013) and *Untitled (Charlotte Rampling)* (2013)—two stern headshots. On the subject of these images, Heagle turns taciturn but seems to imply that the two actors have both inhabited quite strong roles through their careers, like a protective shell or armor; the actors' facial expressions seem to present a public persona rather than an intimate, internal view of the subject.

Vanity, masculinity, and violence are tied together in a single painting of the beautifully colored bird with a horrific call in Heagle's *Peacock* (2013). As with suits of armor, the brightly colored plume of the peacock both attracts and repels—it is, of course, this duality, inherent in all of Heagle's work, that is so compelling. The beauty of her work is that she makes all these contradictions fit together so easily.

Holywood

Paul McCarthy and Damon McCarthy: *Rebel Dabble Babble*; Hauser & Wirth, New York.
Paul McCarthy: *WS*; Park Avenue Armory, New York.
Published July 9, 2013; *CultureCatch*.

James Franco is finishing a joke. "*Natalie* Wood . . . get it? What kind of *wood* doesn't *float*?"
Everyone is very hung over this morning, but fortunately Franco sent his Maybach Landaulet
and driver to whisk us to Chlamydia, the new Bobby Flay café in Chelsea, where we are
drinking revivifying Bellinis and an assortment of other smart cocktails with Vito Schnabel,
Slavoj Žižek, Natalie Portman (or possibly Keira Knightley, or Keira Knightley's body double),
Sasha Grey, Heath Ledger, Michael Lee Nirenberg, Lena Dunham, Chloë Sevigny, and a Thai/
Puerto Rican pre-op transsexual who Franco introduces as "Pinball," all of whom are sweating
slightly and staring at Billy Cyborg passed out in a bowl of muesli. Inexplicably, the table is
cluttered with untouched Chinese take-out containers and bottles of Evian, and there are piles
of silver glitter and confetti everywhere. Nirenberg orders it all removed immediately. Skrillex's
mash-up of One Direction's *a cappella* version of Justin Bieber's cover of Mudhoney's "Touch
Me I'm Sick" is playing inside the bar, drowning out other, probably more interesting,
conversations at other tables.

Last night Franco and Nirenberg suggested we see Billy Cyborg and the Hate Fucks
play at a new avant-garde theater in Bushwick called For Rent, which resembled an abandoned
warehouse, exquisitely detailed with defenestrated windows, exposed, sparking BX cable, and
what seemed to be piles of dead cats in the men's toilet, where I went with Jared Leto, Stoya,
Harry Styles, Bjarne Melgaard, and Nirenberg to do a couple of pre-show rails. Billy Cyborg
is the front man for the band, formerly known as Billy Robot and the Botched Abortions,
which was legendary for its Ambient/NuMetal/Dancehall/Ska/Gospel-fusion music as much
as for their notoriously short (usually 3-minute) sets during which the band was usually candy-
flipping, drunk, or just passed out on top of each other. Billy is also a part-time adult film
actor who met Franco on the set of *Deep Inside Brian's Ass* or *The Spurt Locker*. At last night's
awesome performance, the band, who had all eaten a handful of E, formed what could only be
described as a "cuddle puddle" downstage on top of their mute instruments, while the drum
machine played itself for fourteen minutes. Haunting.

I am wearing a black t-shirt I borrowed from Franco this morning that says "God of All
Fuck," optic yellow aviator glasses with very cool holographic skulls in the lenses, and forsythia-
colored store-torn jeans (and matching jacket) by Pucci. I'm barefoot, having accidentally left
my shoes in the Maybach.

Žižek is discussing the new Paul and Damon McCarthy show, *Rabble Dabble Babble*.
"I find this work so much stronger than the grander *WS* project at the Armory, the brilliant
retelling of Walt Disney's Snow White story. But where *WS* leaves us asking ourselves
that timeless question, Who would you rather fuck: Wilma Flintstone or Betty Rubble?,
McCarthy's work here probes deeper into the meaninglessness of American culture."

Pinball chooses this very inopportune moment to call for more Bellinis. I notice that the
name on the black AmEx card she proffers reads "ALEC BALDWIN."

"As I was saying, McCarthy's deconstruction of the myths behind the great Nicholas
Ray's *Rebel Without a Cause*, with all that longing, intrigue, unrequited love, and blow jobs,
is the perfect metaphor for American culture. It is like Coca-Cola! Is it not that in the case of
caffeine–free Diet Coke that we almost literally drink nothing in the guise of something?"

At the mention of coke, Billy Cyborg snuffles a little and lifts his head from the muesli bowl. I was getting a little worried that he may have actually *drowned* in it and was kind of working, like, unsuccessfully, on an alibi. Lena Dunham takes a napkin, spits on it, and starts wiping soggy bran and confetti off his chin. Grey, carrying a Black-Cherry-Bomb-Red Gucci clutch, speaks quietly into Dunham's ear and heads off to the back of the café; Dunham stage whispers "shark week" to the table, informatively.

"What I am referring to, of course, is Nietzsche's opposition between 'wanting nothing,' in the sense of 'I do not want anything,' and the nihilistic stance of actively wanting Nothingness itself. Following Nietzsche, Lacan emphasized how, in anorexia, the subject doesn't simply not eat anything; rather, he actively wants to eat Nothingness itself. The same goes for the famous patient who felt guilty for stealing, although he didn't effectively steal anything. What he did steal was, again, Nothingness itself. Along the same lines, in the case of caffeine–free Diet Coke, we drink Nothingness itself, the pure semblance of a property. This example makes palpable the link between three notions: that of Marxist surplus-value; that of Lacan's *objet petit a* as surplus enjoyment, a concept that Lacan elaborated with direct reference to Marxist surplus-value; and the paradox of the superego, long ago perceived by Freud. The more profit you have, the more you want; the more you drink Coke, the more you are thirsty; the more you obey the superego command, the more you are guilty. In all three cases, the logic of balanced exchange is disturbed in favor of an excessive logic of 'the more you give, the more you owe,' or 'the more you possess what you are longing for, the more you are missing and thus the greater your craving,' or the consumerist version, 'the more you buy the more you must spend.' This paradox is the very opposite of the paradox of love where, as Juliet put it to Romeo, 'The more I give, the more I have.'"

Franco, seeing that Žižek's diatribe is going nowhere, pipes in, "You know, originally, *Rebel Dabble Babble* was a concept that I was developing with Damon McCarthy, Paul's son. It was conceived as a film and film set. You saw where the HOLLYWOOD sign is *inverted*? At the, you know, *beginning* of the show? Whose idea was *that*? Mine."

Pinball, now sitting with six Bellinis in front of her, says, "Yeah, but I think you ripped off a lot of material from Richard Rush's *The Stunt Man*. It had all the same elements: sex, sadistic directors . . . um, impressive, uh, stunts . . . Now *that* was a really great movie about making a movie. Fuck *Fassbinder*. Fuck *Herzog*."

"You have," interjects Franco. "Like I was saying, I dropped out of the project—too busy with my, uh, blogging—but I think that the ostensible theme of the show, the, like, concept, as it were, about the interrelationships between the characters in the movie, and the, um, actors in real life is pretty important. I like how the McCarthys developed the performances . . . how they appropriated a lot of really interesting performance pieces from Vito Acconci and Bruce Nauman, and, um, Diane Arbus . . . and, like, put it through a meat grinder."

"I thought we were discussing Coke?" a puzzled Žižek asks, staring somewhat awkwardly at the now-snoozing Billy Cyborg, whose head is in his lap.

"Watching McCarthy's performance is a bit like eating meat," continues Franco. "I mean, I love meat . . ."

Pinball's eyebrows arch, forming perfect, inverted "V"s.

". . . but," ignoring Pinball, "I'm not sure that I want to go to the slaughter yard. That is where Paul and Damon take you."

Žižek, who has clearly lost his train of thought, adds, "McCarthy's work is a near-perfect example of all that has gone wrong with American culture. It provokes physical revulsion, but it is not mere provocation; it is intended as an all-out assault—as he calls it, a 'program of resistance!' He himself has said, 'I can see much more clearly now that we are living in the middle of this kind of insanity, and it runs itself. And the really scary thing is that we are not conscious of it anymore. It is a kind of fascism. The end goal of that kind of capitalism is to erase difference, to eradicate cultures, to turn us all into a form of cyborg, people who all want the same thing.'"

"Betty Rubble," I say to the suddenly quieted table. "Definitely Betty Rubble."

Pretty in Pink

Cary Leibowitz: *(paintings and belt buckles)*; Invisible Exports, New York.
Published October 11, 2013; *CultureCatch*.

> In the beginning was the Word . . .
> —John 1:1

> On our way to a single pictorial audience! We are the Plan, the System, the
> Organization! Direct your creative work in line with Economy!
> —El Lissitzky, UNOVIS street flyer, 1919

> So funny it just occurred to me I haven't thought about suicide in weeks.
> —Cary Leibowitz

In or around 1920 or '21 the painter and propagandist El Lissitzky painted a small, unassuming gouache picture for reproduction in a magazine or journal with the words "ROSA LUXEMBURG" lettered in, then painted over, to make a once-declarative statement (political solidarity with the case of Rosa Luxemburg) instead a quiet, self-effacing comment, though unintentional, about the absurdity of making art a weapon or tool of politics. El Lissitzky knew even back then, in another century, before Wikileaks or Edward Snowden, that he was trafficking in shit way above his head.

Both Lissitzky and Luxemburg were highly literate, Jewish, and, with Lissitzky growing up in Vitebsk, from slightly rural cultures. Cary Leibowitz is smart, Jewish, and from Connecticut. Here the similarities draw to an end. Like Lissitzky, though, Leibowitz has a tendency to make paintings that make bold, concise statements, written in the clear syntax of good propaganda, which can turn on a dime into self-deprecating, revealing "notes of a painter."

Since the late eighties, when he virtually pioneered the "school of abjection" along with artists like Kay Rosen and Mike Kelley, who used the painted word as an art form the way Woody Allen used film in the seventies, combining self-analysis, Catskills humor, and a trenchant, deadpan hilarity of the sort that obviated the humorlessness, text-based art of the previous generation of artists working with language—Wiener, Kosuth, Huebler, et al. Leibowitz is an intensely introverted, private person, yet his art would seem to belie this, giving voice to statements (which "work in line with [an] economy") like "Sorry I thought you said spaghetti" (*Sorry I Thought You Said Spaghetti*, 2013). A rather Tourette's-like sputtering—like the awkward houseguest saying "I hate spaghetti!" mishearing, perhaps, a more acceptable pasta offering. A sense of longing for connection, on either a personal or physical level, albeit a kind of desperate Looking-for-Mr. Goodbar kind, comes in the slice-shaped panel of "isn't it great you like pizza i like pizza" (*Isn't It Great You Like Pizza I Like Pizza*, 2013), a bar pick-up line nuanced just this much above "Air? Air is great! You like to breathe? I like to breathe too!!"

The immaculate surfaces of Leibowitz's paintings, which often go unremarked-upon if not totally unobserved (indeed, he is such a practiced painter he makes it look easy), give visual form to the superficialities of the dialog. This plays against the deeper realms of the psyche that he both explores and exposes. Playing with form and semiotics, Leibowitz presents the disconnect we often experience more and more between what we hear and what was actually said. A kind of interpersonal Orwellian doublespeak.

Color plays a greater role in this work. In the past it was an aspect of Leibowitz's painting that either veered toward the decorative or was treated with offhand, aesthetic caprice. In *(paintings and belt buckles)*, the walls are painted the same color as the panel grounds, in a color called "Sweet Taffy Pink"—a nod to the inane Ralph Lauren or Martha Stewart swatch book color names like "Un-Teal We Meet Again" or "Sea Foam Green"—suggests the seaside candy of tourist beach towns, a noxious, nostalgic treat that usually tastes like scented candle wax. The matching wall and panel color creates an effect of the pictures blending into their surroundings like geeky wallflowers at a high school dance. A calculated effect, not doubt, personifying in paint what Leibowitz actually feels sometimes in life. There is a fine line between art-as-therapy and mining one's internal life as material. Leibowitz manages to do the second with amazing results. At the Armory Show last spring, Leibowitz exhibited a large outdoor piece that read "I Need to Start Seeing a Therapist"; that would probably be a good thing for Leibowitz, but possibly a tremendous loss for the art world.

Saturday Night Special

Michael Williams: *Paintings*; CANADA, New York.
Published November 30, 2013; *CultureCatch*.

INT. BELLYLAFFS COMEDY CLUB—EVENING

HOUSE BAND [Jay-Z/Kanye West]: I ball so hard muthafuckas wanna find me, first niggas gotta find me / That shit cray / That shit cray / That shit cray / Ain't it Jay?

MUSIC FADES

SIDEKICK [Tracy Morgan]: Give it up for Jay-Z and Kanye West, Ladies and Gentlemen . . . an now, you have probably seen his recent special *It Aint Gonna Suck Itself* [Applause] . . . Bellylaffs is pleased to present one white boy who really does ball hard . . .

HOST [James Franco]—enters stage right: Thank you Tracy! Thank you! [Applause] Thank you! It's true, I really do ball hard. Very hard. Mostly by myself . . . [Laughter/Applause] . . . Thank you . . .

HOST: So this guy, who has never been sick a day in his life, calls his boss. He says, "I can't come in today, I'm sick." The boss says, "No problem, take the day off. I'm just curious, though, how sick are you?" The guy says, "I just fucked my sister!"

AUDIENCE: [Applause/Laughter/Dog pound fist pumping]

HOST: But seriously folks, we have a really great show tonight . . . We have children's book author Sasha Grey [Applause], Heath Ledger, special guests Billy Cyborg and the Rape Babies, Slavoj Žižek [Applause], and my first guest tonight Mr. Jerry Saltz [Applause] . . .

CUT TO DESK/COUCH

HOST [at DESK/SIDEKICK and JERRY SALTZ on COUCH]: [Reading INDEX CARDS] You probably recognize Jerry Saltz from his recent appearances in *Ghetto Gangbang* and *Spring Gashbreakers* . . .

SIDEKICK: [Laughing] No, Dog, you got tha wrong cards . . . [Audience laughter]

HOST: You're right! [Shuffles Cards] That's Sasha Grey! You may recognize our next guest from his recent appearances on *The Rachel Maddow Show* and Bravo's *Stars of the Venice Biennial: Where Are They Now?* . . . Please welcome . . . Jerrrrrry Saaaaaaltz . . . [Applause]

JERRY SALTZ (Himself): Hi Jim . . .

HOST: Thank you for coming! Good to see you . . . [Host brushes CURIOUS WHITE POWDER from JERRY SALTZ's lapel] I see you found [Makes air-quotation gesture] the powdered-sugar doughnuts in the Green Room [Off Audience laughter] . . . but seriously, you recently appeared on CNN to talk about former President George Bush's new paintings . . . [Audience boos and catcalls]

JERRY SALTZ: Yes, I think he is a terrific artist . . . a far better pictorialist than Adolph Hitler. [Audience boos and catcalls]

HOST: [Off Audience] Ouch! Sorry, Jerry! Hitler? [Audience boos]

HOST: [To Audience] What? Too soon? [Audience applause]

HOST: You describe his paintings as being "painted in the weight room and painted in the shower" . . . Now, to me, that sounds like . . . [making coughing sound, fist covering mouth] . . . coughcoughhugehomohugehomohugehomo . . . [Audience howling with laughter]

HOST: Anyway . . . you are here to talk about Michael Williams's new show . . . I saw it last night and found it to be hilarious! [Settles at DESK with LAMINATED CARDS WITH PICTURES] Look at some of these . . . [Flipping through stack of LAMINATED CARDS WITH PICTURES] Here is one: *Ikea Be Here Now* (2013) . . . and this . . . *Hundreds of Dollars in Meditation Equipment* (2013) . . . and this one is called *It Came Out of My Paint Tube* (2013) [Audience laughter] . . . Now, I am not an art critic, but I think it's pretty safe to say my three-year-old daughter could have painted some of these . . . [Off Audience] . . . if she had been born with fetal alcohol syndrome . . . [Audience boos] . . . What? Too soon? [Laughter/Applause]

WOMAN IN AUDIENCE/HECKLER: You suck!

HOST: Shut up, Mom, you're still drunk . . .

[Laughter/Dog pound fist pumping]

HECKLER: No, you shut up . . .

HOST: Wouldn't it be really great if, like, a group of four or five guys raped her right now? Like, right now?

SIDEKICK/JAY-Z/KANYE WEST EXIT STAGE LEFT INTO AUDIENCE

HOST: Sorry, Jerry, you were saying . . .

JERRY SALTZ: I was stunned into something like a stupor by Williams's work. No matter how closely or long I looked at these eleven large colorful paintings, I could not gain a purchase on their surfaces. His new work delivers a sort of tranquilizer bullet to one's ability to detect haptic presence. A viewer knows there's paint on the canvas, and yet when one tries to focus on it through the multiple overlays of images and abstract fields, the paintings continually come into and then fall away from actually feeling physical. Philosopher Maurice Blanchot has written about such paradoxical "inaccessibility" as something being in "infinite pursuit of its own source." I know that I felt like Williams's new paintings suspended me in an optic warp that kept me probing their processes . . .

HOST: Let's take a quick break. When we return we have a special guest who knows a thing or two about "probing" . . . Sasha Grey will join us and read some excerpts from her new children's book *Don't Tell Mommy!* . . .

COMMERCIAL BREAK

HOST: Welcome back! In case you are just joining us, we're chatting with Jerry Saltz and [Gesturing toward Slavoj Žižek] Slavoj Žižek who has stopped by to talk about Michael Williams's new work. Thanks for stopping by Slavoj.

SLAVOJ ŽIŽECK (Himself): Thank you. I am sleeping with Lady Gaga.

HOST: Um, ok then.

JERRY SALTZ: As I was saying . . . Though not every painting works, the whole show is good, and three stand out. *Ikea Be Here Now* (from 2013, like all the work on view) centers on a naked man in glasses standing in front of a house, a ladder behind him. Another nude figure, maybe a model holding some sort of page that the naked guy appears to be holding, is also present. I saw what looks like a sawhorse, possibly a carpenter's plane, another naked figure, and someone with a backpack. The high-keyed, eye-popping Day-Glo color is just this side of truly gaudy. In the crowded-to-the-point-of-blissful-confusion *Honk If You Don't Exist*, you might spot images, patterns, polka dots, stripes, clouds, and street signs. Soon, you give up trying to name what you're seeing, and then these aggressively pictorial works turn very abstract. *It Came Out of My Paint Tube* is actually ballsy enough to have a big Philip Guston–like shoe smack in the middle, along with a cute cream-colored sun and a cow with an ear for a body. I think there's perspective and illusionistic space in this cartoony thing, but that could all be me, trying to make sense of how it's organized.

HOST: . . . a *cow* with a giant *ear* for a *belly* . . . stop it . . . you're killing me . . . [Audience laughing with HOST]

SIDEKICK: That shit's cray Dog!

SLAVOJ ŽIŽECK: Do you know I am also sleeping with Marina Abramović? Many times.

JERRY SALTZ: All the paintings here create the same kind of visual hit as billboards, placards, brightly colored advertisements, or internet images. In a number of them, the painterly incidents and cockeyed space can't overcome the cartoony drawing, funky bad-boy chaos, garishness, or the occasional plainness, and those are the paintings that don't entirely come off. In this show, Williams is evincing his familiar influences and visual kin—artists like Guston, Bonnard, Vuillard, Peter Saul, and R. Crumb, plus some Chicago Imagism and California Funk. But in the most successful ones, Williams adds the complexities of artists like Peter Doig, Carroll Dunham . . .

SLAVOJ ŽIŽECK: I am sleeping with Lena Dunham, as well.

JERRY SALTZ: . . . and Sigmar Polke. Instead of trying to get between photography and painting, like Doig does, Williams looks like he's trying to get between painting and the digital world, like Wade Guyton. The connections to Polke and Dunham come in the form of Williams freeing himself and allowing the painting to tell him what to do to it.

HOST: [Interrupting] Well, Ladies and Gentlemen, there you have it! I take back most of what I said earlier about a retarded goat being able to paint these! [Applause/Laughter] Still to come: Heath Ledger, Jennifer Lawrence, and Justin Bieber join Jay-Z and Kanye West for a musical tribute to the Village People . . . wait, Tracy? [Looks out at Audience] Jay? Kanye? Mom?

Cut to COMMERCIAL

The Walk Home

Julian Schnabel: The Brant Foundation Art Study Center, Greenwich, CT.
Published January 22, 2014; *Artslant.*

> Must we learn again the simple, forthright experience of actually seeing a
> painting?
> —William Gaddis

> In the end, we cultural theorists are the coroners of history, writing our
> forensic reports on a marble slab table about a murder victim—painting.
> —Dr. Hope Ardizzone, Cultural Theorist/Author

One might arguably make the case, after viewing Julian Schnabel's retrospective at The Brant Foundation Art Study Center, that he is the heir to Barnett Newman's painterly legacy, for no artist since Newman has placed such importance and urgency on the act of painterly gesture. Possibly a stretch, though Schnabel has never shied away from the grand gesture or statement, but given (or despite) the expansiveness of Schnabel's thirty-year career he does come very close to Newman's ideal of an Artist.

Newman believed that to create oneself through the process of making an object is an ethical act of decision making and passion. In 1947 he outlined this philosophical position in a short essay titled "The First Man Was an Artist." Newman wrote that early Homo sapiens had become something more, something human, in this way, by asserting themselves not through the making of objects for *use*, but through the creation of objects for poetic, aesthetic expression, which he said was the purer, superior act. Through this secondary approach to creating objects, Newman argued that one became "formed," differentiated from others, feeling a sense of purpose in the world. "Man's hand," he said, "traced the stick through the mud to make a line before he learned to throw the stick as a javelin." It is therefore more human, (in Newman's language "superior"), to draw a line in aesthetic wonder, as it demonstrates Man's tragic separateness from others in the world through so doing. "In conclusion," he said, "we must get back to the true nature of painting to understand that it involves thought, that it is the expression of intellectual content."

In 1947 these ideals held a sense of urgency, a sense for which it is virtually impossible to find an equivalent in today's art world. In the second half of the twentieth century—the age of Pop, New Realism, Minimalism, Post-Modernism, Gutai, *Arte Povera*, etc.—few artists pursued Newman's edicts about the primacy of Idea and Action into Mark as the *sine qua non* of pure painting. Newman called his marks—his vertical lines—"zips," giving them a new word in the vocabulary of painting; he felt the act was that important. It is reasonable to argue that, though he hasn't come up with any special name for his mark making, like Newman, Schnabel considers the act of applying paint to surface an act of primal urgency and importance.

Schnabel's career began in the late seventies when he was propelled to notoriety by his broken plate paintings—a series of large-scale works that involved broken ceramic dishes set into a tessellated canvas. When they debuted at the Mary Boone Gallery in 1979, the paintings sold out even before the exhibition's opening night. That is pretty much the way that Schnabel's apocryphal biography typically begins, continuing on to filmmaking, photography, interior decorating, etc., etc. It is perhaps a less cynical way of seeing Schnabel's work to remember that the pieces at his first show at Boone were simple, usually monochrome, gestural paintings on old drop cloths, such as *Portrait of God* (1981) and *The Mutant King* (1981). The connection to Newman is not as specious as one might initially think. Around the time he painted these last two works, he visited Annalee Newman's apartment in New York. He said of this visit, "There were some inspired Newman paintings there. They weren't beautiful in the sense of luscious, masterfully painted incidents. Their beauty was a trace of an investigation into a musical analog . . . they were a palimpsest, a collection of signals that triggered an emotional and intellectual vision that resides in and outside of painting."

The best examples of his work in this retrospective are his Olatz series from the early nineties, with the name of his wife written in blobs of white; the Big Girl (2001) paintings, all featuring a girl blinded by a horizontal mark; and *Rebirth I: (The Last View of Camiliano Cien Fuegos)* (1986), picturing a pair of disembodied eyes peering out of abstract forms on a Kabuki backdrop of cherry blossoms and a summer sky. In these pieces, as well as his others, he distances us from his subjects through his paint; he instead draws attention to the act of the painter, and by extension to the importance of the painter, causing the subject to recede before us. We approach what we don't immediately recognize or understand and use our own primitive tools and methods to apprehend and understand. Others have adopted similar strategies: Basquiat, Baselitz, and Keifer come to mind. We find, however, that when it comes to painting, Schnabel has gone so off-book when it comes to making a painting that these artists seem like rigid formalists by comparison.

The paradox of Schnabel, wrote Raphael Rubinstein in *Art in America* in 2011, "is to be at once highly visible as a cultural figure and deeply invisible as a painter." It is in paintings like *Accatone* (1978) where we can see the presence of Schnabel the painter disappearing and the painting taking on a life of its own. The hastily sketched, decapitated, and dismembered figure on a Corinthian plinth struggles against a field of red, worked wax—a signature ground for early Schnabel, which has a small ledge cut into the ground, giving it a haptic sense of dimensional space. This simple, yet rich, image helped usher in a new school of painting in the late seventies (Bad Painting, typified by Neil Jenney, Lois Lane, or Susan Rothenberg) and harkens back to that first artist drawing buffalo and horses on some cave wall. Through oil, wax, and plaster Schnabel has fashioned a man, inscribed in a state complete immobility, unified by the multiplicity of its own possible variations. One is left to complete the picture, to fill in the gaps, not sure if it is a man contemplating the infinite space around him or an entirely new creature altogether.

For Schnabel, it is probably harder to arrive at that prelapsarian condition of painting than we might imagine. It is the condition of our times that irony, deconstruction, and appropriation feel more like our natural state than the sincere gesture of painting a figure and giving it grounding in space. For all the overblown dialog of Schnabel as celebrity artist, when encountering works like *Accatone,* one finds an artist capable of rendering art of a very high order indeed, one of empathy, form, and space.

The Recognitions

Michel Majerus: Matthew Marks Gallery, New York.
Published February 21, 2014; *CultureCatch*.

> I create, you copy nature.
> —Pablo Picasso, in conversation with Balthus

> Even the paintings looked dead . . .
> —Margaret Atwood, *The Handmaid's Tale*

> The audience has a taste for shit.
> The critics have a taste for shit.
> —James Franco, *Actors Anonymous*

> *Wie man dem toten Hasen die Bilder erklärt*
> —Joseph Beuys, *Action,* November 26, 1965, at the Galerie Schmela in
> Düsseldorf

James Franco's body was found yesterday in the toilet of a club called Cisboi, so we are at one of the Gagosian galleries tonight sitting shiv and waiting for Marina Abramović and Willem Dafoe to read excerpts from Franco's many books [*James Franco: Dangerous Book Four Boys, A California Childhood, Actors Anonymous, Palo Alto: Stories*]—the "we" being Michael Lee Nirenberg, Billy Cyborg, Jared Leto, Amy Adams, Oscar Murillo, Matthew Barney, and Ellen Burstyn, most of whom were with me last night when we went for drinks at the Groucho Club, dinner at el Bulle (fish tacos, something called Bichon Frisé Ceviche, and churros y sea urchins chocolat—where I misplaced the keys to the Ducati), dancing at a club called Boy or Toy (where I misplaced the Ducati), and then back to someone's apartment where we hid the guns and credit cards in the Sub-Zero freezer and then finished off a very large bag of crack and candy-flipped Molly, Meow Meow, and Nyquil—hence the not knowing *exactly* which Gagosian we are at.

"Shiv-*a*" interrupts Billy Cyborg. "We are sitting shiv-*a*, not shiv. You fucking moron."

"What's the difference?" I ask.

"Franco is Jewish. You sit *shiva* for Jews. Not *shiv*."

"So, like, was he a Jew or not?"

"What. The. Fuck. Do. You. Mean."

"Well, was he a *Jew* or just Jew-*ish*?" This seemed like a pretty reasonable distinction to make.

Billy Cyborg, who had been tweeting pictures of my cock, which he had somehow managed to take last night (possibly when I was "looking for my keys" in the toilet at Toy, with a lively Portuguese exchange student who was interested in an "internship"), gets bored and asks Philip Seymour Hoffman for a morphine lollipop since he has run out of cigarettes and there was no-fucking-way-now he was getting any from me after the whole shiva thing. Sometimes he forgets he is just a plot device. Skrillex's mash-up of The Pussycunts version of

Pussy Riot's cover of Throbbing Gristle's "Maggot Death" is playing softly in the background. There wasn't an autopsy or coroner's report, but Page Six, which is usually pretty reliable about these sorts of things, noted that Franco had died of autoerotic-asphyxiation, which is almost impossible to believe, since I know for a fact that he didn't even have a *license* let alone know how to *drive*.

You see how black the sky outside is? I wrote it that way.

[Editor's Note (typewritten on yellow Post-It): "Great job so far! But did you actually read the press release? Here it is. Call me! Let's have a drink tonight! ;)"]

[Attachment]: The exhibition includes over twenty-five paintings and multimedia installations by the late Berlin-based artist, whose promising career was cut short by a plane crash at age 35. Majerus samples from popular culture and art history, redeploying canonical styles alongside graphics borrowed from youth subcultures and the commercial mainstream. More than any artist of his time, Majerus exemplifies what art historian Daniel Birnbaum calls "painting in the expanded field," his prolific oeuvre reflecting the prepackaged newness and hybrid spaces of the Information Age. By incorporating the visual vocabularies of next-generation technologies and 1990s consumer culture, Majerus expands on the appropriation art of the 1980s through his pioneering use of digital methods of production, altering the very space of representation itself.

SOMEBODY WANTS TO BUY ALL YOUR PAINTINGS!
1994
Acrylic on canvas
31 1/2 x 35 x 3/4 inches; 80 x 89 x 2 cm

We were in a rush to get to the performance, so I am stuck wearing a borrowed vintage Halston Ultrasuede tuxedo with a hand-embroidered cummerbund, with an equally vintage Powerpuff Girls t-shirt on underneath. Even though I am incredibly hung over, I still look ok. I used to care a lot about how I looked. I don't so much anymore. Maybe it's because I'm so handsome. I am wearing fluffy, pink slippers by Steve Madden that look like little bunnies with long, floppy ears that have gotten wet and limp from the snow and have begun to droop a little. They look a little scared.

your bad taste
2002
Enamel and silkscreen on aluminum
155 1/2 x 256 inches; 395 x 650 cm

"Settle please." The director says. "Marina Abramović's performance is about to start."

There are little bottles of Evian and silver glitter everywhere, and someone has turned on a fog machine. Respectfully, all of the artwork in the gallery has been covered with black velveteen drapery.

Someone has written *"I smell the blood of les tricoteuses"* in the guestbook with a Mandarin-Blood-Orange Crayola crayon.

The gallery is freezing, and the white Mario Bellini chairs we are sitting on have little icicles growing underneath. I can see my breath. Bjarne Melgaard (who is editing his Grindr profile) and Jerry Saltz (who is posting Billy Cyborg's tweeted photos on his Facebook page) extricate themselves from a story Hayden Panettiere is telling Greta Gerwig about losing her virginity to a half-Puerto Rican half-Vietnamese "little person" who had "a huge one, though curiously shaped, like a pig's tail!" who had, apparently, also "gently licked all the blood and tears away, after."

Willem Dafoe is, except for being covered in gold leaf, naked, and curled up adorably in a little ball on the floor, asleep. Marina Abramović begins reading from Franco's autobiography, in a deep, haunting voice:

"In my younger and more vulnerable years, my father gave me some advice that I've been turning over in my mind ever since. "Whenever you feel like criticizing anyone," he told me, "just remember that all the people in this world haven't had the advantages that you've had." He didn't say any more, but we've always been unusually communicative in a reserved way, and I understood that he meant a great deal more than that. In consequence, I'm inclined to reserve all judgments, a habit that has opened up many curious natures to me." She stops reading, and a single glycerine tear rolls down her cheek. Haunting.

Lindsay Lohan passes me the new Coldplay CD, laid out with three giant rails of blow, spattered with blood, which is dripping from her nose. "I hear she has AIDS," Billy Cyborg whispers to me as I am about to hoover, and, when I hesitate for a second, grabs the CD and licks it, blood and all. "Just fucking with you!" he cackles.

pornography needs you
2001
Acrylic on canvas
119 1/4 x 131 1/8 inches; 303 x 333 cm

[Editor's Note (handwritten): "Nice job so far, but this part could use more "beefing up." Are you ever going to call me back?!! Did I do something wrong? :) PS: DID YOU READ THE PRESS RELEASE EVEN??]

Billy Cyborg has fallen asleep and is drooling in my lap. Jennifer Lawrence is telling Ethan Hawke about a recent abortion and how much she is looking forward to seeing *Sharknado 2*. Mira Schor, Deborah Kass, Michael Zansky, and Lena Dunham are whispering quietly in the row behind me; Vito Schnabel, Slavoj Žižek, Natalie Portman (or possibly Keira Knightley, or Keira Knightley's body double), Sasha Grey, Chloë Sevigny, and Damon McCarthy form a vague penumbra of movement and sound in the background. Dafoe, who was quietly snoring, snuffles and rolls over. Marina Abramović moves gracefully across the room to the recumbent body of Franco, who has been wrapped in 1200-thread count Egyptian cotton sheets, covered in Boy Butter, honey, and oregano, and placed on a Frank Gehry Eager Beaver cardboard table.

LONG TRACKING SHOT—We move in and:

Kristen Stewart begins, with great, dramatic effect, to read one of her early poems. "This is about James's first experience with . . . love:"

> I reared digital moonlight
> You read its clock, scrawled neon across that black
> Kismetly . . . ubiquitously crestfallen
> Thrown down to strafe your foothills

. . . I'll suck the bones pretty.
Your nature perforated the abrasive organ pumps
Spray painted everything known to man,
Stream rushed through and all out into
Something whilst the crackling stare down sun snuck
Through our windows boarded up
He hit your flint face and it sparked.

Skull
2000
Enamel on aluminum
98 1/2 x 49 inches; 250 x 125 cm
[SCENE MISSING DELETED]
[Editor's Note: (handwritten on Post-It in purple glitter ink): "Call me?"]

Alec Baldwin and Theodora Richards quietly get up and leave, the open door blowing silver glitter around, the DP getting apoplectic, and a swarm of production assistants with small brooms scurry around the room brushing the offending particles away. Ronan Farrow, or maybe Rooney Mara, begins to softly cry—in the dim lights it is hard to tell. Jay-Z and Beyoncé motion for a PA to bring more little bottles of Evian and Spam-and-cucumber finger sandwiches from the back room, but there aren't any left.

I notice that there is something that looks like thawing dog shit on my left bunny slipper.

The DP has set up the next shot, and the sound guy is ready. "Rolling . . . Rolling" a chorus of PAs chant in unison.

Tron 4 (grün Pantone 375)
1999
Silkscreen on canvas and wall painting
Wall painting: 118 x 118 inches; 300 x 300 cm
Screen print: 56 x 48 inches; 142 x 122 cm

[Editor's Note: (Written in Black-Cherry-Bomb Red Lipstick on M/S): "DON'T *EVER* SPEAK TO ME AGAIN, YOU FUCKING MONSTER."]

Willem Dafoe, now apparently wide awake, and wearing a . . . diaper, is hopping around like a frog while Marina Abramović, who has finished her reading, begins lighting Yohji Yamamoto scented candles and asking the audience if anyone would "like to see a *real* dead body" as the house lights come up.

It is clearly time to leave. I slip out of the front door unnoticed. I think I have learned a lot of valuable lessons. Actual emotion washes over me in giant waves as I walk down the frozen street, my bunny slippers, which are now drenched pelts, cracking the ice under my weight. I could offer a million reasons, but they would all be false. The truth is I'm a bad person. But that's gonna change. I'm gonna change. I think I'm really going to miss Franco a lot.

Fade to Grey

Jasper Johns: *Regrets*; Museum of Modern Art, New York.
Published March 20, 2014; *CultureCatch*.

> The image is dead. The icon is dead. The painting is dead.
> —Patricia Cronin

> Keep everything on the surface, even with the knowledge that the surface
> fades and can't be held together forever—take advantage before the
> expiration date appears in the nearing distance.
> —Bret Easton Ellis, *Imperial Bedrooms*

> Art asks: How do we know anything about other people? The tension
> between an artist's public and private roles is a constant preoccupation
> to the audience. The artist is challenged to dwell within this conundrum
> and elaborate most fully the questions of how to articulate the private in a
> public forum, and whether the private life will be able to find an image for
> itself that can stand up in this forum.
> —Dr. Hope Ardizzone, *Anatomy of Art's Murder*

> During this test you will be shown a series of inkblot images. Look at each
> inkblot for a moment then select the appropriate response(s). At the end of
> the test your responses will be analyzed and scored, and a summary of the
> test evaluation will be presented to you.
> —Instructions for an online Rorschach Test evaluation, 2014

Friedrich Neitzsche once defined regret as a state that man, as opposed to the superman, inhabited, due to the flawed nature of his reasoning. He posited that man never made a single mistake, but always erred twice. He used as an example a gentleman who sought to ingratiate himself into society by throwing a lavish ball. Appalled at the wastrel excess and expense, the next time he gave a dinner too sparse, thus embarrassing himself a second time. Regret, like water filling a scuttled ship, rises to fill the void between our misguided attempts at autonomous action. Regret is inherently personal and specific. One could regret the loss of something, on one hand, or, on the other, a surfeit of unwanted things.

The Museum of Modern Art is currently showing Johns's most recent body of work: paintings and works on paper, predominantly in grays and blacks, all riffing on the same image: a "portrait" of the late painter Lucian Freud, sitting with one leg tucked under him, on an old-fashioned iron bed, clutching his head in his hand, taken by Francis Bacon's friend Richard Deacon. In June 2012, Johns encountered the photograph reproduced in a Christie's auction catalog. Inspired not only by the photographic image, but also by the physical qualities of the object itself, Johns took this motif through a succession of cross-medium permutations.

Johns has often cloaked the personal meaning of his works in a protective coating of irony, often referencing High Art through the vehicle of the ordinary. From the 1950s through the mid-eighties, Johns eschewed pinning specific meanings to his cryptic images, through references to American poetry, Egyptian steles, decorative patterning, flags, alphabets, targets, and numbers—what he called "things the mind already knows." "For me [the meaning] is within the picture. The word is in the picture. I think you'll have to interpret that for yourself. It's certainly in the painting, but so is the rest of the painting in the painting, and the image that's in the painting. It's not meant to be a sign of something not in the painting. Regrets belong to everybody, don't they?"

In the past few years, Johns seems to have taken stock, beginning with his late-nineties *Catenary* paintings, and returned to the simplicity and clarity in his paintings that was the strength and hallmark of his best works. In these current paintings he plays with mirror images of the photograph of Freud. "I don't know why I decided to double it," Johns said of these pictures. "It's curious because there's one with it doubled one on top of the other—a completely different use of space. I found it interesting—the forms, the negative space where he'd torn the picture." Where the twin images adjoin, they form a skull, a reference to mortality that has appeared often in Johns's works, as well as forming a sort of Rorschach Test drawing reminiscent of Andy Warhol's Rorschach paintings. In most of the works Johns has silk-screened "Regrets, Jasper Johns" (a phrase he had previously made into a rubber stamp to answer correspondence in an efficient way). The simple phrase carries a hint of Johns's Southern roots. One imagines Truman Capote declining an invitation to a social engagement—"Sorry darling, regrets"—or Cole Porter's *Miss Otis Regrets*.

Both the artist and the painting struggle against the urge to reveal themselves in their entirety; we see an artist struggling to communicate with sincerity, yet also with studied calculation: "Myths develop. I think people make things up. There's nothing I want to set straight about the record." Johns has worked out his composition and imagery through studies, such as *Regrets* (2013), a charcoal, watercolor, and pastel work on textured paper. Here the mixed media function in relationship to paint the way an understudy does to an actor— allowing Johns to imagine the possibilities and incident of paint, a dress rehearsal for the ultimate pictures. We see the results in *Regrets* (2013) (in oil), with Johns using his previous signature crosshatching to replace the paper's texture, heightening the effect of color in a portion of the figure of Freud. In the end, through the distancing effects of Johns's process, he allows himself to be "painted out of the picture"—in the way that he did with his targets and flags. Johns allows the paintings to once again stand apart from their creator, with an eye to posterity, letting the viewer into his pictorial space, not his personal one. In some ways, these might be some of Johns's greatest works—and, at 84, Johns is in that rarified club of octogenarian artists like Picasso and Matisse, whose late works were both a "fuck you" and a gift to the history of painting.

Body of Evidence

Maria Lassnig: MoMA PS1, New York.
Published April 2, 2014; *CultureCatch*.

> Man is the measure of all things: of things which are, that they are, and of things which are not, that they are not.
> —Protagoras, quoted in Plato's *Theaetetus*

> Both the motor and sensory homunculi usually appear as a small man superimposed over the top of the precentral or postcentral gyrus, for motor and sensory, respectively. The homunculus is oriented with feet medial and shoulders lateral on top of both the precentral and the postcentral gyrus (for both motor and sensory). The man's head is depicted upside down in relation to the rest of the body such that the forehead is closest to the shoulders. The lips, hands, feet and sex organs have more sensory neurons than other parts of the body, so the homunculus has correspondingly large lips, hands, feet, and genitals. The motor homunculus is very similar to the sensory homunculus but differs in several ways. Specifically, the motor homunculus has a portion for the tongue most lateral while the sensory homunculus has an area for genitalia most medial and an area for visceral organs most lateral. Well known in the field of neurology, this is also commonly called "the little man inside the brain." This scientific model is known as the cortical homunculus.
> —*Cambridge University Dictionary of Medical Diagnostics* (Dr. Philip Kennedy, Editor, 2013 edition)

> I am a camera with its shutter open, quite passive, recording, not thinking . . . some day, all this will have to be developed, carefully printed, fixed.
> —Christopher Isherwood

Despite your best efforts and beliefs to the contrary, your life is a series of random events and experiences; you are merely in different rooms, at different times, in different places, with different people. Things around you are in a state of change—you are the only constant. John Updike wrote, "We walk through volumes of the unexpressed and like snails leave behind a faint thread excreted out of ourselves." Maria Lassnig is someone who understands that these lipstick traces, tiny gestures, and human stains are of the utmost importance—the way we document our existence. For seven decades she has attempted to reconcile existential frailty and paint, creating a body of work that is both innovative in philosophy and style, as her retrospective at MoMA PS1 shows.

Lassnig was born in Carinthia, a rural Austrian state, in 1919, and attended the Academy of Fine Arts in Vienna during the Second World War, a time when the Nazis had banned Expressionism as "degenerate" art and promoted a nationalistic form of social realism. Partly in reaction to this, and due to "[a desire] to go beyond skill, beyond the security of the real, into uncharted territory," Lassnig developed an expressive form of self-portraiture she termed the "body awareness technique." Drawing from time spent in Paris in the 1950s, where she met André Breton and absorbed elements of surrealism, automatic writing and painting, and existentialist philosophy, Lassnig returned Austria and embarked on that voyage into "uncharted territory." She created a series of abstract portraits; exteriorizing their interiority, they were stripped of their most identifiable physiognomic features of eyes, nose, and mouth. Executed with palette knives instead of brushes, (for example, *Head*, 1956), the paintings become assemblages of material created with crude instruments, prefiguring Lassnig's later interest in machinery and prosthetic devices in her work.

In her self-portraits, Lassnig's fantasies and anxieties manifest themselves through a cast of mythical, monstrous, cyborg, and alien characteristics. The metaphoric use of technology in *Language Grid* (1999), with a head attached to a metal grate, sitting on an atomic structure of a body, gives us a rebus of imagery served as explanation of a personal, psychological state. She wrote, "I called my body awareness 'paintings,' then 'introspective experiences'; later on I did not call them anything at all . . . I have only abandoned this 'content' when outside events were stronger than I was, when I encountered love . . . death . . . oppression."

It would be difficult to categorize these paintings into distinct "periods" as with Picasso or de Kooning, because Lassnig's painterly decades are not so much a development of style or concepts as they are snapshots of the artist at different ages, exploring differing notions about her "felt self." Her figures are like the motor sensory homunculus, a distorted view of her view of herself, yet one that feels more exacting through its skewness (*untitled*, 2002). Her figures usually have eyes and noses, with seeing and breathing being something one might be aware of while working, but as she aged and began to lose her hearing, Lassnig began to leave the ears off her portraits (*Momento Mori*, 2002).

In a work called *Small Science Fiction Self-Portrait* (1995), the earless and hairless artist peers through a rectangular screen, a prescient imagining of an Oculus Rift, with eyes wide shut. She melds imaginary technology in a metaphorical way—this isn't science fiction like *Star Trek* and *Terminator* as much as it is *Black Mirror* or *Blade Runner*. In a painting called *Illusion of Missed Motherhood* (1998), an alien fetus emerges from the artist—a meditation on Lassnig's choice to not have children, as well as the artist's feelings of being excluded from her own artistic historical moment. In a note she made after watching the movie *Alien*, Lassnig said, "Only a woman and a cat survive the apocalypse." Through a combination of vestigial appendages and phantom limbs, Lassnig creates a psychological modern Prometheus, Frankenstein's monsters of the soul.

Lassnig lived in New York for nearly a decade, at first coming on an artist's residency program, then living in the city during the height of anti-figurative and anti-painting conceptualism of the seventies, when she experimented with film (of particular note are *Palmistry*, 1974, and *Shapes*, 1972). This switch of medium might seem odd, considering the greater body of work her paintings comprise, but at her core Lassnig is a documentarian—a realist in the tradition of Christopher Isherwood. She is both a camera and an x-ray machine. A later self-portrait, *You or Me* (2005), could be Lassnig's version of Picasso's *Self-Portrait Facing Death* (1972), the crayon and pencil nightmare of the artist looking in a mirror at his spent body. Pierre Daix said of his last visit to Picasso that he held the drawing up next to his head and that he did not blink. "I had the sudden impression that he was staring his own death in the face, like a good Spaniard." Lassnig, like Picasso, faces mortality head-on. In *You or Me* (2005), she confronts the viewer, naked (bald, flattened tits, shaved vulva) with two guns, one at her temple and one pointed to us, surrounded by an electric blue and green aura. It is a punk gesture, one of undisputed attitude. Juxtaposed against the sagging flesh of the artist, though, it is a measure of pure spirit. Lassnig shows an artist not going quietly into that good night, but one who will be leaving still kicking against the pricks.

Bête Noire

Susan Bee: *Doomed to Win/Paintings from the 1980s*; A.I.R Gallery, New York.
Published April 20, 2014; *CultureCatch*.

> Most paintings, the instant you see them, they become familiar and then it's
> too late.
> —William Gaddis, *The Recognitions*

To be Modern was, sooner or later, to become kitsch, that is, familiar, a cliché, an agreed-upon collective meaning. Clement Greenberg despised kitsch, yet all the most avant-garde of movements, from the Impressionists to the Pop Artists, eventually ended up, to some degree, kitsch decorations. To be "Post-Modern," especially in the 1980s, was a high-wire act, walking a tight rope between aesthetic cynicism and irony; dabbling in kitsch, was, out of necessity, a net.

Susan Bee is a painter who, though working in a period of appropriation (à la Mike Bidlo or Cindy Sherman), managed to navigate a course of painterly activity that circumnavigated the knowing irony of most eighties painting and instead created a distinctly personal idiom in her work, through references to painters like Andrei Rublev, Georges Rouault, Vincent van Gogh, and Edvard Munch, as well as film makers like Otto Preminger and Billy Wilder. A return to kitsch is an attempt at sincerity, at referring to something, once genuine, which contemporary society or culture lacks. Sincerity is a critique of the inauthentic.

Black-and-white film stills are the pictorial basis of the majority of Bee's pictures; the high-key colors, energetic patterns, and fluid painterly drips and pours render these works both visually and psychologically complex. In the works, figures move about, interacting in *mise-en-scènes* reminiscent of Preminger's *Laura*, the action happening in the complex space she frames in the painting. There is a tension in the way the abstraction plays against the figuration, which was the hallmark of *film noir*—Bee replaces the shadow play of the *noir* interior with tumultuous or rhythmic patterning.

Bee says about these works, "I have become very taken by the idea of theatricality and artifice [in my painting]. I am creating these paintings as spaces for a drama to take place. The figures are actors and actresses in a stage that I am setting up for them to play out their roles. The film stills I'm referencing are dramatic . . . I remain intrigued by the dangerous women and the desolate men in the film noirs . . . I emphasize the dynamic between the figures whether they are pressing against a windowpane or pressing up against each other."

In paintings like *Pickpocket* (2013) [not in exhibition], the windowpane doubles as both a set for the action, as well as a nod toward Piet Mondrian. The window screen or grate that the woman presses her face to is like the barrier in a confessional. She can hear, smell, and—where their hands touch—feel the male protagonist on the other side, but, even though the screen has large openings, they both have their eyes closed and, thus, cannot see each other. The barrier between the characters is psychological—with eyes wide shut, they are their own blinds.

In *Hands Up* (1983), a couple laughs over a cocktail, while a Pollock-like skein of paint swirls around them. Separated by a black line, a woman with a gun is either lurking stage left or outside a door, outside their space. Once again, one sees the influence of the *film noir* sources Bee uses. In the film *Laura*, we are introduced to a world of glass (bottles, glasses, the clockface), of fragile and precious objects on display, in a closed world (Waldo's apartment) within another closed world (Manhattan). Everything is suspended, and there is a sense of waiting, of time arrested. Since Laura is already dead, there is no future indicated, and the narrative will be a return to the past. In *Hands Up*, the return to the past is noted by the appropriation of Pollock's signature style, though in transforming his abstraction into a theatrical décor, Bee also subverts the modernist ideal of the concrete gesture in favor of narration and psychological depth. In *Portrait of the Artist as a Young Pig* (1983) Bee uses Petunia Pig as a stand-in for the painter, layering the illustrative Petunia over an expressionist *odalisque*. It is of note that Bee's painting pre-dates the 1988 film *Who Framed Roger Rabbit*, the neo-*noir* comedy that mixed live action with animation to great effect.

Susan Bee's characters may be trapped in tight situations and dark spaces, but we get the sense that everything will turn out okay in the end. They are doomed to win, or, to paraphrase Jessica Rabbit, "they are just drawn that way."

Mallrats

Walter Robinson: *Figure Studies*; Lynch Tham Gallery, New York.
Published July 2, 2014; *ArtSlant.*

With exuberance and dark wit Walter Robinson has explored America's fascination with the seedy underbelly of urban life for more than three decades. His work has drawn from Film Noir, pop advertising, and trash literature; in the 1980s he dipped into a pool of film stills, paperback book cover art, and pinups (in that age before digital porn), in line with artists such as Robert Longo, David Salle, and Cindy Sherman. Unlike Longo and Salle, who made their images more distilled and sanitary through large-scale studio production, or Sherman, who dove headfirst into making the noir-schlock masterpiece *Office Killer* (1997), Robinson steadily kept his hand in the mix, developing a painterly touch that belied the appropriationist strategies of the decade.

The eleven new paintings and works on paper in Robinson's show at Lynch Tham are based on middle-income, middle-American store advertising for Target, JCPenney, Macy's, and Lands' End, source material particularly relevant to Robinson's work. Through simple depictions of clothing such as the neatly folded *Long Sleeve Plaid,* (2014) or the van Gogh inspired *Lands' End Boots from $25* (2014)—items that Warhol might have said everyone would wear—Robinson creates an eerie darkness. The shirts are precisely tucked in, like police evidence; the boots kicked asunder. These paintings suggest that in our current moment in time both school shooter and victims might be shopping at Marshall's.

Robinson's figurative paintings address the audience they are "selling" to. The implicit stance in *Lands' End Swimming in Confidence* (2014) and *Target Dresses Cardis and Wedge Sandals* (2013) is utopian, proposing a happy, healthy, and harmonious world of ever-changing patterns, seasonal colors, and interchangeable, endlessly consumable product. Robinson's brushwork is integral, informing his ability to draw from these ready-made images a sense of painterly depth that transforms the banality of the advertising image into something seductive on a deeper level.

In *Target-D Signed and Shaun White* (2013), the strongest work in the exhibit, four boys with skateboards and Beatz headphones smile out at the viewer. The imagery on two of the boys' t-shirts is carefully abstracted, drawing our focus into the painting, and we don't notice right away how staged and frozen the boys' expressions and postures are. The contrast between the potential menace of a group of young Justin Biebers, and the delight that Robinson takes in the painting of them creates what Marcel Duchamp called a "delay" in painting—we are drawn into the image, but our eyes wander the paths of the brushwork and color. Robinson wrings poetry out of pandering of advertising. It is as if he were a forensic cultural detective, using his brush like a lab scientist dusting for fingerprints. In this case Robinson is using paint, gently probing for the clues and meanings imbedded in the images he reproduces.

All the most avant-garde of movements, from the Impressionists to the Pop Artists, eventually ended up, to some degree, kitsch decorations. To be "Post-Modern," especially in the 1980s, was a high-wire act, walking a tightrope between aesthetic cynicism and irony; dabbling in kitsch, was, out of necessity, a net. Robinson's works on paper are an appeal to pleasures of consuming, in particular *Lands-End Sleeve Flannel* (2013) which shows three plaid shirts, folded and neatly arranged in a row, suggesting that they might be small, medium, and large. Here Robinson is both critical and complicit in this bid for pleasurable consumption. He has often trafficked in kitsch, and in this show in particular, his critical relationship toward the iconography of commerce and his love/hate relationship with popular imagery adds up to a success in measures that few painters working today can match.

The Shape of Things to Come

Henri Matisse: *The Cut-Outs*; The Museum of Modern Art, New York.
Published December 15, 2014; *CultureCatch*.

In the early months of 1945, Matisse wrote to his daughter that he had gone as far as he could with painting in oil, intending instead to focus his efforts on a large-scale decorative project using the cut-out paper technique he had employed to make sketches and maquettes for his mural and theater projects in the early thirties (*Red Dancer* [1937–38], and *Two Dancers* [1937–38] for Diaghliev's *Rouge et Noir*). "Painting seems to be finished for me for now . . . I'm for decoration—there I give myself everything I can. I put into it all the efforts of my life." Although he had already been employing this technique for years as an adjunct to his paintings, it was not until the mid-forties that he turned almost exclusively to cut paper as his primary medium, introducing a radically new operation that came to be called a *cut-out*. The Museum of Modern Art has devoted an entire exhibition, a mini-retrospective of sorts, to this final chapter in Matisse's work.

Matisse's last few works in oil, *Red Interior, Still Life on a Blue Table* (1947) and *Still Life with Pomegranates* (1947) (not in exhibition), lend some understanding to Matisse's increasing turn to flat planes of color, juxtaposed with incredible subtlety. When looking at many of the first works in the exhibition, such as studies for the illustrations in the book *Jazz*, and *The Cowboy* (1943), the economy of means that Matisse employs, coupled with patience and restraint, begin to emerge. For example, one can see the tangible traces of his minute shifts of colored paper; Matisse used sewing pins to place and arrange his papers, a move inspired by his wife's dressmaking patterns. By 1948, with Matisse's work on the Chapel of the Rosary, a large-scale architectural décor, we can see that what was once a means of arranging studies has become a method of direct painting.

Videos that accompany the pieces in the gallery show Matisse at work, surrounded by dozens of sketches he is rapidly hewing from large sheets (*Pale Blue Window (Second maquette for the apse window of the Chapel of the Rosary)*, 1948–49). In another work, *Little Girl* (1952), Matisse describes a girl walking in a woods or park. The figure is orange, with light blue hair, pulled back with a darker blue headband, and green, jagged shapes represent trees or bushes. Around this time Alberto Giacometti had become interested in Matisse's work. The apocryphal stories about this often point out the irony of the resolutely figurative Giacometti becoming interested in Matisse as he became almost totally an abstract artist. But given the severity of *Little Girl*, one might see how Giacometti's almost surgical reductivist strategies might find inspiration in Matisse's similar approach.

The exhibition's strongest works *Blue Nude IV* (1952) and *Acrobats* (1952) show Matisse mastering the method that he invented. Both the by-now-iconic Blue Nudes and the pencil studies for *Acrobats* show an increasingly precise vocabulary of shape being turned into complete stories of images. Though by now it is almost taken as gospel that these final works are "masterpieces" of Modern art, it is by seeing them all together that some trace of Matisse's struggles still remain. After all, pictures such as this were never seen before, and aside from a constant exchange of letters with his son, the New York art dealer Pierre Matisse, and the well-documented conversations with Picasso and Gilot, Matisse worked in a more or less self-imposed disciplined environment. We can look back now at his letter to Marguerite and smile knowing, as he concludes, "Ever since [his stay in Lyon, the previous year] I feel myself no longer affected by the critics . . . and who knows how what I am doing at the moment will be judged in 25 years?"

Tick, Tick, Bang

Various artists: *The Forever Now: Contemporary Painting in an Atemporal World*; Museum of Modern Art, New York.
Published February 16, 2015; *Artslant.*

Between 1942 and 1963 Dorothy Canning Miller was the curator of the highly perceptive and ultimately influential *Americans* shows at the Museum of Modern Art. Beginning with *Americans 1942: 18 Artists From 9 States* and ending with *Americans 1963*, Miller presented the work of artists such as Hyman Bloom, Robert Motherwell, Jay DeFeo, Robert Rauschenberg, Jasper Johns, Lee Bontecou, and Frank Stella—artists who would ultimately be the defining contributors to the mid-century American art historical canon. After a gap of nearly a half-century, MoMA once again is reviving this tradition with Laura Hoptman's *The Forever Now: Contemporary Painting in an Atemoporal World*, an exhibition of seventeen painters representing current trends in painting.

In contrast to the US-centric exhibitions of the past, *Forever Now* emphasizes the concept of "a-temporality," a phenomenon of culture defined by the science fiction/cultural theorist William Gibson, who used the term to describe a cultural product of our moment that paradoxically does not represent through style or content, or through medium, the time from which it comes. According to Hoptman, "A-temporality, or timelessness, manifests itself in paintings as an ahistorical free-for-all, where contemporaneity as an indicator of new form is nowhere to be found, and all areas coexist."

It is an interesting conceit to an exhibition to, largely, evade the criticism of categorization by pretty much saying "everything is in play here." However, if there is one overarching theme that patinates the work in this exhibition, it is the effects of the late eighties blue-chip Neo Expressionism (read: Basquiat, Schnabel, Penck) and post-internet image reproduction, largely the currency of the moment. While much has been made of the fact that most of the artists in this exhibition are currently enjoying a moment of market rush—Mark Grotjahn, *Untitled (Circus No. 3 Face 44.20)* (2013); Joe Bradley, *Man Made Dirigible* (2008); and the punching-bag of this sort of painting, Oscar Murillo, *7+* (2013–14)—these artists and their work are made almost criticism-proof, as most of the discussion of their works focuses on the market rather than the works themselves. In fact, judging by the paintings in this show, these works support the benign sort of response that Peter Schjeldahl gave in *The New Yorker* magazine, a capitulation that they weren't really bad enough to bother talking about. (On Joe Bradley, Scheldahl opined, "How little can a painting be and still satisfy as a painting? Very little, Bradley ventures. After straining for a sterner response to the works, I opted to relax and like them." On Josh Smith: "As with Bradley, resistance to Smith is understandable but, in the end, too tiring to maintain.")

There is good painting here, though—and it shows that work that flies below the radar of the contemporary fascination with auction prices is being made. Amy Sillman, *Untitled (Head)* (2014) and Charline von Heyl, *Carlotta* (2013) are excellent examples. Yet these two artists seem out of place in an exhibition of "atemporal art." In fact, both these painters are very much of their time. Their use of tropes and methods are both in reaction to and a result of a deep understanding of art history, the place of painting in it, and a careful response to it. By saying that their work represents a sort of free-flowing, dissociated activity does a great disservice to work that is both necessary at the moment and of historical value to the future.

Ultimately this show hinges on the work of two painters: Michael Williams and Nicole Eisenman. Williams and Eisenman have a preternatural grasp of the contingency of painting and use humor and intelligence to critique painting while expanding the uses of it. Williams, like von Heyl, is what we might call a student of the Martin Kippenberger school. While von Heyl understands completely the politics of painting, Williams appropriates from Kippenberger the idea that the art process does not end at the art made. His works are remnants of a process that best resembles a frat party of the art making process. His works defy criticism, or at best, elicit formal responses. This completely misses the point. His use of children's digital paint programs, blue-collar tools like air-brushes and spray cans, and "Bad Painting" circa 1978 styles, show a wealth of techniques—an arsenal with which to undress the Emperor.

In Eisenman's "big head" paintings (*Guy Capitalist*, 2011), one perceives a deep understanding of the history of both "art" and perhaps what we call "art history," as well as a sense that humor, on the level of High Satire, is the tool most appropriate for returning the artist as critical thinker, as well as maker, to the arena of painting. While many of the artists in *Forever Now* use reproduction, appropriation, and stylistic role-play in their work, we do not get the sense that there is an end game. In Eisenman's work a variety of elements come together, and the idiosyncratic humor (for example, the little African figure collages and the Mid-Period Picasso hand smoking a cigarette) are attempts to bring ideas into play through stylistic absorption rather than through mere appropriation. Eisenman says about the work, "I'm open to everything I see; some objects/approaches resonate and work themselves into the fabric of your think/feeling and then show up in a new incarnation, sometimes in unconscious or sly or ways, sometimes with a wink and nod. And then there are works that become benchmarks of influence. I've got a shitload of those."

There was a time, not all that long ago, but in a period now obscured by art movements with names like "relational aesthetics" and "zombie formalism," when a punk aesthetic was necessary to the making of paintings. One defined one's own work largely by showing what it was *not*. For want of any better term, we might call this The Poetry of Hating Shit. There is an abundance of painters today who still adhere to this practice (Albert Oehlen, Nicola Tyson, and Mira Schor leap to mind), and one hopes that future atemporal painting shows at MoMA will show us, through some art historical wormhole, paintings, like Williams's and Eisenman's, that are more poetry than prose.

The Forever Now exhibition includes works by Richard Aldrich, Joe Bradley, Kerstin Brätsch, Matt Connors, Michaela Eichwald, Nicole Eisenman, Mark Grotjahn, Charline von Heyl, Rashid Johnson, Julie Mehretu, Dianna Molzan, Oscar Murillo, Laura Owens, Amy Sillman, Josh Smith, Mary Weatherford, and Michael Williams.

Kicking Against the Pricks

Peter Williams: NOVELLA, New York.
Published March 31, 2015; *Artslant.*

> And when we were all fallen to the earth, I heard a voice speaking unto me,
> and saying in the Hebrew tongue, 'Saul, Saul, why persecutest thou me? It
> is hard for thee to kick against the pricks.
> —Acts 26:14 (King James Version)

> We have art in order not to die from the truth.
> —Nietzsche

The paintings of Peter Williams have, for a long time, addressed the nature of the body, specifically addressing how one might inhabit such a fragile space in such an arbitrary world. Naturalistic figures inhabited landscapes populated with cartoon imagery, combinations rendered plausible through Williams's skilled, and constantly striving, paint handling. With this background in mind, his latest paintings, all untitled, and all from 2015, come as something of a jolt—or, to paraphrase Bruce Nauman, a baseball bat to the back of the head. Here we find Williams stepping out of the atelier and onto the street, so to speak, with works that speak to political and social issues that he seeks to address.

To say that Williams has focused on the figure in the past is not to say that this current work is divergent from that course—there was a time when we spoke of "the body politic," when our social structure was comprised of bodies, and when we looked at it as a living organism. Similarly, when speaking of painters, we talk of their bodies of work. When encountering these new works of Williams we see painting stripped bare. Gone is the lushness found in his early masterpiece *PORTRAIT OF CHRISTOPHER D. FISHER, FOURTH REICH SKINHEAD* (1996), itself a "political" work of sorts, depicting Fisher, a 20-year-old Long Beach skinhead in blackface; Fisher was involved in a 1994 plot to blow up churches and synagogues in Orange County in an attempt to ignite a race war.

In Williams's new works we see the triumphs and tragedies of a cypher figure, a superhero called The N-Word, against a porcine police force, piggy cops with Cyclops eyes—they lack the ability to see things in perspective—who brutalize The N-Word, but he manages to rise time and again from picture to picture. As paintings, these works occupy a space somewhere between history painting and protest placard, at roughly 24 x 36 inches, in primary colors. In one painting Williams references Eric Garner, who lies prone, being choked out by a cop as The N-Word flies in to either rescue or merely bear witness with the camera in his hands. A text running around the sides of the image reads, "it's ok if they die – they'r [sic] animals." Williams clarifies this reading of the work: "I slowly have come to realize that some of the police in this country think they have permission to kill minorities. They already incarcerate millions and they are, simply put, exterminating the rest. It's shocking that this continues even though there is documentation and videos of these acts of violence. So I feel free to expose this ignorance and make art that bears witness to these events." Williams emphasizes the narrative of the artist (in the form of his alter-ego/protagonist, The N-Word) as participant, not mere victim or spectator in one painting in which the Harlequin vampire figure, the cop (who now has two eyes), and the N-Word embrace. "I cannot be separate," Williams explains, "we are all culpable."

Williams may have seemingly left his usual attention to *facture* at the studio door with these works, but to see these paintings less as Painting and more as Propaganda would be an egregious case of boat-missing. Indeed, there is a sense of passion and immediacy to them that at first look dominates. It is this immediacy, though, that is their strength, and it doesn't come at the expense of the painter's interest in painterly painting. In an era of television's "live footage" and "breaking news" and endless iPhone shots, it is probably more valuable than ever for a painter to document his moment using the medium of his trade. One might be tempted to compare these works with Jacques-Louis David's pen and ink sketch Marie-Antoinette on Her Way to the Scaffold (1793), that tiny last document of the Queen and the Terror—"that sinister jotting," as Jean Louis Soulavie called it. Like David, Williams has tried to turn art to more noble ends through minimalist means; judging from these works, he succeeds.

Williams has grown, both as a painter and as an activist, and seems to have taken to heart Gil Scott-Heron's edict: "You will not be able to stay home, brother / You will not be able to plug in, turn on and cop out / You will not be able to lose yourself on skag / And skip out for beer during commercials." You will also not be able to stay home, Williams seems to add, or in the studio, crafting careful compositions. You must be in the public eye, the eye of the body politic, bearing witness. Because the revolution will not only be televised; it, by needs, must also be painted.

Peel Slowly and See

Bill Jensen: *Transgressions;* Cheim & Read, New York.
Published April 29, 2015; *Artslant.*

There was a time in modern music when the role of the artist changed from being the custodian of cultural knowledge to something more of an autobiographer. We might choose that moment in the late sixties when Lou Reed abandoned the writing of pop ditties about boys and girls, to focus on his own, more personal interests, like boys and girls and heroin. In other art forms this sea change was happening—in comedy, where once jokes were shared, un-authored, between performers in Vegas, the Catskills, and New York City clubs, Lenny Bruce made comedy suddenly personal—talking about race, politics, cops, censorship, and heroin. It is tempting to suggest that in painting this shift had happened decades earlier, particularly in that sub-category of painting called "abstraction." Once artists like Kandinsky, Rodchenko, Dove, and O'Keefe had looked for universal symbols—a folk art, as it were—of the collective unconscious. Jackson Pollock, Barnett Newman, and Mark Rothko, in particular, overturned all that—with Pollock famously eschewing commonality by stating "I am Nature."

It is of some importance to note that while all artists probably became aware of these changes, there were some, like Bob Dylan, who sought to give voice to their own stories, while at the same time acknowledging the deep history of their medium. Dylan began as a folk musician, in the tradition of Arlo Guthrie, and transitioned into the premier autobiographical storyteller of his generation, yet he never completely abandoned the idea of a collective musical unconscious. Bill Jensen, whose career has been devoted to maintaining the ideas of abstract painting, may represent, in a period where we have artists who create "zombie formalist" paintings, a folk tradition in painterly abstraction more akin to Dylan than Reed.

Jensen strives for an ego-less, unpretentious practice devoid of preconceived outcomes, surrendering to the painting process, allowing it to determine the path and destination of his work. His intensive layering and reworking of the canvas results in highly tactile and seductive surfaces: paint is plastered on, scraped off, seeped, dredged, brushed, and smoothed until a certain "presence" is achieved; he attempts to create paintings which, like self-contained beings, affect the world around them—a characteristic he refers to as "emotional density." In the work shown at Cheim & Read, Jensen riffs on subjects taken from Chinese poetry, Michelangelo's Sistine Chapel, the icons of Andrei Rublev, and contemporaries, like Jasper Johns and Carroll Dunham.

The first room in the exhibition holds a mini-exhibition-within-the-exhibition, containing small, exquisitely painted variations on Michelangelo. *Study for Right Hand Panel of Transgressions* (2013) and *Study for Left Hand Panel of Transgressions* (2013) morph Michelangelo's Laocoön-like figures into a writing mass of intestinal shapes *à la* Dunham, against a harsh orange ground reminiscent of fifties-era Francis Bacon. The biomorphic shapes twist and turn, seeming to wrestle, fuck, and fight all at the same time. Jensen's use of the triptych also reminds us of Bacon, who used the classic format to create oblique narratives, while heightening the strangeness of the abstract figure.

It is in the second gallery, though, we see Jensen the folk artist. In *Double Sorrow +1 (GREY SCALE)* (2014–15), *Message* (2011–2014), and *Louhan (Violet II)* (2013–2014), Jensen combines elements of Johns's stenciled, black-and-white puzzles and handprints; Julian Schnabel's signature purple scratched splatters and biomorphic white blobs; and Basquiat's drop cloths covered in studio detritus, coffee cup stains, and smudges. It is not to say that

Jensen's interest in working from the memory of nature, as he has so ably done in the past, is gone entirely—*Single Ch'u* (2014) is pure, vintage Jensen—but rather he has begun to absorb the memory of culture, a shared painterly culture, into his process. In contrast to younger painters like Joe Bradley or Oscar Murillo who merely ape a vapid simulacrum of abstract painting's vocabulary, Jensen incorporates a larger and deeper understanding of the history of his chosen style. If it weren't so seemingly pejorative a term, we might be tempted to say that Jensen performs a generic form of abstraction. If one is tempted to find some reductive form of criticism of these new works, or Jensen's strategy as a whole, and attempt to dismiss it as out of step with the moment, one would do well to go, quickly, and listen to Stevie Ray Vaughn's version of Hendrix's cover of Dylan's "All Along the Watchtower."

The Immigrant Song

Jacob Lawrence: *One-Way Ticket: Jacob Lawrence's Migration Series and Other Works*; MoMA (Museum of Modern Art), New York.
Published May 27, 2015; *Artslant*.

One of the most startling impressions that one takes away from seeing the reunited Migration Series at the Museum of Modern Art is how current the paintings still feel—in a way that Céline still does, or Christopher Isherwood, or John Steinbeck, documenters of a very specific moment of transition, faithfully recording sensitive observations. Jacob Lawrence's cycle of 60 paintings on the subject of the Great Migration, during which 6 million African Americans ultimately left the rural South, is both a landmark work for an artist who was just 23 years old when he began it and a work of historical importance in American art of the twentieth century.

Lawrence, who had dropped out of school when he was 16, was encouraged by his single mother to take art classes and visit museums. He studied at the Harlem Art Workshop, which was in the basement of the New York Public Library branch on West 135th Street (now the Schomburg Center for Research in Black Culture). There he met the painter and muralist Charles Alston who became the first of several mentors who were struck by his talent and drive. Lawrence received a scholarship to the American Artists School on West 14th Street where his fellow students included Ad Reinhardt and Elaine de Kooning. There he soon developed a personal pictorial style, which he called "dynamic cubism," of jagged compositions in bold, flat colors. He befriended and was influenced by writers including Jay Leyda, Richard Wright, Ralph Ellison, and Langston Hughes.

It was possibly the confluence of all these influences that make the Migration paintings so visually compelling over such a large cycle. Comparisons to Giotto or Michelangelo might be easy, but Lawrence was working on small panels, painting in casein almost like an animator filling in the colored "cells" of a film. While his simplified range of shape and color speed us along from panel to panel, he still manages to shift mood and feeling, like different scenes in a film, through superb character direction. In *Panel 4*, which is captioned (Lawrence wrote the captions to all the works and meant for them to be an explanatory verse) "The Negro was the largest source of labor to be found after all others had been exhausted," Lawrence shows a man hammering a spike, in mid-stroke. The spike is oversized but resembles a railroad spike, and the hammer feels heavy. Both these inanimate objects draw our attention, as he has left the figure more of an abstract shape than a human portrait, emphasizing the dehumanization of the people. Incongruously the action takes place inside, in an empty room with one window. With equal simplicity Lawrence gives us *Panel 16*, captioned "Although the Negro was used to lynching, he found this an opportune time for him to leave where one had occurred." Here is the emotional devastation of Picasso's Blue Period: a woman in a red dress slumps over a sharply raked dinner table with only an empty bowl and spoon, a metaphor for the emptiness we feel in her.

Like any good documentarian, Lawrence does not fail to give both sides of the story. A nattily dressed couple looks at us with disdain, if they are looking at all, in *Panel 53*: "The Negroes who had been North for quite some time met their fellowmen with disgust and aloofness." And the final panel, *Panel 60*, which reads "And the migrants kept coming," leaves us in awe of the sheer mass of displaced humanity that was breaking in great waves against the shores of the industrial North.

Three additional rooms in the exhibition include other accounts of the Migration, including novels and poems by writers such as Langston Hughes, Claude McKay, and Richard Wright; photographs by Dorothea Lange, Ben Shahn, Gordon Parks, and Robert McNeill; sociological tracts by Carter Woodson, Charles Johnson, Emmett Scott, and Walter White; and paintings by Charles Alston, Romare Bearden, and Charles White. In an effort to show that Lawrence's work still resonates, particularly in our current moment with regard to race relations in America, the poet Elizabeth Alexander, in collaboration with MoMA, has commissioned ten poets to write works inspired by Lawrence. One of the commissioned works is a children's book about Lawrence by Sharifa Rhodes-Pitts and Christopher Myers. Mr. Myers, an illustrator, said his visits to schools and juvenile detention centers made him realize that children needed to realize that their own lives could give them models of success beyond what they find in the lyrics and videos of so much popular music.

Indeed, it is music that might be the most important element, both as an inspiration to Lawrence and a bridge for younger viewers today. A side room of text, music, and video of the music that was both an influence to Lawrence and a sonic record of the Harlem Renaissance accompanies this exhibition to great effect. Thomas "Fats" Waller, Louis Armstrong, Mahalia Jackson, and Lead Belly provide background material that has the musical equivalent and range of Lawrence's paintings. Billie Holiday singing "Strange Fruit" (in the accompanying video documentary) provides a fitting coda to Lawrence's immigrant song.

Physical Graffiti

Leon Golub: *Riot*; Hauser & Wirth, New York.
Published June 4, 2015; *Artslant.*

> I think of myself as a kind of reporter; I report on the nature of certain
> events. I think of art as a report on civilization at a certain time.
> —Leon Golub

Leon Golub: Riot at Hauser & Wirth, in New York, presents a long overdue opportunity to see Golub's paintings gathered together from several different bodies of work spanning a four-decade period. Showing *Napalm I* (1969) and *Riot V* (1987), Vietnam-era paintings, and several fine examples from his late *Mercenaries* series, this exhibition offers a chance to view Golub's rough-hewn, infinitely tactile, and large-scale works the way the artist intended: full-on, confrontational, and unmediated.

Encountering *Napalm I*, which fills the first gallery, T.S. Eliot comes to mind: "Things fall apart; the centre cannot hold; / Mere anarchy is loosed upon the world, / The blood-dimmed tide is loosed, and everywhere / The ceremony of innocence is drowned. / The best lack all conviction, while the worst / Are full of passionate intensity." Yes, of course mere anarchy is always loose in the world, but if one might select an artist of passionate intensity, that might be Golub—and if there was ever an example of a twentieth-century artist of conviction, Golub was the very definition of it. Why does this work evoke such paradox? Perhaps it is Golub's subject matter and painterly method colliding on the canvas before us.

Created between 1968 and 1969, the *Napalm* series represented a pivotal moment when Golub's subject matter shifted from the mythological to the political, advancing its relevance and urgency in relation to contemporary life. These paintings are the first to reference the Vietnam War and are part of what Golub himself described as an "overt political effort." In *Napalm I*, he depicts the sheer vulnerability of the human body. Two figures are entangled in a rust-stained landscape. As one fights to extricate himself, the other lies mortally wounded with an open, blood-encrusted chest. Golub's treatment of this wound in paint reminds one of de Kooning's wrinkly-skin paint skeins in his *Clamdigger* series of the '60s; paint no longer depicted desiccated flesh, it *became* it. In a repetitive process that required weeks of demanding physical work, Golub dissolved his pigments, soaked the canvas in solvents, scraped away paint with a meat cleaver, and rendered surfaces as eviscerated, porous, and raw as the violence that a human body suffers in scenarios of duress and agony. Our unease is a result of seeing this process—bodies created then eroded, laid out before us. Their faces, death-mask rictuses, evoke no emotion from us; rather, our response comes from the tortured figures wrestling in front of us.

Interestingly, another artist who comes to mind when viewing these pieces is Francis Bacon, roughly Golub's contemporary for a time. Bacon freely appropriated T.S. Eliot's highly theatrical poetry for his own highly theatric orgies of flayed flesh. Like Bacon, Golub's attacks on the figure were clumsy, physical, inelegant—and most of all sincere. Both drew on the Classical, conflict, and, possibly, underneath it all, an attempt to resurrect a type of religious painting, via Grünewald, which both vociferously denied.

Golub struggled through his early Classical phase, his Vietnam period, and (not in this exhibition) a series of head studies of political leaders in the '70s before recognition for his work finally caught up with him. From the late 1970s through the mid-1980s, Golub created his most celebrated works, with the series *Mercenaries, Interrogations, White Squads,* and *Riots.* Depicting scenes of coercion, torture, terrorism, and urban unrest, these paintings portray the aggressors as men who perhaps are not so different from ourselves. In these years Golub focused on power and its abuses, giving particular attention to American military activity in such places as Latin America. It is at this point that Golub turned his painting into a kind of *reportage,* distancing his process in favor of a kind of Christopher Isherwood-like objectivity:

I think of myself as a kind of reporter; I report on the nature of certain events. I think of art as a report on civilization at a certain time. It tells about the confidence of hierarchies, how hierarchy is expressed: who is included and who is not . . . Perhaps for the first time in history, with the exception of Goya and a few others, there is an art that does not celebrate state and church power. If I paint mercenaries, whatever else I am doing, I am not praising state power and the success of arms. I am reporting on the state of our society, how we use force, and how men act out their roles.

Riot V shows a gang of men in paramilitary garb, caught in mid-action—cheering, attacking, recoiling. The image retains an element of ambiguity. We become the focus of the gesticulating, leering group, and, for a moment, become either victims or complicit in the action. These works, though strong, seem mediated—mediated through the source material that Golub collected, mediated through period clothes and weapons, mediated through our own exposure to the same imagery. In some ways, through all this mediation, some of Golub's uncanny ability to depict power dissipates. Not to say that these are lesser painterly achievements, but rather, they are to depictions of power and struggle what a drone strike is to a boots-on-the-ground soldier. Equally lethal, emotionally distant.

The exhibition also includes a selection of monoprints that Golub began in 2000 and continued to create through the last four years of his life. Intimate in scale, these works employ the technique of oil transfer and revisit earlier themes, referencing mythology, eroticism, and violence. They call to mind the monoprints of Eric Fischl, the modern master of the medium. In some ways their lightness and humor provide a tonic for the heaviness of the paintings. The symbol of the sphinx returns in *Alerted* (2003). Part man and part beast, the sphinx is an ideal metaphor for the struggles of humankind seeking both gratification and civilization. A Satyr (*3 Legged Satyr,* 2004) and a sketch of a Centaur (*The Wounded Centaur,* 2004) are a sly nod to Matthew Barney; and two standing figures fucking (*Love in Art School III,* 2004) parodies late-period Picasso à la Tracey Emin.

The painting *Fallen Warrior* (1968) is the masterpiece of this exhibition. Its fallen, broken figure is echoed in the cut and abraded scrap of canvas it barely inhabits. Approximately life-sized, this image combines Golub's early affinity to the Classical with the news of the moment circa 1969. It is timeless, nevertheless, as we see today with ISIS torture and African atrocities. Golub, like Courbet or Delacroix or Goya, managed to create an image of man, who despite centuries of civilization, is still slouching toward Bethlehem.

Written on the Kitten

Jean-Michael Basquiat: *BASQUIAT: The Unknown Notebooks*; Brooklyn Museum, Brooklyn. Published May 6, 2015; *Brooklyn Rail.*

There are some painters who are born great (Picasso), some who attained greatness due to circumstances of their time (David), and some whose work grows in importance posthumously (Kahlo); Jean-Michel Basquiat is a rare case of a painter who managed to fall into all three of these categories. He was a prodigious teenager who came out of the gate fast with his graffiti work, which was timely and poetic and achieved meteoric success and celebrity in the '80s. Now, 30 years on, he is an artist whose work, it seems, grows in complexity and meaning through retrospective and deeper readings. Basquiat fused drawing, painting, pop culture, and music with history and poetry to produce an artistic language and content that was entirely his own. Combining the tools of graffiti (Sharpie markers, spray enamel, and chalk) with those of fine art (oil and acrylic paint, collage, and oil stick), his best paintings maintain a powerful tension between opposing aesthetic forces—thought and expression; control and spontaneity; wit, urbanity, and primitivism—while providing acerbic commentary on the harsher realities of race, culture, and society in the early '80s New York social landscape. *Basquiat: The Unknown Notebooks* at the Brooklyn Museum is an excellent opportunity to evaluate material that has never been placed in a public exhibition.

Right at the start of the exhibition we see the ease with which Basquiat transitioned from tagging walls in the late '70s with Al Diaz under the pseudonym SAMO to filling small children's composition books with block-lettered phrases, pieces of poetry, and found sayings and phrases. Conceptually and visually these books resemble the early concrete poetry of the sculptor Carl Andre, who used words as material, laying them down in careful arrangements on the page, composing, both visually and literarily, snippets of conversations, word snapshots, and diary entries, albeit of an oblique kind. The exhibition contains six notebooks, which have been carefully dissembled to present the work in a more individual format. Although they are displayed non-chronologically, they show Basquiat creating a format and sticking with it throughout his career.

Basquiat's use of language, in contrast to other artists in the '80s like Barbara Kruger, Mira Schor, or Christopher Wool, was largely poetic. He chose words for their descriptive and lyric qualities, sampling found material and combining it with his own word inventions— "leapsickness," "pedxing," "aspuria." Some pages, like this from a 1992 notebook, border on the cinematic:

> AN EPELEPTIC SECRETARY ON TELEVISION / THAT MOBSTER
> STEVE'S GIRL / SCAN / I WANT YOUR PURSE / IF YOU SCREAM
> WITHIN 60 SECONDS ILL BE BACK." Other pages from the same
> folio are lists of phone numbers, shopping lists ("1 STICK BUTTER /
> BACON / 1/2 DOZ EGGS"), or women's names. In a nine-panel work
> from 1984 titled "Melville," Basquiat copied the chapter index from Moby
> Dick, emphasizing the poetry of Melville, by turning the chapter titles
> into poetry: "QUEEQUEG IN HIS COFFIN / DOES THE WHALE'S
> MAGNITUDE DIMINISH? / THE WHITENESS OF THE WHALE.

In addition to the notebook pages, the exhibition includes a selection of Basquiat's paintings with collaged elements. In these works he does not simply scale up the words to fit the canvas, as Cy Twombly or Julian Schnabel might, but rather fills the space with a cacophony of words both discordant and, sometimes, eerily brilliant. For example, in *Untitled* (1986) a torn canvas that resembles a bearskin rug riffs on familiar themes of jazz music, luxury items, and Batman logos. In this vividly colored canvas—as well as in the neighboring oil stick on paper, *UNTITLED (LEONARDO DA VINCI)* from 1982—words are used like brushstrokes; the frenetic, all-over quality suggests a drive toward a sort of disjunctive mapping, rather than the building of a classically unified composition, where seemingly unrelated marks suddenly coalesce in syncopated rhythms. Comparisons were made of his work to boxing and the cool jazz of Miles Davis.

In retrospect, it might have been a little too easy to place his work in the category of Neo-Expressionism, with its bombast and emphasis on direct, experiential painting. Closer looks reveal that his process (no doubt influenced by his working relationship with Warhol) didn't fit quite so neatly into the same camp as Schnabel and Clemente but walked a fine line between high and low culture. In his essay "The Culture Industry: Enlightenment as Mass Deception," the art theorist and social critic Theodor Adorno attempted to analyze the transformation of the cultural sphere in industrialized capitalist society. Adorno argued that as a result of the increasing rationalization of life in a technological society, the cultural sphere becomes one of the areas through which the dominant economic norms are inserted. He posited that this commodification of culture leads inevitably to the conflation of the avant-garde, or high culture, and those lower forms of popular entertainment or spectacle. For Adorno, the end result of this mash-up is kitsch. Perhaps no artist in the twentieth century since Warhol understood how to commodify kitsch into a believable art form as much as Basquiat.

Basquiat indeed has proven to be a greater, more lasting talent than the bombastic propaganda the '80s promised. One of the most beautiful things about this show of works, which in some ways were probably meant to be personal, is that we get glimpses of the private Basquiat. One diaristic page reads like a confession, or an indictment—a poem of almost excruciating poignancy, showing us what this effort cost him:

> THIS IS NOT IN PRAISE OF POISON / ING MYSELF WAITING
> FOR IDEAS / TO HAPPEN MYSELF—THIS NOT / IN PRAIS
> OF POISON / THE NON POISON NON POISONED / SO SELF
> RIGHTOUS / NO ONE IS CLEAN / FROM RED MEAT TO WHITE
> POISON / THIS IS NOT IN PRAISE OF POISON / THE BIGGEST
> BUSINESS / UGLY, FAT LIKE A PIG / THE CUSTOMER IN NEW
> YORK / CHICAGO DETROIT / PSALM.

This is What Tomorrow Looks Like: On Painting

Albert Oehlen: *Home and Garden*; The New Museum, New York.
Albert Oehlen: *"Home and Garden" Annex*; Gagosian Gallery, New York.
Magalie Guérin: *Project Room*; Lyles & King, New York.
Brenda Goodman: *Selected Work 1961–2015*; College for Creative Studies, Center Galleries, Detroit.
Brenda Goodman: *Painting is Not Doomed to Repeat Itself*; Hollis Taggart Galleries, New York.
Erin Smith: *The Right Place at the Right Time*; Amy Li Projects, New York.
Published September 1, 2015; *Artslant*.

Michael Heizer once wittily compared the Fall art season as the art-world equivalent to duck hunting season, with collectors and viewers returning from their summer homes hungry for new art experiences. While it might seem a bit of a stretch, and maybe a little deprecating to the artist ducklings, there is some truth to that feeling of anticipation we have of wanting to see what is going on after the dog days of August.

It is difficult to find overarching themes and styles in much of the current work of the past few years, compared to the '80s (when art "movements" came pre-packaged with names like "neo-geo") or the early aughts when a single artist brand (like Damien Hirst) could fill a dozen galleries with his brand. We are seeing a return to a more intimate, personal type of painting—one that points toward a style that while conceptually vital and disciplined, and drawing upon an array of influences, shows an artist who is primarily a maker of painterly images, ones that are quirky and personal. A good example of this is Albert Oehlen's retrospective (*Albert Oehlen: Home and Garden*) at the New Museum, as well as his concurrent show at the Gagosian Gallery (*"Home and Garden" Annex*). Oehlen, along with Martin Kippenberger and Werner Büttner, were part of a wave of German Neo-Expressionists who, like Rainer Fetting and Salome, sought to reaffirm the primacy of painting. Oehlen and Kippenberger espoused a tongue-in-cheek approach to their work, mixing in a little Duchampian humor, albeit a more schoolboy variety. In the early '90s, though, Oehlen dropped the stand-up shtick and sought a new approach to making paintings. Oehlen went back to basic—a kind of ground zero of painting—where he began working in series, such as his "computer paintings," which attempt to find new ways to examine the type of paintings (like Jackson Pollock's) that defined abstraction in American painting since the 1950s.

It is this sort of DIY, heart-on-the-sleeve approach to picture making that seems particularly relevant now—a kind of visual antithesis to the corporate branding that has dominated much of the art of the past few years. Brenda Goodman, who recently had an exhibition at Life On Mars Gallery (*Brenda Goodman: New Works*, 2015) will be having a full retrospective at the College for Creative Studies in Detroit this Fall, as well as being included in John Yau's *Painting is Not Doomed to Repeat Itself* at Hollis Taggart Galleries. Goodman's paintings resist definition. Unlike Oehlen's work, which retains the framework of serial structure, Goodman chooses to find the image as she paints, lending her work an element of free association, one in which Goodman allows the viewer access to her process. In works such as *Almost a Bride* (2015), the figurative element is grouped with a variety of abstract marks of pure gesture; one gets the sense of an artist who eschews the vocabulary of pre-existing forms, instead putting a premium on visceral connection. There is a rawness in Goodman's work, a stripping down of empty style and trope, that allows us to connect in a way that feels genuine.

Magalie Guérin, whose work is at Lyles & King (*Magalie Guérin: Project Room*), also ascribes to Goodman's direct approach to paint, though, like Oehlen, she doesn't abandon some of the irony and formal structure of her earlier work. In the past Guérin has worked in photography and drawing, allowing for cross-pollination between the two disciplines. Often quoting from other historical works, for example Robert Mapplethorpe photos or the work of Diane Arbus, Guérin played with ideas about authentic gesture and also explored the personal through her appropriation strategies, à la Sherrie Levine. In her new paintings Guérin begins with primary structures—an image of a hat or four-leaf clover—and then explores it through different approaches and painterly processes. While the formalistic approach might yield slight payoff, Guérin instead wrings a wealth of playful, quirky visual excitement from limited means.

Erin Smith is a young painter who will be showing her small-scaled but high-impact work at Amy Li Projects (*The Right Place at the Right Time*). Smith combines gesture and style in a mash-up of visually exciting color and form. Her work combines the layering of images, reminiscent of Gina Magid's fabric paintings, with a painterly touch that calls to mind the walls of paint of Clyfford Still. The painter Mira Schor, whose work seems like a role model for much of the work being produced today, used the term "modest painting" to describe a type of painting that is powerful, intelligent, and free of bombast and empty pictorial rhetoric, when describing what she aspired to as a painter. The term has a rightness about it that seems to fit our current moment, and ideally defines where we are headed.

Zombie Birdhouse

Keltie Ferris: Mitchell-Innes & Nash, New York.
Published October 5, 2015; *Brooklyn Rail.*

A screenwriter bursts into his agent's office. "I have a great idea for a new picture," he enthuses. "We do a remake of *The Wiz*. Only with *white* people!" Clichéd Hollywood joke, sure, yet pretty much on point with regard to current trends in art and music. The mash-up, dub, remix, redux, or whatever you want to call it, has replaced the "appropriation" strategies of the '80s. It has morphed into something called Zombie Formalism that for better, or worse, is now seen as a legitimate art movement.

Mitchell-Innes & Nash is showing the paintings and works on paper of Keltie Ferris. These very large, high-keyed, color-filled canvases are warmly inviting on first viewing. Bright reds and blues dominate. The arching motif is brushy passages of paint, checkerboard squares, and general noodling around with the brush over airbrushed planes of color. The press release notes, "Ferris explores painting as a personal index," and indeed, there is something deeply felt about these works—something likable and genuine that was lacking in much of the work in the *Forever Now* show last spring at MoMA. In the MoMA show there was indeed a zombie-like quality to much of the show's paintings—a feeling of deadness and mere object making. Nicole Eisenman and Christopher Williams were the only exceptions to the walking-dead rule there. Here, Ferris manages to vivify her paintings by following the lead of Williams. In *Story* (2015), she first paints a stack of vertical bands, which are covered by vertical pulls of paint, which are fogged over by a Jules Olitski-like mist of airbrushed pigment, which is then doodled over with scratchy, felt-tip-pen-like green strokes. In *Marksman* (2015) a similar technique references Christopher Wool and Arthur Dove; other works suggest passages of Jonathan Lasker, Ross Bleckner, Gerhard Richter, and Amy Sillman, as well as African textiles and Amish quilts. When these elements come together, as in *Cleopatra* (2015) the result is quite likeable, like an Atari version of a Marsden Hartley.

The problem at the center of this type of art-making process is not the lack of original material. "Voodoo Problems" is a great song. Hendrix is great. Jay-Z is great. Put them together and you have a sonic Reese's peanut butter cup of greatness. Nor is the use of the repetitive mark-making, the quilting together of random paint strokes particularly compelling. Shows of McArthur Binion and Jack Tworkov (at Galerie LeLong and Alexander Gray Associates, respectively) are running concurrently on the same block and offer an instructive lesson on how this material can be based on a much stricter, disciplined approach to great effect. No, there seems to be a greater problem, which might be the fault of we, the audience, as much as it is the artists. We are often accepting of mediums of convenience, things that are good enough rather than more difficult and better. We laugh at memes and YouTube postings, talk to people on cell phones over networks whose sound quality would be mocked by Alexander Graham Bell, and often view art exhibits only on our laptops. Information theory tells us that the amount of bits needed to communicate certain types of content, like the hilarious New York Subway Pizza Rat, on the internet can be much lower, and lower still, as the viewing audience becomes adapted to interpreting content with less data. If we only need to extract the information from a phone conversation, like listening to a computerized answering service from tech support in India when your computer is down, then maybe good enough is ok. Or maybe not.

When looking at painting, specifically post-Frank Stella painting, there has been a similar decline in levels of painterly qualities that sometimes has left us feeling that something has gone missing. Stella himself wryly observed that "what you see is what you see," though in his work he replaced a certain romantic approach to painting with geometry, and in doing so merely replaced a certain appreciation of painterly beauty with the beauty of geometry and color.

All of this is not, in the end, to disparage the projects of Ferris. Indeed, this type of painting obviates criticism to some degree. A more clever review of this show would have consisted of a William S. Burroughs cut-and-paste mash-up of the reviews of Clement Greenberg, Rosalind Krauss, Harold Rosenberg, and Peter Schjeldahl. But perhaps we should take away something instructive from all of this. If television has taught us anything lately, it is that we should fear the walking dead.

The Whiteness of the Whale

Frank Stella: *A Retrospective*; Whitney Museum of American Art, New York.
Published November 23, 2015; *Artslant*.

> Blank Frank is the messenger of your doom and your construction
> Yes, he is the one who will set you up as nothing
> And he is the one who will look at you sideways.
> –Brian Eno, "Blank Frank"

> For now we see through a glass, darkly; but then face to face: now I know in
> part; but then shall I know even as also I am known.
> —1 Corinthians 13:12

> What you see is what you see.
> —Frank Stella

We cannot begin any assessment of the work of Frank Stella without the obligatory quote that has followed his career for over fifty years. "What you see is what you see" was Stella's painterly philosophy distilled down to seven words. If there is a definition of Minimalism that is more succinct, it has yet to replace Stella's as a key to understanding a certain type of particularly American painting in mid-century art history.

At the Whitney Museum we have a chance to carefully review Stella's work, something that has not happened since his last retrospective at the Museum of Modern Art in the 1987. Stella has had either the great fortune, or great curse, of being a painter whose work gained immediate attention with his Black Paintings—strikingly simple, yet endlessly ponderable tangrams of painterly philosophy. Then, according to the sentimental narrative of art historical storytelling, he spent the rest of his career in slow, steady decline as his work began repudiating everything that he had started out to do. It is of great credit to the Whitney that through this carefully curated show we might see how Stella's works did in fact retain certain threads of thought, ideas that slowly matured over time, and how his visual syntax built upon itself, rather than just being jettisoned, when he turned his attention to more complex, decorative, and large-scale work that more resembled theatrical decors.

Stella's biography lends itself to the belief that he was a prodigy, one who began painting at 14, attended Princeton, and then moved to New York in 1958 at the height of a time when Abstract Expressionism had opened up the scene, and Pop Art, Color Field, and Minimalism were both vying for, and to some degree sharing, the attention of a new audience that was hungry for new visual experiences. Stella's appearance in Emile de Antonio's film *Painters Painting* (probably the best source for appreciating that moment in the early '60s when everything seemed possible in painting) shows a young painter at work on his Black Paintings, chewing a cigar, resembling what we might get if we crossed Groucho Marx with Vincent van Gogh, saying, "I want the paint to look as good on the canvas as it does in the can." This little moment of brilliant cinema (the other best scene in the film is a saintly-looking Robert Rauschenberg, seated atop a ladder in his studio, talking about his work like some sort of ethereal Trappist monk) is a key to understanding Stella's approach to making paintings, which was equal parts philosophy, humor, and aesthetics.

It is interesting to compare Stella to Jasper Johns, another anointed prodigy whose early works were immediately injected into art history at almost the same time. If Johns was the John Cheever of American painting, with his Americana (maps of the United States, American flags, gun range targets) thinly veiling a brittle, wounded sensibility, then we might be tempted to think that Stella was the painterly equivalent of Philip Roth. Works before the Black Painting period, like *Mary Lou Loves Frank* (1958), *Your Lips are Blue* (1958), and the regrettably destroyed *Mary Lou Douches With Pine-Scented Lysol* (1958), share something of Roth's sensibility in his writing: a sharp wit, a willingness to embrace vulgarity, and a terse sense of prose that masks a deep interiority. In attempts to turn Roth's books into film, we can see the difficulty of showing visually the character development and transformation that he achieves in his work; we can make a comparison with how much Stella struggles later in his career to illustrate certain concepts through a visual vocabulary. It is wonderful to be able to compare *Mary Lou Loves Frank* with its biting turn of phrase (does Frank love Mary Lou?) to the austere *Jill* of 1959 with its diamond-shaped pattern suggesting living room rugs, pinstripe business suits, good jobs on Madison Avenue, and engagement rings. While the idea of comparing Stella to Roth might at first seem spurious, it is important to remember that throughout his career he did return to literary sources: *Your Lips are Blue* has echoes of Salinger's *A Perfect Day for Bananafish*, and *At Sainte Luce!* (1998) was inspired by stories of the German writer Heinrich von Kleist. With his Moby Dick series from 1986–1997, Stella found a source whose ambition, sense of humor, and visuality (the depictions of the "whiteness of the whale" must have held great fascination for Stella) matched his own. Even in *The Raft of the Medusa (Part 1)* (1990), one of Stella's best forays into sculpture, we can see how he tries to create a sense of narrative through abstract aluminum pours and splashes (à la Richard Serra) and build a sense of drama against the support structure of the sculpture's armature. Like Théodore Géricault, who created a replica "set" of the Medusa's deck when he painted *The Raft of the Medusa* (1818–19), Stella emulates the theatricality of the scene at the moment of rescue.

Beginning with the Black Paintings, then following into the Aluminum Series, the Copper Series (*Plant City*, 1963), and the Irregular Polygon series of 1966 (*Chocorua IV*, 1966), Stella carefully excised the humor and gesture from his work—or, it might be closer to the truth to say he submerged it and replaced certain notions of beauty and aesthetics, which were the dominant paradigm of the mid-'50s, with the pure beauty of color and geometry. We see, though, that through the constant emphasis he placed on his titles, like *Die Fahne Hoche!* (1959) or *Moultonville II (1966)*, that story, set, and setting were constantly there, under the surface, waiting until the 1970s to be made more manifest and integrated into a "whole" of pictorial narrative. At the time, in the mid-'80s, when he decided to tackle Moby Dick, there was a general consensus that Stella's work had become bloated, overwrought, and sinking under the hubris of its creator. It is somewhat paradoxical that that was the same period when painters like Julian Schnabel, Susan Rothenberg, and Anselm Kiefer were being lauded for similar pursuits in their work. In retrospect it is easier, perhaps, to see that Stella had not abandoned his principles or pursuits but was expanding on concepts he had been working with all along.

One of the great needs that painting fulfills, along with certain types of musical performance, film, and literature, is a type of analog experience that cannot be replaced with virtual or digital media. At a moment in cultural history when there are artists who are practicing abstraction with a knowing wink, the "zombie formalists" whose existence is largely intangible by being shown mostly at auction houses, it is important to see Stella's work as a whole—a body of paintings that exist both as objects as well as records of time. Our way of viewing them has changed over the years, and, thus, they are a kind of constant, a measure of how things are perceived, change, and are seen anew. We will always need a place to practice not being distracted, and like a book or a film, painting offers a specific separate place where one can be alone with a mediating object to experience thoughts and ideas that are not your thoughts, but those of an artist sharing their experiences with you. Stella's paintings, and the Whitney Museum's generous exhibition, provide us a place where we can share in his long search for meaning in painting.

Where Darkness Doubles Light Pours In

Mira Schor: Lyles & King, New York.
Published March 24, 2016; *Artslant*.

Paul of Tarsus wrote, "When I was a child, I spoke as a child, I understood as a child, I thought as a child; but when I became a man, I put away childish things. For now we see through a glass, darkly, but then face to face. Now I know in part, but then I shall know . . ." This passage from *Corinthians* comes to mind when looking at the recent work of Mira Schor, now at Lyles & King. Schor's paintings, dark, compactly strong meditations on mortality, power, and language, show an artist wrestling with the big questions. Schor has always been a painter who confronted politics, art history, and painting head-on, and these new paintings don't veer far from that course.

We understand from Paul that what we see is limited—only a portion of the truth, "through a glass, darkly." In *"Power" Figure #30: All that's left is paint* (2016) and *"Power" Figure #24: Language* (2016), Schor gives us dense, layered, dark grounds of impastoed paint, in a range of subtle blacks, illuminated by the delicate tracery of her hand. It suggests an artist who is searching, looking in Plato's cave for deeper truths. Indeed, these two works, which are essentially self-portraits—the first of a large older Mira delicately attached to a tiny, floating younger Mira; the second an Andy Warhol-esque silver-haired Mira reading—are both iconic (à la Lascaux cave drawings) and personal (like Rembrandt's overly intimate, late self-portraits). Yet, we might also interpret these monolithic paintings as a meditation on the role of painting in our current technological age.

The contemporary phrase "black mirror" alludes to the ubiquitous screens with which we are confronted as we watch movies, compose text messages, and, yes, even read this article, though they only become black when they are turned off. In the dull glow of laptops, cellphones, televisions, and Kindles, we see ourselves reflected—and sometimes distorted— through a glass, darkly. The modern looking glass is these myriad screens, all of which mediate our experiences of objects, and most especially, art. Schor's adherence to the medium of paint, that oldest means of visual communication, lends her work a sense of authority, of historical knowledge, that is often lacking in the art world today, where commodity, Zombie Formalism, and intellectually bankrupt appropriational strategies have become the norm.

Schor's most recent body of work presented the figure as avatar, a stick-figure understudy for the artist, in a series of "selfie" self-portraits. In *Death Is A Conceptual Artist* (2015), that figure has become a golem of sorts, its head a skull wearing a translucent shift, with umbilical lines of paint connecting breasts to books or text panel cue cards, and a giant floating flower. The umbilical lines are a deep red oxide, suggesting blood—little lifelines, of knowledge being passed to a new generation, and of tradition being traded at great expense. Schor understands the vocabulary of the millennial generation, yet her work suggests that there are traditions in painting that are slowly being degraded or forgotten—lost knowledge coming at great expense to our shared cultural understanding. *Death Is A Conceptual Artist* is schematic with the pieces of nature, culture, and self all separate but connected. Her paintings are a sly nod to "selfie" culture and her inclusion of text a rebuke to a generation who are leaving Facebook for Instagram because it uses "less words."

Language, as always for Schor, is a thing of utmost importance. Installed side by side are two paintings from 2015, both titled *Flesh*: one, a picture of the Mira figure with an umber cue card panel with the word "flesh" hovering nearby; the other, a pink on gray calligraphic rendering of the word "flesh." Combined, these two paintings read as a Magritte-like image-play or rebus. Schor gives us a fleshy painted word, something intangible made solid through the mysteries of paint. This play on the painted word shows Schor's continued interest in how language and image intersect. Indeed, her work as a writer and painter have overlapped in the past, often morphing into a painterly territory of existential calligraphy. Her interrogations of language as a source of power are captured with Johnsian succinctness in this diptych.

The bulk of the show is given to a series of studies, although that word seems somehow inaccurate, of the Mira figure, sketched at roughly the same size on tracing paper and presented in the chronological order of their making. Schor was partially inspired by a recent show at the Metropolitan Museum of Art of Mangaaka figures from the Kongo. Schor wrote:

The first time I went to see the show at the Met I became quite overwhelmed by the figures, their scale and stance and presence, so much so that I had to leave the room for a while before going back in. I was nearly in tears, of emotion and also excitement. I immediately felt that I had to respond to these figures, at first primarily to their scale and physicality. So after three days I created the first four drawings.

The depiction of power, though its presence is immaterial, has been a source of fascination for painters since, well, there has been painting. Michelangelo, David, Rembrandt, Benglis, Golub, Kruger, and Longo come to mind. Schor plays with the relationship of the figure, immense and monolithic, against the ground, delicate and ephemeral. In *"Power" Figure #8: Hello Dear* (2015), the figure, a death's head wearing a nightgown or dress, carries detached breasts, like Saint Agatha. *"Power" Figure #14: Mira at 19 and Now* (2015) seems like a study for *"Power" Figure #30: All that's left is paint*. Again we have a large figure with a floating, attached, tiny one. The small figure is a redrawing of a self-portrait Schor did at 19. Like Picasso, in his last self-portrait (*Self-Portrait Facing Death*, 1972), Schor gives us a schematic depiction of time at work. The Mangaaka figures which were the catalyst for this group may have had talismanic properties for their creators, but for the contemporary artist, Schor seems to ask, does art still have that power? Schor's drawings are meditations on time and aging, and on the power of art to transform and transcend the temporal.

The scope of these drawings is vast. Schor references an array of fellow artists, a history of stylistic influences, and a lexicon of symbols, both personal and historical, that cannot be apprehended through one visit alone. Here we find the true source of power in Schor's work: an artist who has amassed an arsenal of knowledge, armed with a sense of the importance of traditions and histories, who has transformed the information she has gathered into images of great beauty. One gets the sense while wandering through this show that the true audience for this work has not yet been born.

More Pricks Than Kicks

Philip Guston's Nixon Drawings; Hauser & Wirth, New York.
Published November 15, 2016; *Artslant.*

Although this exhibition of Philip Guston's archly satirical drawings of Richard Nixon was conceived long before last week's election, it could not have opened at a more opportune moment to illustrate Karl Marx's adage that "history repeats itself, first as tragedy then as farce."

Hauser & Wirth has assembled selections of Guston's Nixon drawings, a series that the artist worked on over a period of several years when faced with a tumultuous personal and artistic crisis—changing his style from abstract to representational and changing galleries from the established Marlborough Gallery to his last gallery and champion David McKee—as well as the tumult of the Vietnam- Civil Rights-era Nixon administration. A refugee from the Manhattan art world, Guston moved to Woodstock, and there, along with his new best friend, Philip Roth, finally found a subject worthy of his skills as a political satirist—a modern-day Hogarth and Voltaire.

There is a wonderful moment in Mel Brooks's *The Producers* where the producers, in a bid to lose as much money as possible, create a musical farce specifically *designed* to lose as much money as possible. Seeking the lowest brow, they bring to life *Springtime for Hitler*, a kind of aborted *Sound of Music*. The classic line from the film, Brooks's "That's our Hitler!" stands for that eureka moment when one's expectations of meeting the lowest common denominator have been met. Spoiler alert: the musical is a great success.

Anticipating the anomaly of this body of work in Guston's career, *In Bed II* and *Alone* (both 1971) give us the archetypal Guston figure, a vaguely Tin Tin-ish, round-headed figure, recumbent in a disheveled bed. He is illuminated by a bare lightbulb, the symbol of poverty and loucheness—"I can't stand a naked light bulb, any more than I can a rude remark or a vulgar action," says Blanche DuBois in *A Streetcar Named Desire*—and is suffering under the weight of some heavily painted and heavy-looking objects, like books and sandwiches. Pretty stock stuff for Guston. Up until this moment, Guston had been, if not at the forefront of the Abstract Expressionist movement, at least a pretty faithful member of the cause. Possibly because of his early successes—well-funded teaching positions in Iowa and luminously beautiful abstractions reminiscent of Monet—Guston seemed mired in nothing so much as niceness. A terrible position for an artist to find oneself, especially following his well-received mid-career survey at the Guggenheim. But there had once been another Guston, an early Social Realist painter, whose works, like *Martial Memory* (1941) or *Drawing for Conspirators* (1930) showed both a leaning towards the work of the Mexican Muralists, as well as a leaning, well, Left, as well.

A supersaturated solution, such as a glass of salt water, needs only one crystal to transform. Enter Philip Roth, the catalyst out of Guston's mid-career slump. Roth's satirical writing, heavily infused with a history of being an American Jew, was something Guston (born Phillip Goldstein) may have found invigorating, along with Roth's embrace of popular culture, politics (his *Our Gang*, a satirical novel about a character called Trick E. Dixon), vulgarity, and frank descriptions of human behavior, especially awkward sexual depictions. It is in particular Roth's vulgarity, a quality that bookish and WASPy New York culture found both fascinating and off-putting, that became an important element for Guston. In the context of Roth's writing it is significant to note that our word "vulgar" might connote both the original definition "characteristic of or belonging to the masses" as well as the more colloquial "crude or distasteful." This is crucial to our understanding of Guston's transformative work with Nixon, changing him from what was becoming a popular political caricature to Guston's greatest muse.

Hauser & Wirth have divided up Guston's folios, most of which are simply titled *Satirical Drawings*, into temporal-based groupings, providing us a view of the developing relationship Guston formed with Nixon over the four-year period. In *Nixon in Bed* (1971), which follows the format of Guston's bed-locked figures, we see a Nixon homunculus, not quite defined but in various states of distress. One drawing is inscribed "a case of the measles," showing a spotty Nixon, his body (and we presume by metaphor, the body politic) in a state of sickness. From here Roth's influence becomes more apparent; Guston develops a Nixon character, a figure whose unshaven face sports a huge cock in place of a nose, which, like Pinocchio's, grows longer as Nixon lies. We see this in the series *The Presidency*, with Nixon in the company of his trusted henchmen Henry Kissinger (usually represented by a pair of horn-rimmed glasses, reminding us of Garry Trudeau's *Doonesbury* comic strip) and Spiro Agnew. The adolescent, graffiti-like quality of the phallus-nosed Nixon reminds us of Jon Stewart's recent Twitter spat with Donald Trump, where he dubbed the president-elect "FuckFace von ClownStick."

Nixon's lackeys wear KKK hoods, plot and scheme, and are probed by Nixon's nose. They speak in a hieroglyphic mock Chinese language, swim in Biscayne Bay, and travel to China, or at least a Chinese restaurant, replete with Fu dogs, coolie hats, and rice bowls. *Poor Richard* (1972), the most resolved of the folios, is a play on the fall of Nixon, as well as *Poor Richard's Almanac*, melding the visual and the narrative in clever play. Nixon's dog Checkers is rendered as a cubistic checkerboard, and Nixon's head is transformed into an ancient, pyramidal monolith, decaying under the weight of history.

The exhibition ends with the *Phlebitis* paintings from 1975. Nixon, with an elephantine leg, bandaged and dragging behind him, resigns under the threat of impeachment and slouches off stage to Bethlehem. In the final drawing of the series, Guston shows Nixon on his deathbed—a bit of wish fulfillment, and a little premature. Perhaps Guston was nostalgic for, if not the literal death of Nixon, the Nixon that inspired such an outpouring of work. Guston would create another decade's worth of paintings, relying more heavily on art historical references—great paintings, but bloodless by comparison. Guston's hideous Nixon golem with elephantiasis might be seen more as his *Olympia* than *Death of Marat*, such is the luscious delectation with which Guston paints his Hitler.

Wide Awake in America

C. Michael Norton: *When Paintings Awake*; David&Schweitzer Contemporary, Brooklyn.
Published April 21, 2017; *CultureCatch*.

There was a time, over a century ago, when the idea of a purely abstract painting, one which referenced only the means of its creation, was a far-off goal, a seemingly unattainable dream. In the following decades this idea was tested, tried, worked, and re-worked until the project engendered many and various permutations. Post-modern, appropriational, deconstructed—the list of approaches to this idea is legion; yet there endures some compulsion, some drive that seems hardwired, to create paintings of pure visuality. Just when we think we have come to the end of this story we find new characters waiting in the wings, new gladiators wanting into the arena. In C. Michael Norton's current exhibit at David&Schweitzer Contemporary we see that this project still has viability. Indeed, Norton seems to open new fields of exploration.

In several of the large-scale works here, Norton has managed to synthesize a wide vocabulary of historical references and combined them with innovations and old-school tinkering to present variations on themes that have seemingly endless variations. A particularly lively one is *Things Lost That We Are Not Aware Of* (2016). It welds passages of knifed-on, splattered, and scraped paint, which brings together large yellow "gun" shapes that evoke Claes Oldenburg's "ray guns." Passages of yellow resemble the broken street paint of crosswalks, and taped-off sections look as if pulled out of a late Al Held work. The taped-off sections are particularly suggestive because Norton, like Held, uses various acrylic media that visually "pop" against the rough weave of the linen grounds. There is a searching quality here, and one is left with the feeling that, like de Kooning's *Excavation* (1950), we see an artist noodling around, combining and rearranging passages of paint according to some internal logic.

Similarly in *Einstein's Edge of Winter* (2009–2011) we have a diptych, held together with an underlying lattice structure of Yves Klein's Blue, which seems in the process of either being covered with or obviated by an abraded and scraped white. There is an interesting tension between the strictures of the geometry and the overall randomness of the white. Interspersed and mixed into the white passages are a small spectrum of color, and we are reminded that in the "real" world white is the sum of all color; thus we might choose to see the blue structure as emerging from the void of white, rather than being obliterated by it.

In *Stricken* (diptych) (2016–2017), which is the strongest work in the show, the unequal panels suggest a topographical map, with the left panel having only the barest traces of brushwork resembling a view of city blocks, buildings, and streets seen from above. The right panel burbles and pops, a volcanic stew of viscous pigment, piled and pulled an inch or two above the surface of the linen. Taken together, the painting at first glance resembles the small maps dropped into newscasts on CNN covering Syrian air strikes.

It is of note that at the moment other artists, such as Rick Briggs, Dona Nelson, and Jackie Saccoccio, are applying some of these same strategies in work which bears superficial comparison; however, Norton largely eschews mark making that is not strictly in the service of the painterly gesture—no spills, drawn lines, or embedded objects detract from the knife-edge mark. There is a sense of an internal set of rules driving these works, and it is this aspect of Norton's paintings that seem to tie him to an earlier age. One thinks of color-field painters, or the minimalist structures of Peter Halley, and even to some degree Warhol's explorations in abstraction in the early '80s. Using linen for a substrate, and contrasting it with the synthetic medium, Norton also hints at bringing this painterly abstraction into the ring with earlier artists, giving a sense of historical weight that, say, Anselm Kiefer did in his painting in the '70s. Standing in front Norton's paintings, one has the sense that the artist is playing Dr. Frankenstein with the corpus of art history and breathing fresh life into his creatures.

Love in the Ruins

Anselm Kiefer: *Transition from Cool to Warm*; Gagosian, New York.
Published May 26, 2017; *Sharkforum*.

> The strategic adversary is fascism . . . the fascism in us all, in our heads and
> in our everyday behavior, the fascism that causes us to love power, to desire
> the very thing that dominates and exploits us.
> —Michel Foucault

> What interests me is the transformation, not the monument. I don't
> construct ruins, but I feel ruins are moments when things show themselves.
> A ruin is not a catastrophe. It is the moment when things can start again.
> —Anselm Kiefer

While Anselm Kiefer's painting has always harkened back to an earlier time, when the artist was an important member of the body politic, a large part of his *oeuvre* has largely depended on reading his grand, theatrical works as "political"; however, they do not so much address outright current political polemics, but rather allude to a history that Kiefer himself never witnessed. What has kept Kiefer's work interesting over the years has been watching the struggle, the contingency of his plan, and the odd balancing act of creating vast, expressionist works of art that are awkwardly filled with references to the Third Reich, the Roman Empire, and Egyptian mythology. Irony abounds—had he actually painted his monumental landscapes with their fascist architecture during the Third Reich he would have no doubt been labeled degenerate and the works then destroyed.

Kiefer's watercolors are washy, sensual exercises. Rodin comes to mind in *Extases féminines* (*Feminine Ecstasies*, 2013); Turner's sunsets are another reference point in *aller Tage Abend, aller Abende Tag* (*The Evening of All Days, the Day of All Evenings*, 2014). Kiefer's bookmaking, notating his large canvases and sculptures with text and making frequent references to poetry, support the idea that Kiefer might see his work as a postmodern form of History Painting. Framing his work in our current social/political context, one that includes the increasingly urgent concerns of "identity politics," it might be useful to reassess Kiefer's project as, possibly, a complex form of satire. While Martin Kippenberger might have known how to maneuver better with wit and lightness through this moment, we would be well served to remember that despite his dusty *gravitas*, Kiefer is a painter of remarkable intelligence and visual agility.

In this exhibition Kiefer seems to be excavating themes and imagery from his own past. The title is drawn from a book that Kiefer made in the late '70s, a book of watercolors depicting a landscape and water (cool colors) morphing into the figure of a woman, done in warm hues. Kiefer has always claimed some heroic vision for his work, seeing, like his teacher Joseph Beuys, his work as a part of the "healing" of Germany after the Holocaust. Seen through this perspective the transition of the landscape into a female presence could be read as a visual transformation of the Fatherland into a more benevolent Motherland. In more recent paintings like *Des Meeres und der Liebe Wellen* (*The Waves of Sea and Love*, 2017), lead waves lap over the landscape and are reminiscent of Jackson Pollock's *Full Fathom Five* (1947), as well as Julian Schnabel's recent Van Gogh's grave plate paintings.

In an era where painters are once again mixing art and politics, Kiefer stands in a unique position. While his work does address politics and their eventual obviation of German society after the Second World War, he uses imagery from a historical period in which he was not a witness, in many ways he serves as a forerunner to painters of a younger generation. Like Kiefer, Dana Schutz attempts to address racism in the US using imagery and subjects (Civil Rights, Jim Crow laws, etc.) that also preceded her. Her painting of Emmett Till, *Open Casket* (2016), met with a great deal of resistance when it was shown at the 2017 Whitney Biennial. On the other hand, Eric Fischl, who indeed painted some politically charged "machines" in the '80s, has lately adopted a Daumier-ish style of political caricature, depicting Trump and Co. as clowns and characters from *A Clockwork Orange*. Peter Williams has produced several bodies of work that bristle with rage—depictions of police brutality that are personal and sincere, encouraging sympathetic viewing instead of politically correct smugness.

Kiefer's work also shares an affinity with the later work of Ashley Bickerton; his position as an art world insider allowing him to work on such a grand scale yet remain somewhat the outsider—a member of a society that was trying to forget its past, that chose history painting as his medium. Is it possible to see his work now, through the perspective of our current political climate? Of course. Who better to show the next generation of artists how deep one can delve into a century of war, brutality, and near oblivion and emerge with new ideas, new ways of apprehending the world, new ways of remembering. A recent New Yorker cartoon caption might best sum up what our painters face in our political moment: "Those who forget their past are condemned to refer to everything bad as "like the Nazis."

Things Past: Brenda Goodman at David&Schweitzer

Brenda Goodman: *In a New Space*; David&Schweitzer Contemporary, New York. Published September 24, 2017; *Sharkforum*.

If there is a thread that unites the varied bodies of work that the protean painter Brenda Goodman has produced over her five-decade career, it is the sense of urgency—in the need of the artist to articulate her thoughts and emotions onto the painted surface, but also a feeling of immediacy in the directness of expression, the painterly "hand" manifest in the work.

Even in the Ingre-esque drawings of her work in the 1970s, one senses Goodman's need to capture a moment, a relationship between her psychological characters, and then move on, leaving a generous space unfinished for the viewer to move around in. This restlessness pervades her work, in fact defines it, as she jumps from style to style, figure to abstraction, throughout different periods.

What is most surprising about Goodman's recent work, now on view at David&Schweitzer, is a feeling of quiet introspection, a Proustian sense of contemplation, that pervades the paintings and works on paper, all created in the past year. To anyone familiar with Goodman's work, it comes as no surprise that the imagery, a hybrid of painterly syntax, might require some thoughtful participation to unfold. These powerful, compact paintings reveal themselves slowly, with the contingency of her previous works replaced by a weightier, architectural feel, at once both formally strong and psychologically layered with meaning.

An aspect of the Surrealist movement, which holds greater relevance to many painters working today, was that there were two quite different approaches, stylistically and philosophically, to painting. The first, most iconic, was the "dream illustration" typified by Dalí; the second was a more literary-based "automatic writing" developed by Masson. It was this second, inward-looking manner of working that would have the greatest impact on American artists like Motherwell and Pollock. Goodman's paintings harken back to both ways of working. Most of these works begin with a scarified surface, for example *Lickety Split* (2017), whose underlying mark-making resembles a Mark Tobey or a Masson. It is from this unconscious, random scraffiti she "discovers" forms; but through a process of editing and layering, these forms coalesce and resolve into "head" shapes that in turn form a sort of proscenium or stage, which frames an imagined, internal subconscious scene. The connection to the Abstract Expressionists is manifest in Goodman's process; as she says, *"Lickety Split* I would say is probably one of the riskiest paintings I've ever done because it was a beginning that upon looking at it for a few day quickly became an end and it was done." This ambiguity, in which we are both "seeing" and "seeing into," along with the painter, gives these paintings an internal tension as we unpack the imagery like a matryoshka doll. Goodman embraces wholeheartedly these contradictions; seldom is ambiguity been depicted so clearly.

Goodman's anthropomorphized "stage heads" suggest the trope that Picasso used in his "Guéridons" of the 1920s. Goodman's work in the '70s used the idea of the painting as stage to give space to her morphing characters in scenes, imaginary relationships, and stories. Here, Goodman reinvests the concept further with personal anecdote, drawing on memories of her mother, childhood stories, and references to her partner Linda. In *Tomorrow's Promise* (2017), stage, character, and story conflate. We can almost feel Goodman remembering and reflecting and recording memories through the medium of paint. Godard wrote that the most beautiful and difficult thing in cinema was capturing on film the moment when someone changes their mind. With these new paintings Goodman seems to be on the same search, for an elusive perfect moment, a memory from the past, happening still.

Vir Heroicus Sublimis

Cy Twombly: *Coronation of Sesostris*; Gagosian, New York.
Per Kirkeby: *Paintings and Bronzes from the 1980s*; Michael Werner, New York.
Mary DeVincentis: *Dwellers on the Threshold*; David&Schweitzer Contemporary, New York.
Published April 24, 2018; *CultureCatch*.

> The first man was an artist.
> –Barnett Newman

Before there were fertile grounds growing olives and grapes, before the ages of kings and kingdoms, and long before the shifting of countries and armies when war defined the Valley, the caves were the locus of the wandering tribes who would one day be called "human."

Star-Watcher, whose bright eyes glistened through patches of matted fur, punctuated by scars and untended infections, watched from the cavern's oculus as a rag-tag hunting party set out under the rising sun. Moon-Watcher, taller than the others, with his massive brow and a determined set to his eyes and mouth, thought only of the day's hunt. With the receding of the ice, and the end of the giant lizards, the world had come to look more and more like a giant buffet than a fear-filled world of terror, an alternate world to the safety of the cave. Star-Watcher had once gone along on the hunt. Her spear had brought back the reindeer, rancors, and mynocks that the tribe survived on. The scattered piles of bones attested to her prowess.

Star-Watcher allowed her gaze to linger on the diminishing forms of her cave mates scattering and hiding, awaiting the careless gazelle or dozing nocturnal mynock on a low-hanging branch. She turned back to the darkness of the cave and paused. Drawings of running reindeer and stags, a large cat taking down a buck, and dozens of bison, bears, and tribbles filled the great entrance to the cave. Star-Watcher paused before a large etched and colored image of a rancor. The beginnings of a memory stirred. It had been a long hunt. The tribe was tired when they came upon the massive rancor, and the hunting party, which had started out as a group of seven when the sun had risen, returned with the beast as a party of two. Moon-Watcher and Star-Watcher had lived to tell the tale over the fire, then Star-Watcher, still holding a delicious hoof, scratched the beast into the wall of her menagerie.

Snapping back from her reveries, Star-Watcher searched around the cave. She had secreted handfuls of colorful pigment, which she had dug from the cave, from under trees, or from small rocks she had crushed. She knew the importance, though she did not yet understand it, of keeping track of the hunts. How else would they remember it was Long-Tooth that by himself took the giant mastodon? Or that Moon-Watcher had once brought back three mynocks from the frozen tundra, ending a month-long famine?

Star-Watcher turned her attention to a wall of handprints. At some point she had realized that the comings and goings of the food-beasts could be more accurately predicted by watching the comings and goings of the Second Sun—the Second Sun that also brought the blood. For her, each print represented the waxing and waning of the Second Sun and by her calculation portended a good hunt today, or guaranteed a hungry night. She chose a sulfurous powder from a mynock skin pouch and poured it into her hand. Pressing her other hand to the wall she blew on the yellow powder and then removed her hand. The outline stood out brightly on the glistening cave wall.

* * *

It is an exaggeration to say that the urge to paint is a primordial one, yet the evidence is there if we really want to imagine it. Abyssinian Kings realized the power of a carefully placed mural of a beheaded foe to inspire uncertainty in a visiting dignitary. And while the tales of Livy and Thucydides could be both exalting and terrifying, their existence depended on that thin thread of the teller and the tale. Paper, writing, printing, and broadcasting have made the word more tangible, but even in the metric age, political discourse is weak compared to, say, the image of President Obama wearing Heath Ledger's Joker make-up.

Let us digress a bit from the power of the image on the public and look at the power of the image for the artist. What is it about this most archaic form of language that still holds such sway? First there were cameras; they begat the news photo that begat the newsfeed of Instagram, Facebook, et al. Yet the urge to put pigment to the cave wall of canvas remains.

Several recent exhibitions, though unrelated in terms of style, content, and intent, show the tenacious grip that this art form still holds for painters. Cy Twombly, the Homer of Modern Art, whose cycle on Sesostris is a personalized revision of Herodotus's account of the Egyptian King, exerts a primal pull on the viewer through its arcane pictorial language of scrawls and smears. It is rare to see the work of a septuagenarian, let alone one who is working at the height of his painterly powers (one thinks of Louise Bourgeois or Picasso in this same company). The aging Twombly replicated some of the idea of Herodotus's epic travel adventure by painting these works in several locations, beginning in Gaeta, Italy, and finishing the series in Lexington, Virginia, his hometown. Sally Mann, the American photographer and a friend of Twombly, documented the artist for many years—a sort of Boswell to his Dr. Johnson. We are moved by the power of the images in some small part by seeing the frail artist wrestling with his painterly problems on such an epic physical scale. It is a commonly accepted myth, the artist as hero, struggling with the monumental; it is quite another to see the frail human struggling for real to capture the heroic on canvas. The struggle is often overlooked, however, and possibly unmentioned because many seem to have lost the compassion to look at those human frailties that artists overcome in their desire to create.

* * *

Per Kirkeby's work bears re-evaluation after a fall in 2013 left the artist with severe head trauma and memory loss, which affected his ability to paint. Indeed, one of the most moving passages in cinema is in the opening scenes of *Man Falling* (2015), a film by Anne Wivel, which documents the artist post-accident. We see him looking blankly at his past work, unable to recall having painted it.

Michael Werner presents an exquisitely curated show of the artist's work from the 1980s, with massive slabs of color, skittering brushwork-filled paintings, and pounded and torqued bronzes cast from clay. One finds the work monumental, elemental even, and gives little thought to *who* made it, *who* brought these things into the world. Indeed, given his interest in geology, nature, and biology (talks with the artist largely revolved around trees), it is not carelessness that causes us to take the works as another part of nature; it was the artist's *intent* that we take these works *as* nature. What Wivel's documentary shows us is the artist learning to reinvent his work, and reinvent himself as a painter. While a gulf of nothingness separates the artist from his past, he continues to work, re-learning a vocabulary of forms and narratives. Wivel gives us an intimate portrait of an artist's struggles made manifest through determination; the urge to continue to paint dominates, and though the accident's tragic pause in the artist's life pressed "pause," it is painting itself that pushed "play." Kirkeby's running talk of painting through the film is a rare view of the mind recovering things that he still knows.

194

There are other fine examples of making art in the face of adversity. The trials of Chuck Close are fairly well documented. Close's career is an almost Job-like tale of overcoming physical travail. The dyslexia of childhood pushed him toward image making, though because of the medical condition prosopagnosia, commonly known as "face-blindness," which makes facial recognition difficult, the artist chose to focus exclusively on portraits, in an attempt to "fix" through art what cannot be cured through medical treatment. We can also look at the work of Mary DeVincentis. Her paintings at David&Schweitzer Contemporary create a magical realm in her show *Dwellers on the Threshold*. DeVincentis has a condition called aphantasia, a psychological phenomenon where the subject cannot visualize imagery without external reference. Commonly referred to as lacking "the mind's eye," the subject can verbalize memories and descriptions of people and things but can't "picture" them. In DeVincentis's work we see manifest the process of a painter creating an external universe of internal thinking. Of particular note are the pictures *Dweller on the Threshold* (2017), a Rorschach-like cave or butterfly flanked by Casper-like ghosts; and *Under the Strawberry Moon* (2016), with a couple kissing, dwarfed by a yellow moon. Her works possess some of the uncanniness of the best of Francesco Clemente's imaginary self-portraits, worlds where the internal and external are not so separate.

What these artists have in common, perhaps, is not so special or unique. Medical conditions aside, when viewing the work we are struck by the power of the work, not the strength it took to create it. This, ultimately, brings us back to the fact that this urge to paint is the primordial urge Barnett Newman believed it to be, as he wrote in the essay "The First Man Was an Artist" in 1947. In part it reads, "What was the first man, was he a hunter, a toolmaker, a farmer, a worker, a priest, or a politician? Undoubtedly the first man was an artist."

Newman begins the essay: "A science of paleontology that sets forth this proposition can be written if it builds on the postulate that the aesthetic act always precedes the social one. The totemic act of wonder in front of the tiger-ancestor came before the act of murder. It is important to keep in mind that the necessity for dream is stronger than any utilitarian need. In the language of science, the necessity for understanding the unknowable comes before the desire to discover the unknown."

Newman was describing a being which, for lack of a better term, was "*homo aestheticus*," the next step along the evolutionary line of those bipedal creatures scrabbling over the planet. If these recent shows have anything to tell us 70 years after Newman's thesis, it is that this form of anthropoid is alive and thriving.

* * *

For Star-Watcher it was sometimes monotonous work, all her scratching and coloring. but the boredom allowed her to think of other things, things bigger than the cave. As the ices receded, the tribe had found the bones of other creatures, things that no longer walked the Valley. Who were they? Where did they come from? Where did they go? These questions lingered in the back of her mind as she worked. Her handprint firmly fixed and finished, she carefully rewrapped the pouch, dusted off her hands, and stepped back to admire the outline of her hand. It always stopped her, every time, when she had finished her work. Her hand was there on the wall, yet not there. The bison with the running stags were there too, yet they had been eaten long ago. Yes, the beginnings of new ideas were forming. But it was getting late. The others would be back before darkness filled the Valley; the darkness that was good for the hunter, but not for the prey.

But there was always tomorrow, always the bags of stone and color. Star-Watcher was not yet sure what she would paint tomorrow, but that was still a long way off, and she would think of something.

Men In Rooms: Bruce Nauman at MoMA PS1

Bruce Nauman: *Disappearing Acts*; MoMA PS1.
Published October 29, 2018; *CultureCatch*.

> I talk, you listen
> —Bruce Nauman

> Sculpture is the art of intelligence
> —Pablo Picasso

> No sense makes sense
> —Charles Manson

Dear Dusty. Sorry for the delay. I got your letter and the m/s last Tuesday. My landlord Lana, you met her once I think found me this morning passed out in the hallway, hungover. It's ok. She's seen me worse off. With young girls, or 1 time naked after mistakenly picking up a cupcake I swear to god looked like Hedy Lamarr with an afro. She turned out not to be so nice when I couldn't pay her. One time these 2 German girls came from Hamburg to visit me. I tried to fuck both of them, finally settled on the older one 19 while the other one went to the Brehmer & Cross to wait. I gave her a real pounding, 1 or 2 inches at a time at first, I kept punching at the tunnel, good hard strokes. "Oh god Frank! It's so BIG Frank! HOLY SHIT IT'S PURPLE, FRANK!" she went on and on. Maybe it was all the beer, but I gave her 3 or 4 good long strokes then gave up and ate her out. The girls stayed 4 days and nights until I got bored and then it was 4 or 5 cans of beer and a couple little cans of vodka mix with rum because we were out of vodka just to get them out.

I am going to go by the post office to mail you the new poems, but I want to stop off at the Black Sparrow. There is a new bartender there called Bruce [*First Hologram Series: Making Faces B*, 1968] who used to work days but now he just does nights. He says the tips are better at night and he is trying to save up money so he can move out full time to work on a dude ranch. [*Setting a Good Corner (Allegory and Metaphor)*, 1999] Kid is ok. He is a composer. He doesn't know shit about Mahler, but he brought in a tape recorder that he had a tape on of a symphony he composed. Modern shit, but the title of it was *DEAD DAD* so who the fuck am I to say. It wasn't half bad.

That screenplay shit I told you about was just some "artist" wanting to do a student film. I told him to fuck off because a) he didn't seem to have any money, b) he wants to do *Boners* when I had specifically told him it had to be one of the longer shorts from *Mother's Pussy* and c) I think he just wants to fuck me.

You know that feeling you get when you feel like you've forgotten something like your room key or that something is missing like your soul? Bruce understands that. That is something. Most artists never understand that. The absent, the void, the feeling of nonexistence. Bruce gives form to these things. [*Seven Wax Templates of the Left Half of My Body Spread over 12 Feet*, 1967] Things that are seen, holes the size of a body part, the space under a chair, a beautiful woman vanishing around a corner. In the nocturnal life of the studio, the empty bathtub where you were 2 minutes before. He grapples with the anxiety of the psychological world. Like Victor Hugo wrote on emptiness and inhabiting. Ouasimodo's cathedral was "egg, nest, house, country and universe . . . one might almost say that he had espoused its form the way a snail does the form of its shell. It was his home, his hole, his envelope. He adhered to it like a turtle to its carapace. This rugged cathedral was his armor." There was a big shoot-out last night outside the Sparrow. A real Punch and Judy show. [*Crime and Punishment (Punch and Judy)*, 1985] I didn't actually see it. I heard some shots and figured it was some SLA shit or Manson, or the IRA. Bruce didn't want to go out. He said, "It will be on tv in 10 minutes anyway." Bruce likes his violence secondhand I guess. It's the city does this. Turns real people into animals. [*Leaping Foxes*, 2018] Concrete walls. Endless streets. All the protest signs in Zapruder Park. Fuck You. NO. Get out of my head. All you need is love. [*Human Nature/Life Death/Knows Doesn't Know*, 1983] I had left the racetrack a loser, after the 9th, so clearly my luck wouldn't be improved walking into a riot. Bruce is right. It will all be on tv in 10 minutes.

Tried to look for some symphony music on the radio and passed by the news. It didn't mention the shootings today. I guess it's not a real story unless somebody dies. There are always so many angles on these things, whoever knows what the truth is. Bruce says, "the real artist reveals mystical truths" or some shit. Poetry. Well, I think maybe the tv brought it into the streets. Maybe it's an overdose of Marx. Sometimes I wonder what Hem would have done, then I laugh because we know what Hem would have done. Ha Ha. Oh lovely Mahler.

I am lucky to have you as a friend. I am sending you some new poems. I will have the new novel *Blowjobs* soon. January if I don't get murdered, for better or for worse. We must first look for centers of simplicity in our lives, in our many rooms. [*Double Steel Cage Piece*, 1974] Bruce said the other night "we are just in different rooms at different times, with different people." He knows death and waste and glory and some of the rent paid and courage. And moving toward the sun. He said "frustration is something that gets you into the studio and gets you to work through it. It's not evident in anything that is finished. Knowing when it's enough and you can leave it alone." I hope I remember these things. The cat with a bird in its mouth, the rifle sticking out of the window the screaming clowns the rats at night surryingly oblivious. Walking into the water and becoming one with the sea.

The Palace at 4 a.m.

Giacometti: Soloman R. Guggenheim Museum.
Published December 10, 2018; *Battery Journal.*

> I am a camera with its shutter open, quite passive, recording, not thinking.
> Recording the man shaving at the window opposite and the woman in
> the kimono washing her hair. Some day, all this will have to be developed,
> carefully printed, fixed.
> —Christopher Isherwood, *Goodbye to Berlin*

> A deception that elevates us is dearer than a host of low truths.
> —Aleksander Pushkin

Like Pablo Picasso, Francis Bacon, and Willem de Kooning, Alberto Giacometti (1901–1966) has become something of an icon of mid-twentieth-century existential figurative painting. At once going against the prevailing trend toward Modernist abstraction, Giacometti sought to continue the traditional notions of classical figurative painting during a time when those ideas seemed growingly irrelevant in the century that saw World War I and World War II, AIDS and a cure for polio, the invention of mass television and radio, X-rays and LSD, Pop Tarts and the hydrogen bomb, Freud and death camps.

Giacometti was the son of Giovanni Giacometti, a minor post-Impressionist painter and the older brother of Diego, a sculptor of animals; Diego would later become responsible for the casting and patinas of Giacometti's sculptures. From the beginning of his career Giacometti seemed uniquely destined to record the transitions, vagaries, and intellectual ideas that surrounded him after his move to Paris in 1922. Like his father, Giacometti began as a painter, particularly influenced by both Cézanne's revolutionary notions of fracturing the picture plane, as well as his nervous, stenographic brushwork. Giacometti's career has been traditionally divided into two separate "periods," the first, a decade-long affair with André Breton's Surrealism, began a fertile period of sculptural investigation, which allowed Giacometti to shed some of the more overt influences of Cézanne, Cubism, and probably most significant, the work of his father. Sculptures such as *Woman with Her Throat Cut* (1932), *Hands Holding the Void* (1934), and *The Palace at 4 a.m.* (1932) reflect Giacometti's assimilation of Breton's notions of the unconscious, as well as delving into some of the more "dissident Surrealists" who were influenced by Michel Leiris and George Bataille. Throughout the 1930s Giacometti made some of the most iconic of his "object-sculptures," which, like the paintings of Juan Miró, merged the figure and abstract elements into a new vocabulary. Even at their most abstract, as in *Cube* (1934), these works are imbued with figurative elements. The hand-smoothed surface of the object belies its aspirations as a Platonic Solid, recording the countless, obsessive hours spent ameliorating it into its final form. The philosopher and art historian Georges Didi-Huberman noted that *Cube* marks the transition between Giacometti's Surrealist and Realist periods, including his interest in portraying dimensionality, the relation of the figure to geometry, and what Didi-Huberman termed Giacometti's "abstract anthropomorphism." *Cube* is both a foreshadowing of Giacometti's changing style of portraiture, as well as a memorial to a type of "handmade" sculpture that would almost cease to exist 20 years later.

Giacometti's interest in literature is somewhat undocumented; James Lord noted that the only books he ever saw in the studio that Giacometti shared with his wife Annette Arm were spy novels, which he read during insomnia-plagued nights. However, a form of narrative structured some of his strongest works. The nightmare dollhouse of *The Palace at 4 a.m.* with its moveable elements evoke the haunted rooms of the fractured collective human condition in the aftermath of the war. *No More Play* (1931–32), a marble game board that resembles a cemetery, is "played" with wood and bronze "pieces." The marble is cratered with indentations and holes, and a smooth center panel containing a tiny grave divides the board. With no discernable rules of engagement, *No More Play* becomes a sadistic twist on children's games, as well as a metaphor for a society that was slowly learning of the horrors of the front.

It would be Giacometti's second act that would solidify his position as a major figure of twentieth-century painting. During this second period of his career, he abandoned the more literary pretensions of Breton and returned to portraiture after the Second World War. It began, he told Breton shortly before his exit from the Surrealist camp, with a desire to just "paint a nose on a face." Giacometti's return to the figure was of course more complex. He said, "In the street people astound and interest me more than any sculpture or painting. Every second the people stream together and go apart, then they approach each other to get closer to one another. They increasingly form and reform living compositions of unbelievable complexity." Like Alain Robbe-Grillet and Christopher Isherwood, Giacometti's work privileged the idea of the modern artist as recording device.

Figure Between Two Houses (1950), like *Cube*, is a transitional work, incorporating the geometry of the structure with a signature Giacometti "stick figure." The figure crosses between two box-like houses, which are connected with an empty road or bridge. The composition of the sculpture, coupled with its size and scale, resembles a mid-century television console, with a figure moving across the screen. Giacometti, like Bacon, encased many of his figures in a cage structure. Bacon derived his from well-known photographs of the Nuremberg Trials, and Eadweard Muybridge's grids. Giacometti, unlike Picasso who delighted in watching comedies and catch wrestling on television, eschewed having the device in his studio. One wonders if *Figure Between Two Houses* was merely a one-off formal device, or just the technology of contemporary culture seeping into his work. While he didn't watch television, he did love going to the movies, and his last girlfriend Caroline styled herself after the "stars" of the '60s.

While the action of *Figure Between Two Houses* implies movement and life, the head trapped in a cage in *The Nose* (1949, cast 1964) speaks to Giacometti grappling with understanding death. Revisiting the figure-in-an-environment format of his Surrealist work *Suspended Ball* (1930–31) and *Palace*, Giacometti inserts a head, cragged like a lunar surface, the mouth a rictus—it was man transformed by death. Having witnessed firsthand a traveling companion die in 1945, Giacometti wrote in 1946 of the transformation of the body in death: "His nose lengthening, his cheeks grow hollow . . ." This back and forth between depicting the living under attack by entropy and death would consume the next two decades.

The apocrypha cannot, with any degree of certainty, be separated by mere fact. Chiseling away at both paint and plaster, his circle of subjects narrowed to mostly women he knew personally—Annette, his mother, Caroline—and a few men he was close to, such as Diego (*Bust of Diego*, 1964) and Ely Lotar (*Head of a Man (Lotar 1)*, 1964).

He also worked with the occasional writer, such as James Lord and Gene Genet, who came to record him recording them. His anxiety-filled process created a demanding job for those sitters. Giacometti demanded stillness, as well as direct eye contact while he worked, and the deer-in-the-headlights expression on his subjects' faces was the result of the endless hours of posing as much as any existential dread. The Guggenheim ends the exhibition with *Dog* (1957), one of the most moving depictions of an animal in art, with Picasso's painting of predatory cats of the period being the inverse. For an artist who had so focused his eye on the human subject, it is something of a paradox that *Dog* might be his most humanist sculpture, describing in its bent and hungry form the despair that Louis-Ferdinand Céline would portray in *Journey to the End of the Night*: "That street was like a dismal gash, endless, with us at the bottom of it, filling it from side to side, advancing from sorrow to sorrow, toward an end that is never in sight, the end of all the streets in the world."

Guided By Voices

Hilma af Klint: *Paintings for the Future*; Soloman R. Guggenhiem Museum.
Published December 15, 2018; *Battery Journal*.

> What is beautiful . . . which springs from the soul.
> —Wassily Kankinsky

> Death is so abstract.
> —Andy Warhol

> BELIEVE
> —The private message Harry Houdini said he would send to his wife,
> during a séance, after his death, to determine the legitimacy of a medium.

> During the days when I was living alone in a foreign city . . . I quite often
> heard my name suddenly called by an unmistakable and beloved voice. I
> then noted down the exact moment of the hallucination and made anxious
> enquiries of those at home about what had happened at that time. Nothing
> had happened.
> —Sigmund Freud

In 1969 the German painter Sigmar Polke painted a work entitled *The Higher Powers Command: Paint the Upper Right Hand Corner Black!* (1969). The picture he produced was just that, an empty canvas with a black triangle in the upper right corner, and to ensure the delivery of the punch line, he painted the command underneath: *Höhere Wesen befahlen: rechte obere Ecke Schwarz malen!* in an old typewriter font, as if the edicts from above were dictated and sent out like any other from the Head Office. What at first might seem to be merely taking the piss out of yet another "style," like Pop Art, AbEx, or Socialist Realism, *Higher Powers* symbolized a strain of spiritual abstraction that was distinctly German. Polke would himself dabble in the spiritual in art during the 1970s, via mushrooms, meditation, and the mindlessness of media. Whether or not Polke's audience saw the joke in 1969, it was a knowing nod on Polke's part to the end of a certain type of avant-garde, one built by artists such as Hilma af Klint, where the viewer might believe they were having a genuine aesthetic, if not spiritual, relationship, through the artist, into something greater. Painting had once been a window into other worlds, showing the moral by way of the miraculous. The shorn breasts of St. Agatha, the disembodied eyes of St. Lucy gazing from a tray, or St. Clare, depicted with three balls, which were removed, *post mortem* from her body, and each of which magically weighing the same as the other two combined. These paintings were seen as vessels carrying messages from powers greater than ourselves; the history of Western Art has for the most part been a history of Western spiritual beliefs.

Hilma af Klint was born near Stockholm in 1862 and attended the Swedish Royal Academy of Fine Arts, graduating with honors in 1887. Predisposed to the mystical, she had begun attending séances at 17. This interest in the occult intensified after the death of her sister, ultimately finding kindred spirits in a group of women who called themselves The Five. Like many others at the turn of the century, The Five met to study Theosophy, Rosicrucianism, and Anthroposophy, and to hold séances. The turn of the century was filled with Steam Punk combinations of the religious, technological, spiritual, and scientific. William James, Arthur Conan Doyle, Harry Houdini, Wassily Kandinsky, and Helena Blavatsky were among the notable intellectuals on the same path.

At their regularly held séances, The Five would receive messages from mystic beings, the High Masters, which they would collect in notebooks and drawings. In these states of contact af Klint, speaking for Amaliel, Ananda, Clemens, Esther, Georg, and Gregor, the High Masters, announced plans to build a temple, which would be filled with paintings. In 1905 Georg and Ananda instructed af Klint to begin work on 193 large canvases. Using a psychograph, an instrument that received the dictations of Goerg and Ananda, af Klint embarked on a series of preliminary works, *The WU/Rose Series*, before beginning *The Ten Largest*, a series of large works that were tempera on paper, mounted on canvas, and all about 10 x 8 feet. Subdivided into the themes "Childhood," "Youth," "Adulthood," and "Old Age," *The Ten Largest* forms the core of the nearly 200 *Paintings for the Temple*. The earliest of these were painted under the specific instructions of the High Masters, though as the work progressed af Klint, as any prophet usually does, began interpreting more loosely the messages received. Af Klint's holistic approach to painting allowed her to use the picture plane as a receiving device. Drawing on her background at the Academy, where she studied botanical and anatomical drawing, af Klint created mixtures of floral, geometric, biomorphic, and calligraphic forms. Inventing languages for the High Masters, she created a rebus-like vocabulary where a tendril might become a spiral, or coiling calligraphic script; a snail might be inserted for scale reference; two orbs might represent two eggs or solar system diagrams; a set of Pantone-like swatches might be either the ascending colors of the chakra or an elevation of a pyramid. Platonic solids become organic forms.

A case has been made for af Klint's *Ten* series that these works might be the first purely abstract paintings, beating out Kandinksy by six or seven years. This Tesla vs. Edison postulation precludes one fact: to af Klint, these were *messages*, about *important things*, not abstract forms; they represented content, just not content recognizable to us. Af Klint, a Late Victorian intellectual, had every reason to believe that the psychograph was communicating real messages, scientifically, from beings who inhabited a different time and space continuum.

Af Klint exhibited her works outside of her group only once, and, the construction of the temple aborted, she stipulated that the paintings not be shown until 20 years after her death. In a Houdini-like move, af Klint vanished for decades, her works magically reappearing in 1986 in an exhibition in Helsinki. There is a strange, Billy Pilgrim-like feeling to these paintings, which seem to have come unstuck in the fabric of art history.

Af Klint, like many artists of her period, was, to Clement Greenberg, "in search of the absolute." He continued, "The avant-garde arrived at 'abstract' or 'non-objective' art and tried in effect to imitate God by creating something valid solely on its own terms, in the way nature itself is valid; in the way a landscape, not its picture, is aesthetically valid. Something *given*, independent of meanings." In *Group IV: The Ten Largest, No. 7, Adulthood* (1907), we see af Klint wrestling with this notion, creating a new vocabulary, attempting to translate form into language. The biomorphic elements, a large yellow pod carefully annotated with Roman numerals, like a page out of a medical book, is combined with wallpaper-floral swirls. It is as if af Klint is trying to show us something magical and strange, and giving us a vernacular reference for context. In *Group IV: The Ten Largest No. 3, Youth* (1907) one is struck by the sense of modernity of the color, the candy-colored egg shapes, the zany spirals; the all-over composition feels like the opening credits to an Otto Preminger film, or the background for a Bugs Bunny dream sequence. What is of great interest is to imagine what might have been, what influence these works may have had, had af Klint chosen to share the High Masters' messages rather than tuck them away like a dowry. For all their modernity, they now carry with them the scent of lavender and moth balls.

If Post Modernism has taught us anything, it is that the history of art is a multiverse in which ideas and images appear and cycle at intervals, through different artists, at different periods. The fabric of that history is comprised of the work of many people—the artist, the viewer, the collector, the critic, and finally, the artwork itself. The final tapestry, Art History, is greater than the individual threads and ultimately is a never-ending work in progress. The business of art is a collective work, which goes on from age to age, no single artist defining a period, no critic telling the whole story of their time, with any degree of certainty. No age has the final word. We can only interpret an art in the light of our own time and cultural understanding; other generations will add their perspectives, as well as remove the bits they no longer understand.

Art historians love apocryphal stories about painters: Pliny's Parrhasius and Zeuxis, Vasari's Leonardo and Raphael, Greenburg's Pollock, Schnabel's van Gogh. Af Klint was paid a visit by the Austrian educator and fellow spiritualist Rudolf Steiner in 1908. Steiner critiqued her work, advising her to move away from her spiritual inclinations and to work from her own ideas and intuition, a basic tenant of the Steiner school system. Af Klint abandoned her work on the Temple paintings and stopped work altogether for the next four years, resuming painting, but never with the same interest. One is tempted, though, seeing *Group IX/SUW The Swan No . 17* (1915), a severe yet very beautiful painting of concentric, colored circles, which seems steeped in Constructivism, Orphism, and Der Blaue Reiter, to wonder what might have been had af Klint not let things of the spirit come first.

Hesitation Marks

Judy Glantzman: *1979–Today*; Betty Cunningham Gallery.
Published January 10, 2019; *CultureCatch*.

> What the painter adds to the canvas are the days of his life. The adventure of
> living, hurtling toward death.
> —Jean-Paul Sartre

> I hope that my painting has the impact of giving someone, as it did me, the
> feeling of his own totality, of his own separateness, of his own individuality.
> —Barnett Newman

Abraham Lincoln wrote that "men, like trees, are best measured down." This phrase immediately jumps to mind viewing the current exhibit at Betty Cunningham Gallery, a retrospective of the work of Judy Glantzman. A painter of great sincerity and intelligence, who has been working in New York, creating a personal vocabulary and style for four decades.

The reference to trees, of course, was Lincoln's metaphor: one should reserve judgment on our fellow humans until they are dead, have finished their story. In Glantzman's work, though, trees are also an important medium. Carvings of hands, *Reach* (2017), grouped in help-me clusters on plinths, are poignantly beseeching, being at once eerily generic, like something found in a reliquary, and at the same time oddly personal, each hand seemingly modeled from life. While bearing a passing resemblance to the sculptures of Nicola Tyson and Georg Baselitz, with their roughhewn carving, Glantzman's sculpture feels far more complex and strange—Pinocchio adrift on the Raft of The Medusa.

In the '80s, her work addressed AIDS; in her more recent work she paints of loss, conflict, and war. It is now hard to remember, but in the '80s death often came slow, slow and painful, as plagues often do. In our current age death happens quickly, randomly, anonymously. The bomb in the plaza, the gun in the school yard or at the movie theater. Glantzman's approach in her current work mimics the contingency of the subject. She writes, "I am looking for 'shorthand' symbols that speak of war. The large collages are very physical, so the intuitive process has a lot to do with tearing and layering. Chance plays a big part in the collages. I want the work to 'show me,' so I often glue things together that happened to fall together on the floor."

There is something ironic about recent movies having provided a greater glimpse into the work of painters. Julian Schnabel and Willem DeFoe's Van Gogh, and Stanley Tucci and Geoffrey Rush's Giacometti, show the anxious work of the painter trying to connect with a subject. Glantzman follows this tradition, and in *Untitled* (1993) the scraping, layering, and erasing come together slowly, cohesively, revealing the thought process of the artist. The ballerina dress perhaps a nod to Degas, or maybe a niece, it doesn't really matter. It is a compelling work, iconic in its simplicity.

Hands reappear in some larger works from 2016. In *Dark Prayer* (2016) a turvy-topsy array of school portraits, globes, capsized boats, and clasped hands portend both helplessness and hope. Glantzman loses some of the intimacy of her single-figure works when she ups the action on canvas, but what we lose is offset by the cacophony of scratchy notes and sketches, the urgency of a reporter writing on another horror. Glantzman may seem an unlikely documentarian, but perhaps we miss the point if we assume the work is merely political commentary. She says, "I come from a self-portrait orientation . . . The more I am in it, the truer it is. And the more I am in it, the less it is about me—even though in truth it is all about me." In Glantzman's work the political is personal.

Dandy in the Underworld

Dana Schutz: *Imagine Me and You*; Petzel Gallery.
Published January 24, 2019; *Battery Journal*.

> The Surrealists waged the most extreme warfare on the containers of an
> autonomously developed cultural sphere. The contents got dispersed.
> —Jurgen Habermas, *Modernity: An Incomplete Project*

> For Freud our sexual desires as male or female, our confidence in language as
> true or false, and our security in the image we judge as perfect or flawed, are
> fantasies.
> —Jacqueline Rose, *Sexuality in the Field of Vision*

Dana Schutz might once have seemed an unlikely candidate to fill the role of Baudelaire's "painter of one's time"; her early work, knowingly funny, played within a framework of contemporary tropes, sitcom storylines, and post-modernist strategies. While often lampooning High Art, her greatest strength was an uncanny knack for finding the deep psychological impulse hiding in plain sight, in quotidian scenes of everyday life. Baudelaire wrote, "Nearly all our originality comes from the stamp that time imprints upon our sensibility." When he wrote this, mid-nineteenth-century Parisian artists were experiencing the apocalypse of the Franco-Prussian War, the rise and fall of the Commune, unstable economies, class systems undermined by industry, and industry driven by rapidly developing sciences. Poincaré's theories, Flammarion's celestial maps, Pasteur's discoveries, Thénard's paint. Replace "Trump Era" with "Third Republic" and one might see Schutz as the Painter of Modern Life for the Instagram Age.

Schutz infuses the personal onto popular images, using a variety of styles. Her early work felt like an artist at play, in a serious way, rummaging through art history for the parts to create a new kind of painting, one where simple subjects, like nudes and portraits, resulted in highly charged, psychological studies. Like Manet, Schutz's strategy ran aground, with *Open Casket* (2016), when the contract between the artist and the public shifted during a time of media saturation.

In her recent work at Petzel, *Imagine Me and You*, Schutz incorporates many of the tropes of her early work—the *Chaplinesque Treadmill* (2018), the sitcom Surrealist setup of *Washing Machine* (2018)—but she seems to suddenly break through these narratives to create works that feel more intense, more personal, a little haunted. André Breton wrote, "It is incumbent on us to try to see more and more clearly what is transpiring unbeknownst, in the depth of the mind." Schutz lays bare, in a few works, that sense of searching, of plumbing the depths of weirdness and emotion. *The Visible World* (2018), like *Treadmill*, the most literal works here, both show figures "on the wheel" of Modernity, always wanting, never getting.

Trouble and Appearance (2018) and *The Wanderer* (2018) are the kind of paintings one sometimes encounters where the wealth of visual reference is woven into a simple, iconic image. In both works the protagonist is a roundheaded, vaguely Charley Brown-ish, avatar of a Wall Street businessman. In *Trouble and Appearance* he has a suit and tie and a briefcase. In *The Wanderer* he has lost the suit, and probably his license, as he now sports a tracking device on his ankle. He inexplicably carries an umbrella and slogs through a sea of tiny crabs. Here Schutz's paint goes off to wander on its own, daubing, dragging, swirling, wet-on-wet;

monumental little constructions of pigment are woven together, physically weighty. The figure in *Trouble* is menaced by a spectral figure of a woman, a surreal apparition, like something out of a Picabia or Jorn. Schutz plays the paint light and insubstantial, in contrast to the earthbound handling of the businessman.

In *Touched* (2018), the strangest painting in the exhibition, a bust-length portrait, part Dokoupil, part *Cake Wars*, grimaces, as if in response to the gouging of her breasts. The painting is so tactile, so disquieting, it mesmerizes, not the least for its incongruity. To quote one other nineteenth-century writer, Vincent van Gogh, "My brush stroke has no system at all. I hit the canvas with irregular touches of the brush, which I leave as they are. Patches of thickly laid-on color, spots of canvas left untouched, here or there portions that are left absolutely unfinished. In short I am inclined to think that the result is so disquieting and irritating as to be a godsend to those people who have preconceived ideas." Schutz is an intrepid guide, a postmodern *flaneuse*; we get to stroll with her through the labyrinth of her psyche, and possibly our own collective cultural unconscious.

www.ingramcontent.com/pod-product-compliance
Lightning Source LLC
Chambersburg PA
CBHW051510030726
47592CB00006B/2188